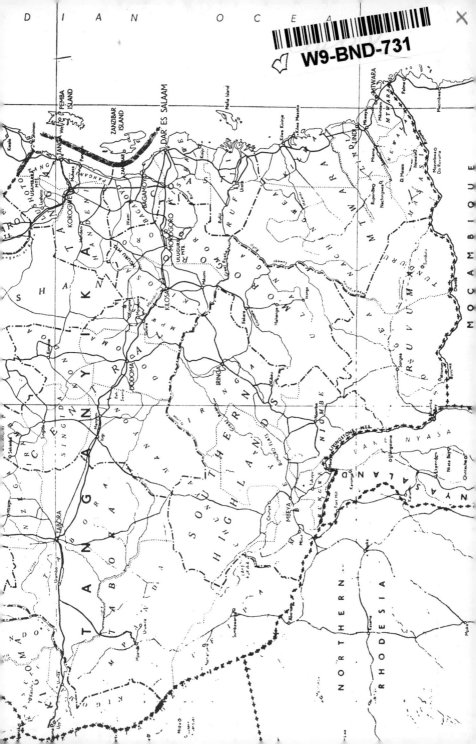

W9-BND-731

Not Yet Uhuru

Not Yet Uhuru

the autobiography of

OGINGA ODINGA

© Oginga Odinga 1967

SOMERSET COUNTY COLLEGE
LIBRARY
North Branch, New Jersey.

HILL AND WANG · NEW YORK

© Oginga Odinga 1967
All rights reserved
Library of Congress catalog card number : 67-26850
First American Edition October 1967

Printed in Great Britain

In the course of our struggle against foreign rule and for independence the decisive contribution was made by the people of Kenya: the unnamed thousands and tens of thousands who acted at crucial times in the national struggle.

When the political temperature was highest the KANU Youth and Women Wings were the greatest single force of our struggle and its nerve centre. Youth wingers at the Coast were led by Msanifu Kombo and Okondo Onyango, in Central Nyanza by Ochola Achola, Ooro No, Were Olonde, and Otuge Omuoso, at Kiambu by Wairoho, at Naivasha by Kigathi, and by Sammy Maina, Akoko Mboya, and Oduya Oprong in Nairobi. The Women's Wing created the political consciousness which sent the women to the polls, and it is they who voted to sweep our first independence government into power. In Nairobi, Margaret Kenyatta and Anna Wanjiku were among the 'Mama' Uhurus' who did splendid work. Central Nyanza women were championed by Magdalina Aboge and Nyangisa Ojino, Owino Ong'ongo, and Mama Uhuru Alima of Mumias, Kakamega District.

The youth and women wingers galvanized the people on whose support we rode to victory; they were never afraid of bullets, tear-gas or jail.

I dedicate this book, the story of my life and political struggle, to the youth of Kenya, my country. As the spirit of the youth carried us through our hardest days in the fight for independence, so on the youth depends the shape of the new Kenya.

Contents

vii

Contents

Illustrations

ix

Acknowledgements

Now that the writing is done I am faced with a task which I fulfil with pleasure, but find by no means easy. I wish to acknowledge with thanks the help of those without whom I would not have undertaken this book. Many hands helped to make these pages, and the degrees of contribution vary. Acknowledgements themselves appear casual and say little about the individuals whose criticisms, suggestions, research findings, technical assistance, and ideas, often expressed in casual conversation, rendered me invaluable service. Those I here mention by no means exhaust the list but, as I have said, I do not find it easy to record in full my indebtedness to friends and colleagues.

My talks with the late Carey Francis, my old teacher, recalled for me a wealth of experience that I was able, in retrospect, to distil and evaluate. My elder brother Abisai, about whom I should say much, Odhiambo Okello, Othigo Othieno, and Rading Omolo provided me with valuable information and advice.

I drew from the experience of many elders among whom Paul Mboya, Simeon Nyende, Anindo Nyakachunga, Timotheo Omondo, Paul Olola, Elijah Masinde and Canon Jeremiah Awori were of great assistance. I am indebted to Tom Okelo-Odongo, B. F. F. Oluande K'Oduol and Odhiambo Masiga, who worked as my private secretaries, and to my good friend and legal adviser, Pranlal Sheth.

I would consider my acknowledgement incomplete without special mention of D. O. Makasembo who played a leading part in the political struggle in Central Nyanza and

xiii

in Kenya as a whole. His untimely death in a motor accident has left a gap which will remain unbridged for long.

The Principal and Secretary of Maseno School kindly allowed me to refer to school records. I must mention with gratitude the work done in typing the manuscript from tapes and in final form by Carolyn Okelo-Odongo and Emma Pinto.

I have told frankly the story of my life and political activity, admitting my mistakes and miscalculations, and trying to write about the early days without too much hindsight—though this might be difficult for anyone to shed completely. I have tried to show that there have been consistent threads running through our struggle from the early years until the present, and that my own policies, though they have travelled a long way since I became involved in village affairs in Nyanza, have been consistent too. I am deeply perturbed that in Kenya today those who sacrificed most in the struggle have lost out to people who played safe in our most difficult days. For the story of the Emergency years I must acknowledge with deep appreciation the information divulged by Bildad Kaggia, J. D. Kali, Kamau Gicholi Githua, and James Beuttah, which they told for publication for the first time. Achieng Oneko gave me information about the early days of KAU, and Jonathan Okwiri about Piny Owacho.

Most important, I am immensely grateful to Ruth First, who has not only edited the manuscript but has also given it shape. This is one of the tasks for which the writer alone bears ultimate responsibility, and in this I am no exception.

Nairobi-Kisumu
June 1966

Not Yet Uhuru

CHAPTER ONE

At the Feet of the Village Elders

AMONG the Luo of Central Nyanza, the forecasters had said of the White people 'If you touch them the skin will remain in your hand because they are very soft. But they will come with thunderstorms and they will burn the people.' Omuodo Alogo was the chief elder of my village and he told me he had seen these people, some of whom were as white as snow, some as red as fire, and that they had an instrument that harboured the thunder, and that hit from afar. When these people first came (the story goes), the elders had warned that we should never, never try to fight them because their weapons were better than ours. They would be intent on devouring our land and our wealth but we should be wary of them. If they asked for cooking flour we should give it; we should give whatever they requested, even animals. But we should study their lives and their minds to know exactly what they wanted. We should never fight them. But we knew that when we had studied them our children would probably be able to get rid of them.

Not that we saw many Whites. The first White man I saw was the missionary Archdeacon Owen. This was the time of a plague outbreak. The children of our village were taken to be inoculated. We were very frightened, for we thought we might die. We allowed the Archdeacon only to touch us, and then ran home as fast as we could. We were lucky we did not catch the plague, for that year it claimed many of our relatives and neighbours. The villagers were told that to stop the plague we should trap the rats, cut off the tails and send them to the Chief's *baraza*. From there, I learnt later, the rats' tails were bundled in tens and sent to Kisumu headquarters; on the walls of the Commissioners' offices hung charts of the monthly rat returns. It was in these years that the government started to collect taxes from our people: taxes and the orders to produce rats' tails have always been associated together as the arm of government reaching out to our villages. When the time came to take a register of taxpayers, government clerks were sent to the villages. Our mothers had news of the approach of these awesome strangers and they hid the children in the bush and brought us food there. We children were curious and we crept out to gaze secretly at the encroachers. We watched them take a papyrus reed from the roof of each hut and cut it neatly in two. When the reeds were tied in neat bundles they represented the registration of that *boma*. One bundle was given to the elder for him to take to the Chief's *baraza* when he paid in the taxes; the other set of bundles was taken away by the clerks as a tally of the taxpayers of the area, a sort of carbon copy of the registration. The clerks who came with the Whites for the tax registration were not people of our tribe; they spoke Swahili and we called them *Okoche*.

We connected Whites and Government with five main things. There were the inoculations against the plague from which the children ran in fear. There were the tax collections. There was the order to the villagers to work on the roads. There were clothes, *kanzu*, the long robes copied from Arab garb at the coast, given free to the chiefs and elders to wear to encourage others in the tribe to clothe themselves in modern dress. There were the schools, which came later, and to which, in the beginning, only orphans, foster children,

2

poor nieces and nephews and never the favourite sons were sent, for the villagers distrusted the pressure on them to send their children out of the home and away from herding the animals; and the more alert objected to the way the Christian missions taught 'This custom (yours) is bad, and this (ours) is good', for they could see that the children at the missions would grow up to despise Luo ways.

One year there were instructions that we should go to the Chief's Camp to be vaccinated against smallpox. The District Commissioner was to be there that day and I was curious to see him, for though I had seen my first White in the person of Archdeacon Owen, it had been a fleeting encounter. A friend and I went towards the Chief's Camp, hoping for a close-up view of the White Commissioner, but as we approached a headman caught us and took us by force to the vaccination centre.

The first time I saw a bicycle was the day we children were given baskets of *sim-sim* and maize to take to the Kadimo Indian shopping centre, about twelve miles from our home. Chief Olulo Nyadenda in a white *kanzu* rode by on a bicycle, passing us so quickly that I was reminded of a snake. He was followed by the District Commissioner flashing past, and they went on to the shops ahead of us. There I had my first glimpse of an Indian. It was astonishing to hear an Indian speaking in Dholuo. His body looked as soft as a baby's when it is newly born. When the Indian came to carry my basket I thought he would never manage to lift it, his body looked so soft. The *sim-sim* I carried to the shop fetched about 25 cents, and with this money I bought a length of material to be used as a loin cloth. When I returned home I did not, of course, wear it to milk the cows. I took it off and hung it on a wooden peg outside the granary. While I was milking, an animal came along and ate my loin cloth. I had had my first piece of clothing for less than a day.

My attempt to calculate my age is associated with clothing.

3

My parents were not educated and they did not register the date of my birth, so I have had to work backwards to estimate it. I remember an old man Elijah Bonyo had a khaki jumper, with a red buttoned flap at the back. Years later when I met Bonyo he told me he had this jersey in 1918. At the time I remember him in the jersey with the flap I had begun to look after our animals, which would have made me a small boy of six or seven years. I can work out my age by association with other events, of course. Immediately after the 1914–18 war there was a severe famine. My mother went away to search for food and I was left to look after my younger sister and a small brother. I fetched vegetables from the bush and cooked them until my mother returned. I must have been at least six years old to have been able to take charge until our mother returned and as the famine was between 1918 and 1919, I think I was born between 1911 and 1912. My mother told me I was born during the short rains which begin normally between September and December. So I place my birth at October 1911.

My home village Nyamira Kango is in Sakwa Location Central Nyanza District, near Lake Nyanza (formerly Lake Victoria: we in Kenya dropped that name in 1964), which is the water link between Kenya, Uganda and Tanganyika. Nyanza Province in the west of Kenya lies across the equator. To our west are the lake and Uganda; to the east the Rift Valley Province with its thick White settlement; and to the south Masai land and Tanzania. The former, Nyanza, which included Western Province and Kericho, has always been known as Kenya's granary and labour pool. The Luo are more agricultural than other Nilotic people, but we keep many cattle and fishing is important along the shores of the lake. Five peoples live in Nyanza: our neighbours are the Baluya, Kisii, Kuria, and the Kipsigis, who live along the high ridges.

My great-grandfather was Rapondi, son of Wenwa. He

4

fathered four sons, among them my grandfather Rayila. According to our clan history Rayila was not a well-to-do man. Nor in fact was his father, nor others further back in our lineage. My father passed down to me the story that Rayila was too poor to afford cattle for a wife. He worked on his plot of land to grow just enough to feed himself. He was lucky to meet a widow who had left her children in her husband's home and come to relatives in Sakwa: my grandfather decided to marry her because for such a woman the dowry was low. So Rayila married Omindo, daughter of Otengo of Konya Kajulu, and together they worked in the fields to raise animals for her dowry. Of this marriage there were six sons and two daughters. Rayila combined providence with frugality. He had a premonition that a great famine was approaching so he and Omindo dug a deep hole in the centre of their hut, where they buried a pot and stored a portion of the grain from every harvest. The famine did come and the neighbours were astonished that this poor man could feed his family. We children had this story recounted to us for the moral that without the land none of us could survive, and we should not fail each morning to go to work on our plots.

Rayila's sons were Oburu, Ngire, Omuodo, Otengo, Amolo, and Ajuma. It was the last-born, Ajuma, who married my mother, but Ajuma died shortly after the birth of their second child. My grandfather had taken a second wife after Omindo and by this marriage had produced three sons, Ochieng, Odinga, and Rayila, named after himself. When Ajuma died his half-brother Odinga took my mother into his household, according to the tradition that the widow is cared for by her brother-in-law. Odinga had two previous wives, so my mother became his third. I was born of that union. In all we were three brothers and two sisters in our mother's house.

Of my uncles, Oburu was the administrator, a liberal and

popular man; Ngire was a strict disciplinarian who dealt ruthlessly with mischievous, gossiping women. Omuodo was a man of justice, chosen by his brothers as a leader to judge village cases and solidify the people of the village; it was Omuodo above all who was the unifying force among his brothers and their respected chairman. I was Omuodo's favourite. I had always to be at his feet. He called me to bring his fire for smoking, to fetch his food, and we ate together in his small office-house. Omuodo was the leader not only of our family but of all the families in our neighbourhood. He was stern and ruthless when dealing with transgressors, and I pitied those who fell foul of his judgement, but though he was strict and quick to act against the lazy, he showed no partiality towards his sons or those of his brothers, but laid down the law fairly against relatives and outsiders alike.

In among the thick hillside vegetation of the Sakwa area lie fields of maize and millet, and clusters of homesteads of thatched huts. Our village, like all Luo villages, was neatly fenced about by euphorbia trees or 'Ojuok' as we call them. Inside the circular village were twenty neatly built huts, forming a concentric circle within the fence. In the centre were four small huts which we regarded as the headquarters of the elders of the village. The one in the centre was the *duol* or office of the Jaduong Dala, or chief elder. He was Omuodo Alogo. Next to this hut was the office of Odinga, my father; then that of Oteke, the uncle of Omuodo Alogo; and the fourth belonged to a friend who had married one of our sisters and come to live in our village. Each hut in the village represented one woman. Elder Omuodo Alogo had six women, Odinga had five, Oteke had three, and so on. In all there were thirty-six children in the village. Omuodo Alogo was regarded as owner of the village, leader and lawmaker and the giver of orders. He had to consult with the other elders, and they formed themselves into a kind of

6

village cabinet to regulate village life and maintain discipline.

Head of our family, head of the village and accepted as leader of the surrounding villages was Omuodo Alogo and by virtue of his leadership our home became the headquarters of our area. Many people called on us each day. They came to discuss a problem with Omuodo Alogo or to attend a meeting he called. Though Omuodo's father and grandfather had been poor people he was well-to-do by African standards. He was also generous and refused no one in need of a dowry who had no animals of his own. He gave frequent beer parties and from the songs about him I knew he was praised for his charity, wisdom, and far-sightedness. I was with Omuodo during the 1918–19 famine called the *Kanga*, and I have never forgotten his actions. He would fetch me late every night and take me from granary to granary to examine the food stocks. When we found a granary with little left in it he would direct me to a granary which had plenty, and we would replenish the almost exhausted store. When I asked why he did this he said we should be kind to those who had nothing. Women with many children had greater need, and to prevent argument over food shares, he thought it best to arrange a re-distribution himself, by night. When it came to disciplinary action Omuodo was cruel and ruthless, but when he was ill people came long distances to see him and wish for his speedy recovery. He died one evening in 1934 and many people came to mourn, taking off all their clothes and daubing themselves with ash—the dress of mourning—in ceremonial tribute and respect for Omuodo. The weeping and wailing went on all night and I recalled the grim scene for many years.

Life in our village followed an even routine. The elders woke first each morning, got their pangas ready and went to prepare their plots for the work that would follow that day. The children were awakened by them as they were leaving for the land, and our first duty was to milk the cows. We delivered the milk to the huts where the women, with the young girls at their side, were waiting to churn the butter. When we boys had done the milking we tied the animals near the granaries and ran to our houses to drink milk with *kuon* (a millet flour bread that is red in colour) which had been prepared the day before. Then we went to the land to dig the ground cleared by our fathers. Sometimes we worked in groups, at other times we worked our fathers' individual holdings. While we dug, the very young children were in charge of grazing the goats and the sheep. At about ten o'clock our fathers left the land and returned to the village. An hour or so later we boys had to return home to release the cattle from their stakes and take them into the grazing field. This was the time we enjoyed, for we arranged between ourselves for some of us to tend the animals while the rest took part in games. We wrestled and raced one another. If there was a pond nearby we swam. The elders were always at a distance supervising us, watching to see if our animals strayed into a garden, and when we neglected our duties they appeared among us to chastise us. By midday the women had returned to the village to prepare our food and cultivate the vegetable plots, assisted by the girls. In the afternoon the elders went back to the lands to clear the areas we would have to dig the following day, and some of the boys were taken with them to learn how best to clear the bush. In the evening we brought the cows home and milked them, leaving the milk in the churns for the next morning's butter. Then we had to clean and sweep the village while our fathers sat in their offices and watched us at work. It was in the evenings that our fathers would meet the elders from nearby villages. The women would bring beer and the men would drink it as they talked, exchanging the news, whether anyone had gone on safari, and they would discuss the work they were planning for the village for subsequent days. The

8

women were ready with the food at about seven o'clock and the elders sat in their respective offices to be served with it. The children from each hut had to carry the food to the elder and this was the time that the sons joined their fathers to enjoy the food prepared in the various huts. Some women had cooked vegetables, others fish, meat or chicken, and all taken together there was a variety of dishes. But the elders were strict about our eating, encouraging us to eat more *kuon*, or *cassava*, rather than meat, and reprimanding the boys who ate greedily. When the evening meal was over we sat at the feet of the elders, for now they would gather in the office of the chief village elder and discuss the problems of the village. We boys listened attentively. The elders might instruct us about our duties, or they might tell stories.

The stories of the elders were one of our two sources of education in the village. The other source was the harpists who played an important role in the community. The harpists learnt at the feet of the elders and expressed the peoples' philosophy in musical and poetic language. The Luo people live around the lake and their harpists drew imagery and source of inspiration from the water. Through their songs the harpists chanted words of inspiration to the warriors; praised famous wrestlers; admired beautiful girls; recognized keen farmers whose granaries were always full. Their humour was entertaining. They acknowledged men who were experts at courting, and through whom others managed to secure wives. They praised men and women who had achieved distinction in the community. They condemned thieves, lazy people, cowards and people with bad habits. In the community the harpists were a recognized institution awarding approval to individual and communal achievements, and admonishing and reprimanding those who did not come up to standard.

The greatest among the modern harpists, Otuoma, warned that we fight for water and land and that our aim is to attack the enemy's heart and defend our eyes. But, however victorious we may be, there is always an end and our brave ones pass away leaving behind only their names for us to remember. He sang that water was the source of inspiration, wisdom, and life and he used the analogy of water as the source of transmitting understanding of current affairs. A rough translation of a part of one of his songs runs as follows:—

The sea, how great are you
that your message suffers no blow
for the tide, so faithful a servant
conveys your power and presence.

True, is it not true, that
the tide, so efficient and sure,
at your shore does surrender
the mighty message to the mountain.

Between the mountain peaks does the
message signal the affairs current
to the wilderness so quiet and steady
and the wind takes over the performance.

From the wise, calm and great doctor
the wilderness in other words they say,
summons the wind to move with the
message for our ears to receive.

At about nine o'clock, after hearing the elders, we went to bed, leaving the elders talking among themselves. Young boys and girls slept together in their grandmothers' houses, and we were told stories of the past. The older boys went to sleep in the *simba*, a dormitory built near the gates by the grown-up boys who were yet unmarried. Boys grown too big to live in the houses of the old women stayed in the dormitory house and there became acquainted with girls from other villages, and had dances at night. We were never allowed to drink anything alcoholic, only milk or thin porridge, and the elders were strict about this. Generally young people who had to be disciplined for failing to fetch firewood, or failing to milk the animals or work in the gardens were singled out by the elders. But they were not reprimanded directly; the elders would report the child to his mother and she would have to call him to order. If the mother resisted the disciplining of her child she could be driven out of the village, and kept out for some time, even for months. I can remember this happening in our family. I had neglected our animals one day but notwithstanding that my mother gave me food that evening. My mother was considered far too protective towards a boy who had done no work and we had both to spend three days out of the village, my brothers were left alone and our gardens untended. This was an admonition that could not be taken lightly. In our custom this is not really a harshness directed against the women, but an insistence that women are the custodians of the children, and their educators: if the children misbehaved it was their mother who had to be shown the error of her ways.

Women took second place in the conduct of many affairs but they also had an important role to play. They were the custodians not only of the children, but also of the granary, and theirs was the responsibility to conserve food for times of drought and famine. The clans were named after women in recognition that they are the mothers of the children and thus the founders of the clans. No marriage could be solemnized without the presence of the mother as well as the father, and even in the case of divorced and separated couples, both parents came together once more for the marriage ceremony of their children. Older women who became wealthy as a result of their diligence were consulted on many questions and in some instances there were women chairmen of elders' councils. We were taught that a good statesman would not give precipitate judgement, but would defer his decision; when an elder said 'I must consult the pillow before I make a judgement' it was understood that he would discuss it with the women.

Each clan—there were about two dozen in all Luoland—was a gathering of sub-clans and had its own chief (*ruoth*). The *ruoth* worked closely with the *ajuoke* and *jobilo* (the prophet-diviner), the warrior leader, and the council of elders. Each clan was entirely self-dependent. It had its own territory and its own leadership and in the old days had acted independently in war. Outstanding *jobilo* or warrior leaders were recognized beyond their own clans and tribe but there was no paramount leadership of the Luo. A chief did not issue orders. He sounded out the elders, met them in consultation and when he said 'This is my decision' he was announcing not his personal verdict but an agreed point of view. His function was not to lay down the law, but to consult and arbitrate to learn the concensus of opinion, and to keep the unity of his people. Elders were men of substance and integrity, and recognized as outstanding individuals. Even when they came from leading lineages they did not inherit leadership but had to demonstrate it. Diligence yielded prosperity and brought respect, but riches alone did not count for leadership, and a rich man who was offensive was not respected.

In the village the authority of the elders was much respected, indeed it was never challenged. The elder gave the signal that the season for clearing the fields, planting, weeding or harvesting had begun. The elder was the first man in the village to build a granary, and the first wife of the head of the village was the woman who gave the signal to bring in and store the harvest. No villager would have dreamt of opening a season without the initiation of the work by the elder. No one was permitted even to taste the maize from the land or bring it for cooking before the chief elder's first wife had cooked her new season's maize and eaten it in her house. It was a bad omen and a breach of village discipline not to wait for the chief elder to act first, and the land elders—the *jodong gweng*—regulated all activities connected with our land.

The Luo regarded the land as their mother, and the tribe as a whole was the proprietor of all the land in its area. Within the tribe, clan or sub-clan the individual laid claim to a *shamba*, or several, depending on his diligence, but he used the land for the benefit of his family only as long as he lived in the community; as soon as he left to live elsewhere the land reverted to the community and was allocated to the nearest neighbour or given to a newcomer joining the community. A piece of land left uncultivated for a season could be used for grazing by anyone in the clan, without his having to ask permission or pay a fee. (Even animals were strictly speaking not private but community property, and a man who was unable to raise animals for his dowry would ask for help from a relation or a neighbour who was under an obligation to help him acquire a wife, for marriage was considered a community obligation, and children the gain of the community as a whole.)

Common ownership of the land was accompanied by a system of communal cultivation. You had your own plot but you helped others dig, plant, and weed theirs and your turn to be helped came round in strict rota. When the village worked your land you supplied food and water; when you helped others they fed you. This is where the role of the village elders in regulating the work of the seasons was so important. The system was known as *saga* farming. Communities of anything from two to five hundred people, headed by the elders, decided which shambas would be farmed each season and then plot by plot, from those alongside the river to those extending to the hill tops, all would work side by side. This concerted farming could work only if it was highly disciplined, which it was; it was understood

13

that all should take part in the work; the midday meal was carried to the fields so any malingerer who was not at work on the shambas would not eat that day.

Land disputes that arose were always settled by the *jodong gweng* who manipulated our flexible system of land tenure and made adjustments for individuals within the community with the consent of the community. There were many who lived and worked on the land of friends, neighbours, and relatives. If there was a shortage of land in any one area, people could move to live among another clan, on its stretch of land.

Under the system of Luo land tenure and saga farming, individual land ownership was not entrenched, and co-operation was a spirit in which the people were deeply steeped. It might be said that this traditional Luo farming was halfway to socialism. Shambas were allocated so that there should be equal sharing of the land near and far from the river, equal allocation of plots suitable for different crops like cotton and maize, and a sharing of plots that could be worked in the different seasons. The very dispersal of plots worked by one family was deliberate and a form of equality.

This was ignored by government land consolidation teams when they started work in the fifties. The opposition to the teams and to government agriculture policy in general, lay in the fact that plans for reforming our agriculture flew in the face of our most deep-rooted practices. Land consolidation meant the gathering of all a man's land fragments into a single holding and their registration in individual title deeds; the cardinal principle of Luo land ownership is that land was transferable for use in the community. Whereas, under the traditional system of farming, all, even newcomers to an area, were accommodated and allocated land to farm, people feared that when the land was consolidated and they could produce no direct claim to a shamba, they would have nowhere to live. The way that improved farming methods, and even land consolidation for more economic use of labour on the land, could work, would have been by consolidating and registering the land not of individuals, but of the clan or sub-clan as a whole. But the government did not try to understand the Luo method of land allocation, or the rhythm of our saga farming, and the people were resentful and suspicious of anything imposed by government.

My first experience of the government of Kenya was in our home when my cousin, Migaya Oburu, the government-appointed headman, came from attending the Chief's *baraza* to tell people the government's orders and requirements for our locality. Omuodo Alogo had himself been asked to act as government headman, but he had refused, saying that he had no wish to be sent about by the Whites as a little child. He deputed his nephew Migaya instead.

The District Commissioner was remote from the people. He lived in Kisumu and we heard about him as the head of all the chiefs, but the people never or rarely saw him. The Provincial Commissioner seemed like a king, so far away and exalted that we doubted his existence. As we heard there was a King and a Governor, so we heard there was a Provincial Commissioner: we knew little about him. The government was feared rather than respected. Agricultural instructors came to inspect our fields for cotton, but they never taught us anything. They only asked questions and if we did not answer quickly or did not give them the answers they wanted, they beat us with a hippo whip. Veterinary inspectors came too, but they wanted to be respected as chiefs, and they accepted as good and loyal only those villagers who gave them beer parties and presents. As a boy I watched from a distance the goings-on at the *barazas*. The Chief was harsh in both his language and his treatment of the people, and did not hesitate to slap an elder if the man did not stand quickly or sit where he was told. Any instructions given to the people were accompanied by beatings. The *askari kanga* was cruel and weighed heavily into the people singled out by the Chief. When the District Commissioner was due at a *baraza*, the atmosphere was tense and the people were frightened. As the Commissioner approached all had to stand and if you were slow to rise to your feet the askaris might seize a chair and hit out with it. Sometimes people were beaten to a point of helplessness and near death. The Government, I decided, had come not to help us but to instil fear into us, and, out of fear, obedience. The Commissioner was remote, yet his power was felt. It was the chiefs and the headmen responsible to the Commissioner who moved constantly among the people. The *milango* had the duty of collecting taxes and carrying orders from government to the people. The Chief's main duty was to report to the *baraza* and to ensure his villagers' attendance there.

My memory is still clear of one *baraza* which was bigger than all the others, flocked to from far and wide. It was held about 25 miles from my home at a place called Lundha in Gem Location. It was said that the great roars of the people 'This land is ours' had made the sheep and the goats break loose from their tethering posts and run into the bush. Politics had begun to rise in the country in about 1920.

The author (*right foreground*) talking to Ker Joel-Omer at his village house in Sakwa, Central Nyanza.

The author (*left*) in Maseno school uniform, 1934. On the right is Fanuel Akolo.

Mrs Mary Juma Odinga.

Aneurin Bevan speaking at a Bombay reception during the author's visit to India, 1953.

CHAPTER TWO

The Rise of Politics

In the beginning Britain was more concerned to collect spheres of influence than colonies in East Africa, but the process of the first becoming the second was inevitable. In the scramble for Africa that started in the seventies of the last century, Britain and Germany parcelled out shares of the territories they coveted and handed them over, in the initial stages, to chartered companies. This was to be a cheap and easy way of holding territories against outsiders. For Britain, Uganda was vital: she was the key to the lake system of the interior and the headwaters of the Nile, and was a basis for expansion northwards to the Sudan and Egypt. When the chartered companies wanted to pull out of the East African territories because of the cost of holding them, Britain had to step in to declare a protectorate over Uganda in 1893, and over Kenya (then East Africa) in 1895.

The decisive event in opening up Kenya was the building of the railway. This reached Nairobi in 1899 and Lake Nyanza two years later. It was not long before White settlement was encouraged as the only way to carry the financial burden of maintaining the railway and the administration. At the beginning of 1902 there were half a dozen settlers in the country; by 1903 there were a hundred round Nairobi. That year Lord Delamere, who had been to East Africa on safari, acquired a free grant of 100,000 acres at Njoro, and the same year the prospects of settlement in Kenya were being advertised in South Africa.

Kisumu, the capital of Nyanza, had originally been the railhead for the Uganda railway, and from there passengers and cargo embarked on the steamers en route for Kampala. But later the railway was carried up over the high ground serving the settlers of Eldoret. Kisumu was left high and dry on a branch line.

Nyanza Province was previously part of Uganda and was called the Nandi Protectorate. On 1 April 1902 it was transferred to Kenya, then still known as the East Africa Protectorate, and given its new name of Nyanza. The boundary decided upon by the Foreign Office divided the tribal lands of the Luo and Abaluya peoples. Those made part of Kenya still looked towards Uganda for some time. When Kenya Colony was proclaimed it was the Arabs in Uganda who prompted a wave of alarm among the Luo by warning: 'You are part of a colony, so this means you have no land . . . the land belongs to the King of England. . . .'

Hut tax was collected for the first time in 1900, but it was not until some years after the start of the century that the British system of administration began to take hold of Nyanza. Early visitors took over the name Kavirondo which the Arab caravans had once used and gave the same name to all the peoples living in Nyanza, though they comprise totally distinct groups. The same hit-and-miss method was used by the colonial administration in imposing rulers on the people. The first missionaries to enter Nyanza met Mumia, Paramount Chief of the Baluyha (Nabongo), at a time when the Whites still did not differentiate between the Luo and the Baluyha, and for a time Mumia was recognized as Paramount Chief of all Nyanza. Men from many villages were conscripted to serve the chiefs, and my father was among those taken to form a bodyguard for Mumia. He was dressed in a stiff uniform and taught to drill and salute. His

demonstrations when he was again home among us of how to march in formation, wheel left and right and present arms greatly amused the young boys of our village.

The appointment of Mumia as Paramount Chief over all Nyanza was the cause of trouble when the chiefs of Uyoma rose against this decision and soldiers were sent in to pacify the area. There was shooting at Kisii in 1907 when the people objected to the British sending in askaris to commandeer flour, and seized the containers from the hands of the soldiers and threw them away; and trouble arose again the year after in South Nyanza. But for the most part there were no armed confrontations between the people and the new rulers, who set about moulding the old system to fit their method of administration. Where the people clung to their customs, the penal sanction could always be applied, as was done in instances when the people carried out their marriage custom called *mako nyako* (according to Luo tradition the bride never says 'yes' as consent, but the groom's party has to help her make up her mind by pulling her along to the ceremony) and the groom found himself sentenced to six months' imprisonment, because this tradition was alien to the new religion and the new ways of government.

Our Luo system of government was by consent and after consultation between the elders. As I have described, the clan head did not inherit his position but, once he belonged to the right lineage, had to prove his leadership qualities and use them to interpret tribal tradition and weld the agreement of his people. His strength derived from his closeness to the elders and his people. The British changed that. They did not want leaders in whom the people had confidence, but men who could be used for their purposes. When chiefs and headmen came to be selected, men whom the British found in positions of leadership were frequently by-passed, and others installed over them. We had a dramatic experience of how this was done on one occasion in Sakwa Location.

One, Jasakwa, had gone for a while to live in Kano where he had learned to speak Swahili. When the time came for administration to be extended to Sakwa, he was sent on ahead to his home to clear the way for the Whites. He met the elders of Sakwa and told them 'New people are coming, the White people. They have dangerous weapons. Don't fight them, but try to make a treaty with them.' The elders did not all agree with him, but as they talked the party of British was approaching. The chief sent Jasakwa the messenger to greet them with gifts. But he had decided to cast himself in a different role. 'The Chief says he cannot meet you,' he told the British. 'He is the leader and it is not, he says, his duty to welcome strangers. I myself bring you these gifts.' This interpreter was proclaimed chief of the location. When the people objected, saying 'We have our Chief, the man you have appointed is his messenger and interpreter,' the British would not listen, and there was trouble during which the real Chief and some of the elders were sent to prison.

Interpreters were in a key position to ingratiate themselves, and inveigle themselves into positions of authority. It was the chiefs who were first asked to send their sons among the British to be trained as interpreters, but they refused because they feared to lose their sons. So they sent subordinates who, when they returned, had not only a new language and access to the new government, but also a body of askaris with them to enforce their will.

There was not always a consistent way of appointing chiefs. Sometimes individuals were chosen arbitrarily; in other cases there was some attempt at getting the clan to arrive at a popular choice. In many cases the people were given as chiefs individuals whom they would not have chosen themselves. Above all, the candidates for chieftainship had to be acceptable to the District Commissioner—and District Commissioners often manipulated in the Locations to have their favoured candidates imposed. Administration instructions make no bones about the position of a chief. I quote from a District circular: 'A chief is the direct agent of the government in his location; his position is much the same as that of a district commissioner. . . . All over Kenya every chief has certain general functions and duties which go with his appointment. Among these are activity to maintain a spirit of loyalty to the British Crown, and to inculcate such spirit . . . to see that all lawful orders are obeyed by the African inhabitants of his location. It is the Chief's duty to collect tax in his location . . . he must take a continuous personal interest in the collection of tax.'[1]

Chiefs were no longer the custodians of their peoples' tribal law and custom; they were now civil servants, pensionable, but also subject to instant dismissal by the government. They were the expression of the power of the new government in the village. They could use their position to amass and exercise personal power, something which was previously unheard of among the Luo.

White settlement, White government, and land alienation went hand in hand in Kenya. In 1908 the British Government granted exclusive rights of occupancy to people of European descent in an undefined area of highland country assumed to be unoccupied by African tribes. Later Orders-In-Council and associated legislation precluded Africans from occupying the land as tenant farmers, forcing them to be either wage labourers or squatters. White occupation swallowed up vast areas until, according to Hailey[2] 'About half of the land in Kenya worth cultivating lay in what came to be called the White Highlands.' The African reserves contained a considerable part of the uncultivable land and so was created a landless and poverty-stricken peasantry. Kikuyu country was

[1] Circular of District Commissioner for Meru, November 1941.
[2] Hailey—*An African Survey*, p. 751.

in the heart of White settlement. Vast areas of land were lost to this people which bore the heaviest burden of settler oppression.

From the beginning of White settlement the government, having enticed settlers out to Kenya with generous offers of land, was obliged to provide them with labour. The toll that White rule exacted from Nyanza was labour, not land. Our province became the country's largest labour reserve. When voluntary labour was slow in coming forward, ordinances for contract labour were issued, like the notorious Labour Circular of 1919 under which the government took powers for the compulsory requisitioning of Africans for 'public purposes' and for portering for sixty days of the year. Young men left Nyanza for workplaces far and wide in the country. My elder brother worked on a settler farm, earning 4 shillings a month with *posho* and a second brother worked near Voi on the rail to the coast. The District Commissioners issued labour quotas to chiefs and headmen, and the chiefs were turned into labour recruiters. Chiefs were subject to pressure and bribery to exact more and more labour from their areas and recruiting methods became a major grievance among the people. Chiefs or sub-chiefs, issued with an order for labour, arbitrarily picked batches of forty men at a time from a location, and had them signed up for a six-month work contract under which it was a penal offence to decamp.

During the First World War Nyanza was milked dry for carriers, many thousands of whom never returned to their homes but died of disease in service, though they wore no soldiers' uniforms. It was during the war, too, that land leases were extended for the White settlers from 99 to 999 years. The African harvest of the war victory was anything but a reward. Hut tax had been doubled from five rupees to ten and though it was cut to eight rupees in 1921 the settlers, affected by a fall in world prices, enforced a one-third cut in wages of all Africans. The law for the compulsory carrying

23

of kipandes (every African over the age of 16 to carry a fingerprinted card) had been passed in 1915 and was rigorously enforced in 1921. Complaints of harsh treatment by chiefs and headmen and district officers began to seep through to the government authorities. There was the case, for instance, of heads of clans who were detained at the administrative headquarters for a week on a charge of slackness, and of clan elders who were given a stroke on the buttocks for each hut on which tax had been ordered to be paid and was overdue. A headman who was reported to have disobeyed an order to bring in porters was compelled to carry loads himself.

The beginnings of the African nationalist movement in Kenya must be traced to those years during and immediately after the First World War. Kikuyu and Luo—barely knowing one another and separated from one another by 150 miles—were beginning to rise. In Kikuyu country the stolen lands and the hated kipande were penetrating grievances and their battle to regain their land in the heart of White settlement made the Kikuyu people the spearhead of our national resistance. In Nyanza the people were restive under heavy taxes and compulsory labour, of women and children as well as men; their alarm grew when Kenya was annexed as a Crown Colony and more and more government camps came to be set up among the locations.

Kikuyu elders, led by Harry Thuku, began an agitation for their peoples' rights. Was the reward for their services during the war to be the loss of their land, the imposition of the kipande and the increase of taxes? they asked. In Eldoret James Beuttah, working in the post office as a telegraph operator, was 'borrowing' sheets of government letter paper from post office stock and helping Thuku frame petitions to the government. This was the birth of Thuku's Young Kikuyu Association. On joining, YKA members took an oath binding them not to sell their land to strangers.

24

There were plans too for an East African Association to unite the tribes. Beuttah who had been a telegraph operator in the post office at Maseno visited Kisumu and addressed large meetings. The people raised ninety rupees and sent it to YKA headquarters in Nairobi. Kikuyu, Luo, and Abaluhya representatives met in Nairobi to talk about organizing in defence of their rights.

In Nyanza small meetings were being called at night, for the people were hiding their first sallies into organization. The people were agitated at the East Africa Protectorate becoming Kenya Colony, annexed to the British Crown. A group went to a District Commissioner to say that they did not like what the Europeans were doing, and they rejected the Colony.

'Who asked you to say that?' the spokesmen were asked. 'Who is behind you?'

To this question came the reply: 'Piny Owacho.' (The Country Says.)

Government interpreter Jairo Owino told the District Commissioner that Chiefs Odindo and Ogada were behind the movement. The two Chiefs were summoned to appear before the authorities. But it was neither Odindo nor Ogada, the people insisted, but 'Piny Owacho': 'The Country says'.

Jonathan Okwiri, one of our first teachers, was among those who summoned the great meeting at Lundha at North Gem in Central Nyanza. The interpreter, eyes and ears of the government, told the Commissioner that the people were assembled not for a meeting, but for war. The crowd had assembled when Okwiri and other elders heard that the government was coming with a large force. Over-ruling his protests, Okwiri hid Chief Ogada. When the armed police came they encircled the crowd. Jonathan Okwiri remembers the events as though they happened only yesterday.

'Why are you here?' asked District Commissioner Montgomery, a brother of Field-Marshal Montgomery.

25

'We are here because we are trying to make our future policy.'

'I've heard that you want only war.'

'But you find us in a crowd like this! When we want war we do not gather in one place; we scatter in different places with our spears and clubs.'

Okwiri challenged the police to search for weapons. If they found any they would know the people did want war.

'If I find spears, about twenty, what shall I tell you?' the District Commissioner asked. 'You search. If you find them you will do what you like.'

The police were sent to search the environs of the meeting. They searched for hours, over a radius of about 4 miles, and all the while the crowd remained sitting, under police guard. When the police returned they told the Commissioner they had found nothing. 'But when we look at the crowd,' they said, 'we see these are people who want war.'

The District Commissioner turned to Okwiri and others who seemed prominent in the crowd. 'Tell me what you want to tell the government.'

But the people wanted to meet without him, he was told.

The Commissioner refused to leave the meeting. Jacob Ochola started to recount the peoples' grievances, one by one. Then he stopped. 'But we can't go on with the meeting. Those guns all around us, they frighten us.' The District Commissioner suggested that the police should withdraw 400 yards. They were still too near, said Ochola and he added: 'We have no food for your soldiers if they stay here; take them home and we will send you a letter.'

The District Commissioner said: 'Can you write a letter?'

'You will get a letter in two days,' the chairman of the meeting replied.

The government officials had to leave the meeting.

The police were withdrawn to the government camp some miles away, and a trainload of Kings African Rifles bound for the area (because there had been reports in Nairobi of war brewing in Nyanza) was stopped.

The meeting went on through the night. Ten points were written out for the District Commissioner.

1. We want to have an organization, and a President in our country.
2. We want the poll tax to be decreased.
3. When the District Commissioner comes to collect poll tax let him not take our men to carry the money to Kisumu; he must use his own men.
4. When the District Commissioner comes on tour he must not ask us to feed him and his men with our cattle, our eggs.
5. We don't want forced labour, i.e. to work on the roads for no pay.
6. We want our Chiefs to have power.
7. We want better salaries for the Chiefs.
8. We want better education.
9. We are against the young people being sent to work on the farms.
10. We do not like the way we are being punished, caned for minor offences.

When he received the letter the District Commissioner passed it on to the Provincial Commissioner. The government report for the year said: 'It is evident that feeling ran high among the rising generation.'

The great Lundha meeting which launched the Young Kavirondo Association and from which the government had been excluded took place two days before Christmas in 1921. Nyanza was throbbing with tension and it was apparent that the government had been taken completely unawares. In February Luo people all over Nyanza held a giant *baraza*, at Nyahera, not far from Kisumu. The meeting started at eight in the morning and went on until eight at night, and the people expounded on their ten points. Once again the people complained about the change from Protectorate to Colony, about the high rate of hut and poll tax, about forced labour.

The *baraza* was given its say. But government also warned the missions to order their adherents to stop their political activity, and threatened the deportation of Africans who continued to attend the secret meetings. The Governor, Sir Edward Northey, visited Nyanza himself to warn that mass meetings were dangerous and grievances should be laid before the District Commissioners.

Nearer the capital Harry Thuku was touring Kikuyu and Embu areas voicing the grievances of the people. Thousands flocked to mass meetings to hear Thuku speak. A general strike was called—the first in Kenya and one of the earliest recorded on the African Continent. In March 1922—a month after the government warning in Nyanza against 'agitators'—Thuku was arrested and held at Nairobi police station pending deportation as 'dangerous to peace and good order'. When the people heard that Harry Thuku was arrested they began to protest. Large crowds of people assembled round the police station where their leader was being held. The police opened fire and twenty-five were shot dead.

Thuku was sent into exile and the Young Kikuyu Association was banned. But the people were not cowed. On the surface they might have appeared to be quiet, but they were boiling underneath. They met secretly in the forests in groups of three and four to discuss how to raise money to pay lawyers, how to have Thuku released, how to make representations to reform their banned movement. This lesson in how to organize an underground political movement was to prove vital political experience a critical twenty years later. After some years the Young Kikuyu Association re-emerged as the Kikuyu Central Association (under a government restriction to confine membership to Kikuyu) under Joseph Kangethe and Jesse Kariuki. In 1926 Jomo Kenyatta, to become President of Kenya four decades later, left his employment with the Nairobi municipal council to become KCA general secretary and editor of its paper *Mwigwithania* (Work and Prayer).

In Nyanza the government was alarmed at the emergence of 'Piny Owacho' and sought for a way to divert it. The people never got the political rights or the association that they had demanded. At the instance of Archdeacon Owen, the head of the Church Mission Society at Maseno, the Young Kavirondo Association was turned into the Kavirondo Taxpayers' Welfare Association. Owen himself became President. This was in 1923.

29

CHAPTER THREE

The White Hand of Authority

Piny Owacho became general talk in our village. It was a sign of changing times. So was the great noise I heard overhead one day, a noise that grew and grew as if the whole countryside was being shaken. I ran to hide. This was one of the first aeroplanes to fly over our part of the country.

Most of my days I spent on the hillsides, grazing the animals, among them my two goats and sheep. I had longed for possessions. I appealed to my father, when we were working together in the fields one day, for a small plot to plant my own crops. I tended that piece of ground morning and evening, until it was ready for planting. After harvest time I built my own granary and stored the food I had grown. I kept chickens which I fed by trapping white ants.

I was a thin and not a physically strong boy, but I never surrendered to a rival in a fight. I remember the battle royal I fought over a beautiful dancing stick I had made. I loved dancing and singing and I was often at the gate of my village watching for dancing groups going by. One day I was at the gate with my stick, which I had made handsomely rounded at the top, and I joined up with a dancing group, but one of the party pounced on me and seized my stick, saying that a small boy was not worthy of it. I jumped upon this man, kicking and yelling, but he pushed me off. The group was already moving down the road, but I chased after them shouting 'Give me back my stick. It is my stick and I must have it.' The chase went on for about eight miles. Then the leader of the dancing group repented, or maybe he did not want to have a shouting small boy spoil the entrance of his dancers into the arena. I was bruised and bleeding by now, having made several attempts to snatch back my stick. At last they handed it back to me. I had won, but I had to walk the eight miles home.

One year Abisai Ajuang, my eldest stepbrother, came home from working in Nairobi and began to teach me what he knew of reading and writing. Each night he improvised a lamp of an old rag dipped in cow's fat and mounted on a stick and I began to learn the first line of the alphabet and my first arithmetic table. This was when I was about ten, and the time of the opening of the Maranda Primary School. Some members of our family went to the school and a cousin and I took them food. On the way we talked about learning to write ourselves. A band of evangelists passed us on the road one day, singing about how they, the 'clothed men', had improved the country. I was impressed by their singing and thought that if I went to school I might sing as well, and learn how to 'improve' the country so that I could share in the self-praise. A few years after my stepbrother had begun my home tuition I was taken to Mzee Shadrach Osewe who was running the Maranda Primary School. By June 1926 I had become a boarder at the school. The fees were paid in millet or maize. My father was reluctant to pay but when he visited the school and saw me parade with the school children he became interested. There were times when I played truant from classes, hiding in my mother's house, with my mother acting willing accomplice to my truancy, but my elder brother, Albert Adur, and my stepbrother Abisai routed me out and sent me back to school, on the advice of Mzee Shadrach Osewe who said I was a good student and needed to be trained.

Maranda Primary School had a day school and a boarding section. We boarders numbered about one hundred, and came from all over the province, from North, Central, and South Nyanza. I had a chance to make friends not only with Luo from many different parts but also with Abaluhyas. We were told to hold meetings in the dormitories and to elect prefects who would keep strict discipline. In my first years at school I was elected our dormitory's food distributor. Food at the school was very scarce, and water had to be fetched far from the school, for Maranda is a dry place, and we used to walk near my home, about three miles from the school, to fetch water for cooking. The students had to grind the corn and cook their own meals. Some of us were poor cooks and the food at Maranda was wretched.

At the end of 1927 Maranda pupils were selected to sit the common entrance examination for admission to Maseno school. Maranda is 35 miles from Maseno and its stone school buildings and church; we set out on foot to write the examinations. The Maseno principal recorded my age as ten years, but this could not have been my age, for a boy of ten could not have managed the long walk from Maranda to Maseno; I was nearer sixteen. I hated my first sight of Maseno: the food was bad and we were roughly treated. We were told to go home and collect the fees of 60 shillings, and then to return to the school to be admitted. I had decided firmly against Maseno. I went instead to the home of an uncle on my mother's side, lingering there the whole year, until Mzee Shadrach Osewe fetched me, at my brother's insistence.

Mzee Osewe knew I was not keen to go to Maseno and he tried, at the beginning of 1929, to have me apprenticed as a telegraphist in the post office. Archdeacon Owen took me to the Maseno principal, Mr Carey Francis, to ask for a recommendation for the post office job. Carey Francis seemed to be impressed with me, said I was still young and urged me to study at Maseno. That was the last thing I wanted. The interview closed with Carey Francis insisting that I stay at Maseno, but the following day a friend and I decided to run away. We went to Kisumu where my friend's father worked as an *askari kanga*. By the time we reached Kisumu the news of our flight had reached Mzee Osewe, and someone was sent to Kisumu to fetch us back. My friend's father sent us roughly from him with a good thrashing and we ran from Kisumu to Sakwa in a day, a journey of about 40 miles. I was home again the following morning, exhausted and crestfallen. Carey Francis had heard that we could not pay the school fees so his mother offered me a scholarship of 20 shillings, leaving my father to find the remaining 40 shillings. My father and brothers collected and sold the *sim-sim* they had harvested that season, gave me the 40 shillings and asked me to go to Maseno. I left home, dejected, to give the school a try.

At Maseno water had to be fetched from the river in large tins and carried to the dormitories where the prefects and senior students bullied us to carry extra water for their baths and handled us roughly. But Carcy Francis received me enthusiastically. I was given the school uniform, the teachers seemed to favour me, especially Timothy Omondo, a jolly teacher who sang for us, and I made good friends among my fellow students. I became absorbed in my studies. Carey Francis invited me to his home every evening so I decided to stick out the roughness of the dormitory treatment, and to stay at school to study.

Carey Francis' mother came to live at the school for a while and showed me great warmth. She visited my home in Sakwa and I remember the day Carey Francis took us both to Uganda, and we stayed in a hotel. When Mrs Francis was with us I lived in her house as her loving son.

Mathematics was my best subject, and I enjoyed history. When hockey was introduced I played centre-forward. I

33

liked cutting the grass round the dormitory. I woke early each morning to work in my garden plot before doing my share of dormitory duty. After classes we played games. I was not good at football, but I tried my best. I enjoyed the school sports most of all, for I could sprint, and I was always in the first ten in cross-country runs.

In my fourth year at the school I was appointed junior prefect of the Willis dormitory, and before long senior prefect of Tucker dormitory. The same year I was assistant school captain and food prefect. I cannot forget the time that the food in the store was finished and I forgot to report this in time to the master in charge. That day the students missed their meals and the whole school turned against me; I took to heart the lesson that all responsibilities must be discharged with care. I had an even nastier lesson. One closing day at the end of term there was a little paraffin left in the dormitory store, so I decided to put it in a small *mukebe* and take it home to light our house. The principal met me as I was leaving and asked what I was carrying in the *mukebe*. I told him. That, he said, was thieving; I was in a position of trust and if I had taken the paraffin without asking permission, I had stolen it. 'I am going to arrest you,' he said, 'and take you back to school for punishment.' I was not able to go home. The principal thrashed me four *kibokos* and detained me at school for five days for being a thief. It was not actually stealing but the experience was ingrained in my mind; I have always remembered this lesson that one must never misuse a position of responsibility.

From 1930 to 1932 I completed the primary certificate, and from 1933 to 1934 did the lower primary teaching course. Those were the years my father decided not to continue paying the fees. My elder brother was no longer working away from home as a farm labourer and he wanted me to continue my schooling, so he tried to sell some of his animals, but was unable to raise the fees. I went to Carey Francis

34

with my problem and he arranged for one of the Maseno White teachers to employ me as his house servant. I woke each day earlier than usual to give my employer warm water for shaving, to lay the table and serve his breakfast. I scrubbed the pots in the kitchen, then ran across to the school dining-room for my porridge breakfast, and went to school with my class. At noon I had to leave the class early to prepare the teacher's lunch. This done, I bolted my own lunch and rushed back to school for the afternoon session. At four I served tea and by six, after games, I had turned from student back to servant, laying the table, lighting the lamps, turning back the bed covers, and serving dinner. Only after all these tasks could I eat my evening meal. Over and above this I had still to tend my school plot and keep the grass cut. I found myself rising earlier and earlier in the morning. My day began at three in the morning, sometimes even at two, and by the time I reported for duty as house servant at five I had already done my gardening stint. My wage of seven shillings a month was enough to pay the fees and buy textbooks, and there was even some money left over. Those years gave me a great sense of self-gratification. I was proud of my diligence and my skill in keeping a household. When I slipped behind I would find my name OGINGA written in the dust on the dressing-table.

We were schoolboys at Maseno but we did not forget our homes and our people, and in 1932 we formed the Coast Boys Association. It embraced the boys from the lake areas of Sakwa, Yimbo, Uyoma, South Gem, and Seme locations, and during the holidays when we returned to our homes we set examinations for the rural schools, corrected the papers and visited the schools to show them how to teach and conduct examinations. We formed ourselves in groups to help the old women work in the fields, and to build houses for them. We scraped together money for prizes for the schools which did best in the examinations we set them, and in sports competitions. It was our association that initiated the famous Migwena sports in Sakwa to which, at the end of each year, Nyanza people came from many different parts to take part in athletics, traditional games, and football and to get to know one another. These sports meetings were interrupted only during the Emergency; for the rest they took place until quite recently. Our association went from village to village meeting the elders and talking to them about topical events. Later this association was to inspire even bigger organization among our people, but this is to anticipate the years ahead. I was the founding chairman of the association, and very pleased with our work.

By the end of 1934 seven of us had completed the teaching course. Carey Francis was keen that we should start to teach. I went to see him to say that although some of the students were ready to teach I would prefer to continue my education. Carey Francis was most displeased. He threatened to make me leave the school immediately, and I retorted that if my desire for education was to be the cause of my leaving the school, I would be pleased to go. I packed my bag and left. Carey Francis rushed after me in his car, took me back to the school, thrashed me, and said he would consider my case to continue my education.

This opened the way for several of us to attend the Alliance High School near Nairobi. It was a very different place from Maseno. This was my first experience of a cold climate at high altitude. Again we had to work in garden plots, but much bigger ones. We planted the English potato and the African potato and maize. The school bought the students' crops to help us pay our fees. When we arrived we were given copies of the curriculum and a set of textbooks. The cold spurred me to work hard. Within a year I had worked through the mathematics books set for the two-year course. When I asked the principal for more advanced books he seemed embarrassed. He advised me to buy the books

36

myself. Later he made me a pupil teacher in mathematics and I found myself teaching some of my fellow students and earning a little extra money which went towards paying my school expenses. We learned that different tribal backgrounds were no obstacle to our living together. Inevitably, at the beginning, there were incidents but out of them grew a feeling not of tribal differences, but of Kenyan identity. We learned to live with all the Kenya tribes—the Kikuyu, the Kamba, the Teita, the Meru, the Masai, the people from the Coast and the Kalenjin, although there were very few of the latter at the school at that time.

My first experience of a strike was at the Alliance High School. It was over food. The sugar ration had been two spoons a student but in our second year the principal reduced us to one spoon. Student resentment flared into a strike. The principal summoned the three senior prefects together with Bishop Olang and Wanyutu Waweru, and when they stood before him he singled out Wanyutu Waweru, accused him of being the ringleader and expelled him on the turn. The school was summoned and the expulsion order announced to the students. Then the principal called the senior prefects in one by one and said to them: 'Do you agree to take the food the school gives you, or are you going with Waweru?' Every one of them capitulated. How could the students have deserted Waweru when all had agreed on the strike, I wondered, and I thought of this as our great betrayal.

Just before we had entered the school we had formed the Nyanza Alliance Boys' Fraternal Society. Its aims were much the same as those of the Coast Boys' Association at Maseno, but it was organized on a larger scale and embraced people from North, Central, and South Nyanza. I served as a secretary for a time. Then we changed the Coast Boys' Association to the Kamba Progressive Society, and I became chairman. This association organized students at Makerere College and also our countrymen who were working out of Nyanza.

During our second year at the Alliance High School we were told that some of us would write the Junior Secondary examination and from among the successful candidates throughout Kenya, two students would be chosen to enter Makerere College to sit for the Cambridge School Certificate. Our examination results were announced at the end of 1936 at the Government Central Offices, which are today Nairobi's law courts. No more than four schools entered candidates for this examination, for in those days the Cambridge School Certificate was unheard of for African students in Kenya. I was surprised to be the first called into the office and told I had won a scholarship to Makerere. The Director of Education said: 'You have been successful in getting the first scholarship to study at Makerere and you are required to be a medical student.' 'I'm sorry,' I replied. 'I cannot do medical studies because I have started as a teacher and I want to continue.' The second successful candidate, Joel Ojal, was called in and the same offer of a medical course put to him but he, too, elected to train as a schoolmaster. The Director of Education had apparently to produce a medical student, so a third student was included in the batch to study at Makerere and this was Dr Mbuthia, a brother of James Gichuru, Kenya's Finance Minister. The three of us left Kenya for Makerere at the beginning of 1937.

There was, once again, the difficulty of raising the fees. Maseno school, through my old principal Carey Francis, raised a loan of 180 shillings which I agreed to refund once I was working and earning. We boarded a boat and sailed Lake Nyanza, landing at Port Bell, from where we travelled to Kampala and then to Makerere. The uniforms issued to us at the College were made by convict labour. Some of the better-off students took them to tailors to have them fitted but I wore them as they were. Each student was given two uniforms a year; I decided to wear one and save the other, so by the time I left Makerere at the end of three years I had three uniforms to set me off in life when I started as a teacher at Maseno school.

The going was hard at Makerere. Our principal was an ex-army captain and the morning parade was like military drill. The sports could be gruelling for they included a weekly cross-country run of 10 miles, but I enjoyed this, as did the principal of the college, and indeed games played an important part in Uganda.

The work load was heavy, for we had to study for the Cambridge School Certificate and compress a three-year course into one year for the teaching diploma. Mathematics was once again my favourite subject. Science was taught to us extensively for the first time and I was intrigued by physics. When we sat for the examination at the end of 1938 I found I had finished the mathematics paper by half time. I passed the examination in the second grade but my mathematics performance was specially commented upon, and it was indicated that I had done well. That year the College had ten entrants for the examination and all of us passed, one in the first, two, including myself, in the second and the rest in the third grade. The following year I got my diploma in education.

The students at Makerere came from all over East Africa, and their names now dot Cabinets and government services in the independent states of East Africa. Uganda's attorney-general, Godfrey Binaisa, was there, and Dr Sam Mukasa, the Kabaka's private doctor, also Ali Mushin of Zanzibar, who was overthrown by the island's revolution, and Dr Mutawali and Chiefs Mangenya and Lugusha of Tanzania. The Kenya students included Argwings-Kodhek, George Waiyaki, Walter Odede, Osiema Adala, Webungo Akatsa, Erasto Mbugwa, Mumba, Tsuma, Joel Ojal, Julian Otieno, Ogilo Ogada, Gilbert Odawa, Peter Oranga, Mariko Ombaka and many others.

We formed a select group of students from all parts of

East Africa, cloistered in the classroom and chapel and on the sportsfield, but every now and then we scattered to our homes for the holidays to meet realities from which we were protected at college. I recall an incident when a special coach on the train'had been reserved for our group of Makerere students, but at Eldoret a farmer ordered his two servants to climb in next to us. We explained to them that it was a special student coach, and they went to find their master to tell him. He came striding back to the carriage to hit the student nearest the door. 'Who are you?' he roared. 'Don't you know you are just *mbuzi* (goats)?' Erastus Mbugwa, who was the student sitting near the door, was our school boxing champion but he didn't win that fight.

A large part of my life at Makerere was dominated by religion. I found solace in a frequent reading of the Bible; I was convinced that a man without strong religious conviction and constant prayers could not succeed in life. It was left to the religious denominations to sort out the religious instruction arranged for the students. The Christian Missionary Society organized its own religious instruction, as did the Catholics, and the Revivalists, and there were invitations to the students to join in the worship of all the denominations.

Religion had first been introduced to me at home by my brother Abisai Ajuang, later by the Evangelists at Maranda, especially the headmaster of the school, Mzee Shadrach Osewe, who was one of the great religious teachers in the area. At this time I was fascinated by the historical references in religious teaching, and attracted by the admonitions to godliness and charity towards others, but my religious understanding and personal sacrifice to God and Christ were limited. I did not fully participate. When I was called to Baptism I took the occasion lightly. My Evangelist teachers had asked me to select a godfather and godmother but I did nothing about this, nor did I arrange a baptismal name, and

when the day of baptism came and I was called to the altar
I could produce no name, and no godparents were present.
Canon Pleydell had come to baptize us and he said: 'Go out
in front of that large crowd and look for your godfather and
godmother.' I was at a loss. Stephen Machiala and Lois
Omolo, the wife of Mzee Shadrach Osewe came forward on
the spot and gave me the names Obadiah Adonijah. I was
called to the altar and baptized but I never liked the names;
I never used them though in those days it was important to
be known, if you were a Christian, by your baptismal name.
In the year I was resisting pressure to send me to school and
I was living with my uncle, Mzee Shadrach Osewe, then
inspector of schools in Central Nyanza, he took me with him
as he journeyed from place to place to preach. I carried his
luggage and sang the hymns. I had a good voice and I sang
melodiously and with enthusiasm, and then Mzee Osewe
delivered his sermon. I liked singing in public, I enjoyed the
travelling and the talks with new people. At Maseno school
my religious feeling ran deeper. Carey Francis was the
principal but also my friend and he fetched me from my
dormitory and we prayed together. Now I adopted the spirit
of prayer. A fellow student, Gordon Rogo, and I became
great friends in religion. We went together to the bush to
pray in solitude, to read the Bible, to sing hymns and to pray
to God to help us in our studies. I left Maseno school for the
Alliance High School without Gordon but with the same
religious fervour and at that school I became the religious
leader of the boys. I led the prayers at the meetings of the
Student's Christian Movement and was elected secretary.
We prayed in church in the early mornings and evenings,
and I became godfather to James Osiema who was baptized
at the school. By the time I reached Makerere a few of us
had decided that Sundays were not to be wasted enjoying
ourselves but should be spent in preaching the word of God
to villagers and so a small group of the students went about

the countryside. I remember preaching in the small private chapel of the Kabaka, before the Kabaka and his Queen. Yet I never adhered seriously to any one denomination. I thought of God as common to all the religious groupings and churches and I liked him this way. The Catholic priest at Makerere invited me to his home and tried to show me the truth in Catholicism; we went together to Rubaga, the largest cathedral in Uganda which is Catholic. I listened to the Revivalists whenever they invited me. I was ever ready to attend the services of any denomination. I did not believe in any one of the denominations but had faith in the supreme God who, I believed, would guide me. I tried in my life to live up to the teachings of the Bible. In the beginning religion had meant the Commandments taught to us by our fathers which prevented us from committing serious sin. At Makerere we tried to carry Christ's gospel outside the student body, to the villagers and their children.

But over the years it dawned on me that I had listened to many preachers and they seemed, all of them, to preach one thing in common—the suppression of African customs. They were not satisfied to concentrate on the word of the Bible; they tried to use the word of God to judge African traditions. An African who followed his peoples' customs was condemned as heathen and anti-Christian. Those who lived among and mixed easily with the non-Christians who were, after all, the majority, were themselves dubbed heathen. Tribesmen who kept many animals were condemned as anti-Christian because the possession of many animals meant it was possible for a man to marry and pay dowry for several wives. Any man married to more than one woman was anti-Christian. Villagers who lived in the traditional fenced-in clusters of huts were anti-Christian; if they were followers of the church they would group their houses near the church building, it was thought. I didn't agree with the taking of Christian names, and I have described how reluctant I had

42

been to take them. I formed strong prejudices against European priests who preached unity and love, yet lived aloof from the people to whom they preached.

The Second World War broke out on the eve of my leaving Makerere. We followed the progress of the war closely and argued points in the speeches of Chamberlain, Duff Cooper, Anthony Eden, and Churchill. We turned the school concert into a war game and dramatized the battles then raging, with players representing the allied armies on one side of the stage, and the German forces at the opposite end. The boys who played the parts of the Russian Marshals, Timoshenko and Budyenny, are still known by Makerere ex-students by these nicknames. Many of us had more than a sneaking sympathy for the Germans and we felt justified when, at the end of the war, India, Ghana, and later even Kenya, got their independence as a result of the weakening of imperialism. We students were incensed at the British and French imperial record in Africa, and Hitler was a challenge to that imperialism, we thought. The devil in our midst might at least be removed by a devil we did not know. While the great powers were locked in combat we would seize our chance to break free. Here at last was a challenge to the British Empire on which, we were told incessantly by our teachers, the sun never sets. The scale of killing that we later came to know about was horrifying. But when it came to race extermination, what have the European powers really learnt? we asked ourselves. There would be an outcry about mass murders by enemy forces, but wiping out African people or dropping atom bombs on Japan was permissible.

As I was completing my teacher training course at Makerere, I had a letter from Carey Francis asking me to join the staff at Maseno. I accepted gladly. The time came for us to pack our bags, say goodbye to the principal and staff and take the train back to Kisumu, via Nakuru.

I travelled home to Sakwa by lorry. Two days after my

43

arrival there I was found lying unconscious, suffering, it was thought, from sunstroke. I had violent coughing spells and lost consciousness repeatedly. After a few days one of my brothers, Tobias Ajuma, took me to Bondo by bicycle where we were lucky to find a veterinary officer who was just coming on duty. He was in his car on his rounds of the district, which finished at Maseno, so he took me with him and had me admitted to hospital. A newly qualified Makerere doctor friend of mine, Dr Arthur Okwemba, turned up after three days in which the hospital had not yet diagnosed my illness. It was pneumonia, he decided, and a weak chest did not brighten the chances of recovery. I was unconscious for long spells in the early stage of this illness but remember my brothers coming to my bedside, and also Carey Francis. I stayed in bed for two months, then slowly began to regain my strength. From the hospital I went home to Sakwa to convalesce, but I longed to teach at Maseno.

In time I reported for duty to the school. I told Carey Francis in one of our early meetings that I had been encouraged by my results in the Cambridge School Certificate examination and would like to study further in Britain. Francis had not forgotten how I had insisted on going to the Alliance High School though he had expected me to start teaching in village primary schools, and he told me that the education I had was enough to help those who had none. I did not insist too strongly; I intended to raise this matter again.

There was the matter of our salaries. Before we had left Makerere we had been told our starting salary would be 90 shillings a month. I told Carey Francis this because I knew he had decided to put Makerere-trained teachers on a starting salary of 70 shillings, with an increment of 2 shillings a year. Teachers with lower qualifications had been started on that salary, but Carey Francis insisted we were not to get preferential treatment. He called us together and said that if we rejected that salary he would not have us on the staff; and he called in one of our Makerere group and induced him to accept that salary. I held out. I asked Francis to write to head office in Nairobi; if the instruction was that we were to be started at a salary of 70 shillings we would accept. The reply from Nairobi said that our starting salary was to be 90 shillings a month.

Carey Francis now gave me my teaching instructions. I was to be in charge of standard five *b*. The pupils were divided into two streams. Boys considered to have first-class brains were placed in the *a* stream and the second-rate brains in the *b* stream. I was pleased to be in charge of the *b*'s: I intended to work hard to get the boys in my section to compete with and outstrip those in the *a* stream.

When I began to teach I had already formulated in my mind my own teaching principles, influenced very largely by my experience at the hands of teachers. Classroom academic teaching was all very well, I had decided, but it had to be related to day-to-day life, for a child had to use what he learnt in his own life. I knew too that there was never one way of solving a problem, especially a mathematics problem, but the ways were as numerous as the brains in the class. I compared this with the roads leading to Kisumu. There were many ways of getting to Kisumu, I told my class, except there is only one shortest way; given a chance all the students could find this way. My policy was never to insist that the students mechanically followed my way. I was determined to encourage thinking, rather than learning by memory. In the classroom I now controlled as a teacher, my own school-days were still alive in my experience. Arithmetic had been my first love at the Maranda Primary School and Mzee Shadrach Osewe had always given us the method of solving a problem before the problem itself. We had to follow his method exactly. I had been very poor at this. I would work out my own way of doing the sum and, having obtained an

45

answer, would wait only to hear whether it was correct. On several occasions our answers differed and I had dared to say 'Sir, I think you are wrong'. We had checked the sum together and he was wrong. On one occasion he slapped me hard in the face, telling me to follow the working on the board and point out the mistake there, not to wait till the whole sum was finished. But when I explained my method he had been pleased that my answer had been correct. At Maseno I had had the same trouble because Carey Francis had also been strict about the method to be used in solving a problem. I insisted on solving problems my own way and eventually Carey Francis had left me to my own methods which he found worked as well as his. By the time I had reached standard six Richard Arina was our teacher, a very accomplished mathematics teacher but a strict disciplinarian, and he refused to let me use my own methods but hit my hands every time I tried. I followed him closely enough to avoid punishment but never changed over completely to his methods of working.

As a student I had always disliked the teachers who expected us to learn notes and reproduce them; I was not good at memorizing. The teachers I remembered with warmth were Timothy Omondo who had taught diligently in the classroom but had also taught us general knowledge, about the things we would confront in life. He was earnest but also gay and he joked and danced and played with us when he had time.

But I found at Maseno that the teachers were disciplined like schoolboys. We had to wear uniform. We were called not by our African but by our Christian names. We had always found Carey Francis to be a man of great simplicity who did everything side by side with us. He was good at football; he wrestled with us; swam, like us, without any clothes; when we worked in the garden he stripped to the waist and dug beside us; he even ate with us. He talked about

46

life in the open, yet how low our living standards in the countryside were and how we should think and preach about the life we could lead in the future. But Carey Francis also knew well the attitude of the White settlers and especially of the government, towards African people. He knew the Europeans did not in truth believe that Africans could shoulder responsibility. His training at Maseno was to prepare us to lead a life of acceptance that the Europeans had settled in Africa and we would have to take direction from them. Maseno school was organized so that no African teacher was free to discharge responsibility. Every African teacher was put in charge of a dormitory and made responsible for the welfare of a group of children; but at the head of every three or four groups was placed a White master who had to supervise the African staff member. The same thing was repeated in the classroom: the African teachers were in charge of their classes but over each group of classes was a White supervisor. On the sportsfield the African teacher was responsible for organizing athletics or football but over him was the man with the final say, the White teacher.

I was one of the first to rebel and I took issue with the use of our Christian names. The headmaster was Zadok Okumu but he was addressed as Mr Zadok, and he was flanked by a staff called Mr Richard, Mr Robert, Mr Jacob, Mr Christopher, Mr Philip, Mr Alfred, and so on. I refused to be known as Mr Adonijah, my baptismal name. At Makerere I had been known as Oginga s/o Odinga (Oginga son of Odinga) and I wanted to be known as Oginga Odinga. There were disapproving smiles when I raised this at the first staff meeting. I argued that Mr Edward Carey Francis was not called Mr Edward, and we, too, had surnames. Webungo Akatsa supported me and in a few months I was pleased to see that he had officially registered his name as Webungo Bukachi Akatsa and was from then on known by that name. I suppressed my own baptismal name and never

47

used it. Carey Francis showed his disappointment in me. I reminded him that he had said when we were schoolboys that the use of a baptismal name alone did not make Christians out of us, and I was convinced I would succeed without the name.

By the time Carey Francis left Maseno his former fondness for me had waned. I thought that in his simplicity he was treating the African teachers like little children, forcing them to copy him; he had not hesitated to tell me that I had changed from the man he had once known. I was going through life discontented, he said, grumbling at everything. He recalled a paragraph about me that his mother had written in a letter: 'Look here, Adonijah,' he said, 'this is what my mother predicted for your future: "I visualize that Adonijah's future is bright and he will be a great man." ' Carey Francis' use of that passage gave me food for thought: was he flattering me to try to influence me as he had once been able to?

Carey Francis retired from teaching in my first year on the staff. I had already broken with his approach and had decided that if the African teachers were to be treated differently from the Whites this would be a continuation of European superiority which I had begun to hate. I did not like the way Europeans looked down at us, nor the way they felt about us. Carey Francis had set the example for our dressing at Maseno: a bush jacket with shorts and long stockings. This grew out of his genuine simplicity, and was something I was later in my life to admire and emulate. But teachers did not like this uniform; they wore it to please Carey Francis. I believed that men should feel free to decide for themselves what they should wear. I paid a visit to an African tailor called John Owuor in Kima, Bunyore, and on my return I sported suits. When I went to classes I dressed simply in shirt and trousers I had saved from Makerere, but on Sundays I dressed up in suits. I had bought a big hat and

KAU central committee meeting, August 1952. Achieng Oneko sits beside Kenyatta, and the author behind them, to the right. (*top*)

The men of the Kapenguria Trial outside the courtroom after the declaration of the Emergency in 1952: (*left to right*) Paul Ngei. Jomo Kenyatta, Achieng Oneko, Bildad Kaggia, Fred Kubai, Kungu Karumba. (*bottom*)

A police raid on an African market during the Emergency.

Africans arrested in Nairobi are driven away in cages for police interrogation.

a walking stick so I looked like an English gentleman from Nairobi or Kampala, as I had seen them. Carey Francis delivered a sermon in church in which he said that there were people who conceived an ideal man as one who wore a big hat, walking stick, suit, and tie and pointed shoes. I held out against the mockery. I was showing that I was master of my decision and would do as I pleased. This was a phase of my rebellion.

The traditional Maseno idea of an educated and civilized man was one who skimped and saved on a meagre salary, but did not soil his hands with mean labour. I persuaded my colleague Washington Onger that we should augment our wages by our own labour. We acquired a few chickens and Washington, who was good at carpentry, erected boxes which we covered over with wire. The time came when we invited the teachers to feed on our chickens and eggs. Our example was soon followed; other teachers kept chickens and I can even recall Richard Arina keeping a cow, another departure in the then established way that masters should conduct themselves. Next we joined Zadok Okumu in planting maize and vegetables and soon this was general staff activity at Maseno.

There was room for other reform too. Bachelor teachers at Maseno were forbidden to invite women visitors into their houses. Richard Arina was head of the African masters at the time and if a bachelor had a woman visitor he would call on the house in the evening to warn that the lady should spend the night in the married quarters. This was really treating us like schoolboys. I decided one day to challenge the rule. I refused to obey Arina's order; I was reported to and warned by the principal, Mr Mayor, but I stood my ground and my women visitors spent the night in my house. I had to face a staff meeting the next morning but I spoke up strongly for my stand. The regulations were withdrawn and never reinstated.

There was still the most important question of our supervision by the European teachers. I was teaching my class one morning when a White teacher supervisor came past the window and inquired whether I had arranged all the books in the cupboard. This was my responsibility, I said, and he had no business to interfere. He argued with me and I almost threw something at him through the window, in full view of the class. I was reported to the principal. I won the support of many of the African teachers and from then on the European teachers were told to mind their own classes. The new rule was extended to the dormitories so that we became independent of the European supervisors. But the old regime still continued on the sportsfields. I was in charge of training an athletics team for a sports meeting at Kisumu, and after I had selected the team I omitted to inform the White supervising teacher, who had the final say in the arrangements. This teacher was annoyed and he interfered with the transport arrangements I had made for getting the team to Kisumu and limited the number of boys who were to go. I ignored him and took the team to the match. On our way the White teacher stopped the lorries and eliminated two of the reserves. A teacher travelling with me, Mr Gilbert Odawa, and the team, left the lorry in disgust and walked to Maseno by foot. The White teacher drove past us and rushed to report me to the principal. When he saw me coming to the principal's house to give my version of the incident he left the principal's house by the window. At the teachers' meeting we had threatened to strike, but we won our point without this. The European staff, it was agreed, was not there to superimpose themselves on us. All the teachers were to be treated as equals.

By the end of the first year I was very pleased with our examination results. Almost a quarter of my students were moved into the highest stream. I thought my students were showing signs of thinking for themselves, learning to solve problems and correlating their lessons at school with their general knowledge. I loved teaching mathematics and the students knew that I placed no limit on the time I would spend helping them to solve problems. I became known as the Master of mathematics. Even my sermons were said to be arithmetical and I told the students 'The word of God is like an arithmetic problem. The important thing is to find a solution. It takes some a few lines, others a whole page, but the correct answer is what is important.' I joined the students when they worked on their garden plots and on the sports fields. During my second year, I was made sports master. I took drill and coached students in running and athletics and we won many cups and trophies in the provincial sports meeting. During that year the students went on strike. The principal singled out for expulsion five students whom he regarded as the ringleaders. The expulsion was a grave matter when it was placed before the staff meeting. The teachers thought the boys had been wrong and deserved punishment. I argued against expulsion. The five were the cream of the student body. Their expulsion would deprive them of the opportunity of studying and would ferment in them a bitterness against the school and the community which would take a heavy toll on both. The principal said 'Mr Oginga, ten years ago I would have felt as you do, but not today'. It dawned on me later that he was referring to my inexperience. The principal stuck to his decision and the boys (among them Oluande K'Oduol, later Registrar of our Lumumba Institute in Nairobi) were expelled from the school.

Though the Principal approved of my work at the school he thought me a trouble-maker. He offered no criticism to my face but he began steadily to curtail my scope. I, in turn, began to lose interest in work where I was not permitted to exercise full responsibility. When my friend Walter Odede suggested that I join him on the staff of the Veterinary

51

School I jumped at the opportunity. I applied for the post, was accepted and was asked to report for duty at the beginning of 1943. When first I had mentioned to my Principal my intention of applying for this post he had said he could easily get a replacement for me. But now that the post was mine he tried persuading me not to leave his school, and when persuasion failed he resorted to threats. The boys at the Veterinary School, he said, were third-rate brains who had failed to gain admission to the Maseno High School and they would make little headway in class. When I was not convinced by this argument Mr Mayor said it was a time of emergency in Kenya (during the war) and my resignation from Maseno would have to be referred for a ruling to the Director of Manpower in Nairobi. I warned him that I would leave Maseno school whatever the ruling; if I could not teach at the Veterinary School I would leave the profession altogether.

By now I had grown dissatisfied with serving in a mission school. I liked neither the flattery nor the underhand dealings with the staff. We were supposed to be government servants posted to work in missionary centres, but our terms of service were not satisfactory compared with those who were fully in government service. I was disillusioned about the treatment of Africans by Whites in the mission services.

During my last year at the Maseno school I was paying dowry for my marriage. I had met my wife at a Migwena sports gathering. We looked at one another but didn't really talk. The following afternoon I found her a guest at Bondo in a home I visited. Thus there were two coincidental meetings in two days. I thought to myself 'This girl looks pretty', but I said nothing to her. I asked a friend to find out about her. She was the eldest daughter of ex-Chief Odima of the Alego location, he said, and her grandfather was the late Chief Ng'ong'a. I admired ex-Chief Odima for he was a great footballer. I started to court his daughter. My brother and other members of the family opened negotiations for the marriage. She had refused many others, I was told, and I was sure she would reject me too, but she did not. I did not take the matter seriously until I saw that cattle were being paid over to her family, then I knew that the marriage was sealed. The negotiations in this courtship had proved complicated. My prospective wife's father was in prison at the time, and he had to be visited there and asked for his consent to the marriage. Ex-Chief Odima had been imprisoned for life for stabbing a stepbrother to death in a family quarrel. (By the time of the stabbing incident he was actually no longer Chief; an ex-policeman had been substituted.) We got the consent to marry from ex-Chief Odima in prison and took our first two children to him on a prison visiting day, but he died from heart failure after serving the first three years of his sentence. But this is to anticipate events. We were married on 23 January 1943. I had decided to celebrate our wedding with two ceremonies. The first was immediately after the church ceremony at Maseno school and was held at the Veterinary School where I was about to begin teaching. A party was held in one of the dormitories and friends came from all parts of Nyanza and from Nairobi, Mombasa, and Kampala. After that party we went to my home at Sakwa to celebrate for two days in the traditional way.

The Veterinary School had already opened and was waiting for me, so a week after our wedding I decided that we should return to Maseno. I began that year with double problems. I had the organization of the school to tackle but I had also to cope with my marriage. Our first son was born that October. I behaved like a new father who had a new possession all to himself. I treated my wife as I handled my students. I gave her a timetable by which she was to suckle, wash, and care for the child. For my wife this was the last straw. Like me, she is hot-tempered, though her temper cools fast. But from the beginning of our marriage I had treated her like a child, ordering her to prepare my food, garden our plot, keep the chickens, clean the house, and mend my clothes exactly as and when I demanded. After the birth of our son we had a very harsh quarrel during which I knocked her down. I was shocked by my own action when I thought about it. The following morning my wife left me. She took the child and found a lorry to carry them to her home in Alego. My enemies at the Veterinary School gossiped delightedly. 'Look at him,' they said, 'he can not even keep his own wife; his madness has extended to his house.' I could keep house but I was saddened by the absence of my wife. I went to her home and tried to explain to her mother, but she didn't believe me, having heard my wife's version. I returned to the school a chastened man thinking I was going to fail in this essential aspect of my life. My wife stayed at her mother's home for six months and then returned to me. She seemed to be a changed woman. Perhaps she had got advice at home on how to conduct herself with me, but in the years to come we never had any real trouble. Two more sons were born the next two successive years.

I faced the problem of the baptism of my three sons. I wrote to the priest of the Maseno Church that I would like to bring my children for baptism but it was to be understood that my decision was to baptize them with African names. I was told that could be done but I should choose not an ordinary African name but one connected with the Church like Khama or Aggrey. On the day of the baptism the church was crowded. When it was our turn we went to the altar carrying the children. I gave the name of the first as Ng'ong'a Molo Oburu. The priest, Rev. Simon Nyende, asked what his Christian name was to be. Ng'ong'a Molo, I said. Rev. Nyende advised I should have taken a name like Aggrey or Khama, names associated with Christians. No, I said, Ng'ong'a was a great chief in the country, loved by his

54

people and I have not heard of anything he did which was objectionable to Christians. Rev. Nyende refused to baptize the children and advised me to choose other African names. My wife was angry to be humiliated in front of the large crowd and she stalked out of the Church. I insisted we had to go back and try again. I wrote to the Archdeacon Stanway that my children had been refused baptism because I wanted to use African names. He referred to the Bishop in Nairobi and word came back that there was no clause in the constitution of the church debarring me from baptizing my children with African names. The African padres objected when this matter was placed before the Church council of the district and the argument went back and forth until the Archdeacon ruled in my favour. Still no African priest would come forward to baptize my children. I found a European priest at Maseno school who agreed to do so but I had a fresh problem: my wife would not help me carry the children to church. I enrolled the help of some of my students to carry the children and persuaded Joel Omino's daughter Akinyi to be their god-mother. My wife realized that she could not shame me in front of the people and she repented and joined us in the church. The children were baptized Ng'ong'a Molo Oburu, Rayila Amolo Odinga, and Ngire Omuodo Agola. I was delighted: I had lived up to one of my strongest convictions. But the stories went about that I was abnormal, and strange. Later many people followed my example, including even my former teacher, Richard Arina, who named and baptized his first son, Jamwa.

I began as headmaster of Maseno Veterinary School to find that general education for the students was not taken seriously. The school authorities wanted the boys to be taught a little English and enough arithmetic to enable them to weigh and record the milk and to understand the medicines prescribed in the treatment of animals. The classes could at any time be interrupted for milking and duties in the fields. There were no classrooms, only cattle sheds. There was a hierarchy of control in the school headed by a Scotsman, a considerate liberal man who was in charge of the veterinary services in the whole of Nyanza Province. Assistant to him was my old friend from Makerere, Walter Odede, who had suggested I take this post. Below the senior veterinary officers and the livestock officers were sergeants responsible for physical training and in charge of the labourers, and below them, were the teachers, at the bottom of the ladder.

In the cattle sheds the cattle, the labourers and the dust interfered with the students, and my first plan was for class-rooms, but when I put my scheme to the senior veterinary research officer I found he had been influenced by the clerk in charge, Joel Omino (an experienced civil servant who had been clerk to the Central Nyanza Local Native Council), to believe that Odede and I had wanted to turn the veterinary school into another Makerere. I had to tell Omino to stick to his work as clerk and not try to run a school. We got permission to build classrooms. The work was done in four months. I faced a fresh battle over the curriculum. Casual education was not good enough for the boys, I insisted, they should be trained in veterinary science and animal husbandry but they should also pass academic examinations. The staff members opposed to changes in the school brought matters to a head, and to prove that my scheme for general education would not conflict with the students' practical training in the fields, we undertook to do whatever gardening tasks were set us. I took the students into my confidence about my plan and, working together day and night, we cleared the paddocks until we could convince the senior officer that we could work both in the classroom and on the land. Mr Omino and others opposed to my plan left the staff after a while and I remained head-teacher of the school, conducting the drill and the physical training, and in charge also of the whole veterinary station, the only African to have such responsibility at that time.

The senior posts were vacated and re-occupied by a series of Europeans each with his own views of Africans as teachers and students. A livestock officer told me that at a station like Maseno Veterinary School there was room for only one cock and that I should know that he was the cock, that we Africans were the hens, and that only he could make us produce anything. He told me outright that my brain was actually not meant to think, but to carry out orders. The students were there to salute the staff and do what they were told but not to sit in a classroom learning English that would make them swollen-headed and unable to carry out orders in the fields. Why didn't I teach them Swahili, not English, he asked? My only consistent backing came from the students and all in charge learnt soon enough that if they took action against me they would have a student strike on their hands.

The government provided only the minimum number of books but the students voluntarily contributed sums of money to augment the supplies. On the sports field we had little apparatus but we improvised our own hurdles and poles for vaulting, and our school champion won the provincial sports and the top prize in the Kenya Athletics Meeting. We organized concerts and debates. The boys were told they were free to discuss any problem; I was accused of spoiling and misleading them.

During 1945 and 1946 the senior veterinary officer was a man who did not believe Africans had ability; he did not believe the 'African mind' was 'mature', he did not trust Africans to do anything on their own. When I was at the blackboard in my classroom he would walk in, stop me, take charge of the class and question me in front of my students. In the middle of classes he would order the boys out to work in the fields. One Empire Day he stopped me teaching and

57

told me to explain to the students the meaning of the Empire Day. I loved teaching and was unwilling to lose my post—apart from which I was used to the ways of successive European officials—so I held my patience and told him we were commemorating the greatest Empire on which the sun never set, the British Empire. I knew a little about it, he told the class, but not much more than the boys. He pointed to the map of the world and showed that the red shading represented the British Empire. He turned to the map of Kenya showing European settled areas. These, he said, pointing to them, are the parts farmed by the settlers, a very small portion, and 'this vast area is African land where lazy Africans produce practically nothing. They look at what Europeans have built in their areas, and want to possess it.'

This veterinary officer taught me more about the Europeans than he knew. He called me into his office one day, when I was the only senior African in the Veterinary School and he needed to bend me to his schemes. This was in 1944 when Eliud Mathu had been the first African appointed to the Legislative Council. 'Look here, Oginga,' he said, 'you are very intelligent, but you must understand that your brain is no better than the brain of my six year old son because you Africans have not developed anything. My son can push a wheelbarrow, *and* he can think, but you cannot think because you have not been brought up to do so. When the first European came to Kenya he found not even a wheel. Your people have not invented anything and it will take you three hundred years to reach the level of the Europeans. I am surprised that Eliud Mathu dared to go to the Legislative Council. I know Mathu very well. I know that you are much cleverer than he, yet your brain is no better than that of my six year old boy, so if you are cleverer than Mathu, what can he do in the Legislature with people of vast experience like Sir Francis Scott and Colonel Grogan? Mathu will sit there like a log of wood, doing practically

58

nothing for you. You would have done better to have a European represent you.' The lecture went on: 'Look here, Mr Oginga, I want you to be responsible here in the veterinary school. I want you to assist me. I don't think there is anything you can teach the boys because most of them are dupes who cannot learn. You could help me to go round the *barazas*, to lecture your people in the field how to look after those *shenzi ngombes* (primitive cattle). I don't know your language so you could translate my English and we could train more people than by wasting time with the few dupes you have here.'

This European official, I saw, wanted to turn me into a stooge, to separate me from my people, to make me into his accomplice, to use me in any way he decided. But I had noticed that the first thing these Europeans had to do to use us was to destroy the confidence the African had in himself, and that which people had in us.

Before I fully understood his tactics I found I was involved in his scheme to replace Manowa Ojwang' (elder brother of Oluande K'Oduol), the clerk in his office, with veterinary trained instructor Ngesa, who came from my home location Sakwa. The veterinary officer told me I had best get Ngesa from Sakwa for the job. The following morning he called the staff together and told them in my presence that he had consulted with me, that Manowa Ojwang' was incapable of running the office and would be sent into the fields, and that Ngesa would take his place. I jumped to my feet and told the European officer that he could not commit me to his decision and that I thought Manowa Ojwang' the right man for the office; he left the room in a fury and from that day my battle with him began. He wrote reports that I was unfit to teach in the Veterinary School, that I was a revolutionary teacher spoiling the minds of young men who would otherwise serve well, that I was anti-European and preached against the Europeans in the classrooms. I was not fit to teach in any school in Kenya, he wrote. There were confidential reports sent to Nairobi, but Manowa Ojwang' worked in the office, and so I knew their contents.

By the end of 1946 the senior veterinary officer decided to suspend me from duty; I did not know the stated reason. I had asked for leave to go to Nairobi but he had cancelled my ticket. I defied him, took my ticket and spent my holiday in Nairobi. When I returned he reported me to Nairobi head office and said he had suspended me, pending instructions. In December I was called to headquarters to the offices of the Secretariat. Two senior officials called me into a closed office to give me my instructions. 'You have been called here,' they said, 'because you have been very rude at the Veterinary School, and we have decided that you will not return to Maseno but will be transferred to teach at Kapenguria. We will watch you closely there and if you make mistakes, we will dismiss you.' I asked whether I could return to Maseno to collect my belongings. No, they said, I must proceed directly to Kapenguria, my things would be sent to me there. I told them that I hoped they would listen to my side of the story but as they had already decided to send me to Kapenguria, I could not accept the post. 'Look here, Odinga,' they said, very annoyed, 'it is said here in this confidential report that when you are annoyed you are rude and unbalanced, and this is what we see in you. You must be careful. Your country has spent a lot of money on you to train you to teach and if you will not teach, well, that is up to you. Think about this and tell us what you decide.'

I spent the night thinking about it. The following day I told these officials that I had decided not to go to Kapenguria but to resign from the teaching profession.

CHAPTER FOUR

Rejection of Patronage

THROUGHOUT the first half of my life, the settlers, the real ruling force of Kenya, were a distant horror to me. I was told of the cruelty meted out to the labourers on their farms, but I experienced nothing of this myself. I do recall one painful encounter when I was on the staff of the Veterinary School and was taking a party of students to visit a veterinary station near Kapsabet, near the White farms of Eldoret. A European police officer stopped the bus on the road and precipitately, without reason, weighed abusively into us: the bus was overcrowded, he shouted, the students were rude not to salute him. I was an irresponsible teacher and he was warning me there and then not to use the road again with such a gang of silly boys. The policeman was himself on the way to Eldoret and he ordered our bus to wait at the roadside until he had reached the town, completed his business and returned; only then could we proceed. He refused to look at our letter of authorization. We waited some hours at the roadside until it was his pleasure to let us resume our journey.

On the whole, though, life in Nyanza in the mission schools was protected against these involvements with the settlers. In all I spent twenty-two years of my life in mission schools as pupil or teacher. I was thirteen when I entered a classroom for the first time as a reluctant pupil, attending classes only intermittently, and seventeen years old before I gave myself to lessons with any real application. I learned easily enough but I grew to resent the patronage of Maseno and Makerere as much as the beatings the younger boys were given for inattention, and later—during three years qualifying for a diploma at Makerere College, three on the staff of the Maseno High School, and four more as principal of the Veterinary School—this resentment grew into a rejection of the entire focus of mission training.

The missions dominated African education. The government, by neglecting to provide state schools, left the field to the various denominations which presided over their schools and congregations as though over small empires. Government and missions, especially the Church Missionary Society centred at Maseno, did not necessarily see eye to eye on policy. This was inevitable when the purpose of 'native' administration in the early decades was to milk Nyanza of its labour, to use chiefs and headmen to impose administration on the people, but for the rest to produce as little change as possible, because change was both unsettling and costly. Christian mission teaching, on the other hand, called on converts to model themselves on the way of life of the White evangelists and aspire to their standards. No wonder the settlers and many a government official railed at the missions for producing jumped-up Englishmen instead of quiescent tribal subjects. Yet events proved in the long run that mission activities and policy anticipated the needs of government before the latter itself realized them. The missions produced men who were rebels against the old way of life for a while but were then themselves absorbed into mission and administration. They became tame, middle men, shadows and subjects of White mission men, and any stirrings in them to become independent leaders of their people were suppressed by their allegiance to the mission hierarchy, and the fact that, once educated, they were absorbed into the government machine.

The mission schools supplied the servants of the administration. The products of the schools rose to be clerks, census and tax counters, interpreters, and chiefs. The teaching in the classrooms stressed memory rather than reasoning, repetition by rote instead of thinking and originality, for these were the ideal moulds for docile civil servants. The purpose of education was not to train for independence, but for subservience.

It was also to teach the African that his ways were alien to civilized living. Christianity could not be accepted without the rejection of African customs and religion. White and African religions were not only different, but Christianity had to be recognized as unquestionably superior. The new religion had to be the *only* way of life. In turning his back on old ways to embrace the new, the African was made ashamed of the traditions of his own society.

In this way docile African hangers-on, who deferred without murmur to the moral superiority of all things White and Christian, were enlisted to serve the White government; and an educated leadership group emerged that was separated by a great gulf from the mass of the people. The educated group reckoned prestige by the closeness of the African to the White man and his ways. At first those who wore European clothes were most like them. Then those who went into domestic service—the so-called 'houseboys'—and lived in the house of the White man, or at the back of it, thought they were achieving superiority. Finally the educated who did not only dress and live like the White man, but who read from his books, sang his hymns and shared his inspirations, moved into the highest spheres of achievement. The price for education had been Christianity; now the price for approval and acceptance was deferring not to the African will, but to the purpose of the Whites. Here were sown early the seeds of estrangement of the educated leadership from the people which has bedevilled Kenya's political life for so

63

long. A man could be a leader by virtue of his education, but his very education estranged him from his people and fostered in him the illusion that he need not be answerable to them. Only this can explain the ease with which leaders of later generations of political activity switched policy and party, allegiance and principle without any consultation of their followers and voters.

African society had a very distinct image of leadership. Leadership was generally associated with maturity, experience, steadfastness, and wisdom, and a thorough absorption of the teachings of the elders passed on by them or sung by our traditional musicians. The new education took leadership from the elders and bestowed it on the youth, but a youth which was steeped in the colonial philosophy and that rejected not only the traditional way of life, but also respect for the will of the people. The mass of the people in the countryside may not be educated but they make up the strength of the nationalist movement and they are unwavering in the pursuit of freedom aims. It was one of the strengths of the colonial regime that it could always use the educated class in the civil service, who were susceptible to pressure, to spread faintheartedness and confusion.

The church created other rifts within African society. The schools were originally built mainly for the sons of chiefs, and to train the new generation of chiefs and headmen. This meant that much of the flexibility that Luo society provided in the selection of leadership by prowess and the concensus of tribal opinion was destroyed by a system that monopolized leadership for the educated chief clan, usurped the functions of the clan elders, and made chiefs prone to bribery and other pressures.

The missionaries objected not only to polygamy but also to our custom of having several families make joint payment of dowry. This had been one of the Luo society provisions for the sharing out of wealth and family responsibility, but the new religion, for all the sermons about the brotherhood of man, advocated individualism and not egalitarianism.

In the villages the missionaries drove a wedge between Christians and pagans. The priests would refer to people as either Christians (jo Christo) or *jopiny*. Jopiny means literally 'the countrymen' but when used in juxtaposition with JoChristo it meant those outside the church, the pagans who had not yielded to conversion. In some churches this was not only a dividing line between those who resisted or espoused the new religion, but a political dividing line, too. When the 'Piny Owacho' movement shook Nyanza in the twenties the administration was extremely perturbed by the wave of political consciousness, but it was also gratified that many missionaries cooperated loyally with the government, especially in South Nyanza, to check the movement, and the Catholic Church throughout Nyanza promptly declared the Young Kavirondo Association to be a forbidden organization to all members of this church and community. Indeed the Catholic Union which was formed in 1923 to disassociate from the Piny Owacho movement supported the government blindly on every possible issue, even the hated hut tax because the economic burden of this tax, they reasoned, might discourage the practice of polygamy.

The association of the Church Missionary Society and its head, Archdeacon W. E. Owen, with Piny Owacho is instructive. The founding members and officials of Piny Owacho were almost all CMS adherents: Jonathan Okwiri, Simeon Nyende, Benjamin Owuor and Joel Omino. When the movement, influenced by the surging forward of the Thuku-led campaigns of the Kikuyu, first sparked into life Archdeacon Owen was away in Europe. He was a missionary who did not operate only from church precincts but moved among the people. His was a major influence in shaping political life in Nyanza. He was influential, outspoken, and an outstanding priest-politician. He believed and he taught that you could not separate the church and politics. The church preached justice, he said, and action outside the church in the political arena had to defend justice. Among the priests he trained were Canon Awori (father of W. W. Awori), Jonathan Okwiri, Rev. S. Osewe, and Michael Were and he brought them up to public life as well as in church affairs. Archdeacon Owen was for many years the bugbear of the settlers because he championed the rights of the people of Nyanza, campaigning especially against child labour. But when it came to the challenge of Piny Owacho there is no doubt that Owen blunted the sword of this political movement and diverted it into welfare channels.

Owen converted the Kavirondo Taxpayers' Central Association into the Kavirondo Taxpayers' Welfare Association. The badge of the association was a black and white handshake. The constitution was shown to government and approved by it. It provided for all location chiefs to be *ex-officio* vice-presidents, and White government officials also served as vice-presidents, and could even attend meetings if invited. The aims of the association now included the planting of trees, the digging of sanitary pits, the manufacture of hand mills for grinding maize, the acquisition of beds by members. A hygiene catechism was drawn up and published.

Government reports recorded, after the anxiety caused by the early Piny Owacho upheavals, that the mission community round Maseno was behaving in a 'perfectly correct and loyal manner'. The government recognized that Archdeacon Owen had done much to restrain 'political agitation' and the administration owed him a debt of gratitude.[1] The sting of the Piny Owacho movement was drawn by Owen's intervention. His guidance was what the government wanted.

In 1925 the government instituted a system of Local Native Councils which it hoped would improve even on the missions in guiding the political aspirations of the people.

[1] Report for Central Nyanza, 1924.

The purpose was to involve Africans into their administration to the extent that their political activities would be harnessed without giving them any real power. The chairman of the council was invariably the White District Commissioner. All the chiefs were nominated members, thus constituting a third of the council strength. The Councils were never genuine mouthpieces of the people, but they did absorb into the colonial machine the men of the mission schools who had once voiced protest. Some of the leading initiators of Piny Owacho were themselves made chiefs and were accommodated by the government they had once challenged.

Owen's association with the Kavirondo Taxpayers' Welfare Association ended in the mid-thirties, and the Association later showed some sparks of life but they were intermittent. A new group of leaders came to the fore, chief among them John Paul Olola, founder of the Kisumu Native Chamber of Commerce in 1927. Under his leadership the Taxpayers' Welfare Association even met with the Kikuyu Central Association on the eve of the Second World War and made common cause with this body against de-stocking orders and against the reservation to Whites of the land in the highlands. With the outbreak of war the government toyed with the idea of suppressing the Association because, said the Provincial Commissioner, judging from reading the minutes the Association was 'almost exclusively engaged in political affairs'. The Commissioner thought better of declaring the association illegal because 'this would drive them underground while at the present they are so open as to permit them to invite us to be present' at their meetings.[1] By this time the Association was known by the people as Jo-Memorandum. Kisumu was a hotbed of memoranda. Whenever government officials were approachable a memorandum was presented, beginning with an expression of

[1] Report for Central Nyanza, 1940.

67

loyalty to the King of England, addressing the Governor as 'our father' and politely asking for consideration. Welfare work and local advisory councils would between them, the government hoped, deflect political protest in Nyanza. By creating a vocal group of educated men mission stimulus in the villages had given cause for temporary anxiety, but once the danger was recognized, it was possible to keep the situation under control.

The trouble with mission control, though, was that it was a double-edged weapon. On the one hand it created a category of educated men who were easily tamed because they had lost their moorings within African society; on the other hand it stoked up a revolt in the church that led to dramatic breakaways and the foundation of independent African churches that preached a gospel with strong political overtones.

The first breakaway church was the Nomiya Luo Church founded by John Owalo who, incidentally, had Kenyatta among the pupils in his class when he taught at the CMS School in Nairobi. Owalo had left the Church of England to become a Muslim when he worked as a house servant for a while in Mombasa; he joined a Catholic Mission on his return to Nyanza. But one night in 1907, he preached, God had come to him in a revelation. He, Owalo, had been taken to heaven for the message and then returned to earth to preach the real word of God to the African people. He called his church NOMIYA (in Luo 'I was given' meaning 'I was given God's word'). The new church practised circumcision, laid emphasis on the Ten Commandments of Mount Sinai, and forbade smoking, beer-drinking and dancing. Owalo came from Asembo location not far from Sakwa but he preached far and wide in Nyanza, and he met fierce attack from the established church and the authorities. On one occasion he was called by the District Commissioner to account to a public *baraza* for his actions. 'Leave me to preach,' he told the authorities. 'I'm preaching to Africans, not to Whites.'

Dini ya Roho (Holy Ghost Church) was started in Maragoli location in October 1927 by Jakobo Buluku and Daniel Sande after they had broken away from the American Friends African Mission at Kaimosi. Buluku and Sande preached against a foreign religious leadership and advocated the expulsion from Kenya of the American missionaries. The latter, of course, reacted violently against the new sect. Bishop Lucas Nuhu became the leader of this church in 1940 and has propagated its faith far beyond Maragoli. He now heads the Nairobi branch where he has been a key figure in the organizing of Kenyan and East African Independent African Churches.

Yet another Holy Ghost Church was that led by Alfayo Odongo, who had been appointed by Owen to oversee the CMS congregation during a period in the twenties, and who had visions from the Holy Ghost to found the Church of Joroho, or the Holy Ghost Church. It had been revealed to him, he said, that Africans should found their own church in preparation for their own African government, which was coming. The new government was to be well founded in the church, and a really African government needed a fully African church. Odongo preached and had adherents everywhere in Central Nyanza, and beyond. He preached the prophecy of Matthew XXIV:

For nation shall rise against nation, and kingdom against kingdom; and there shall be famines, and pestilences, and earthquakes in divers places. . . . Many shall come in my name, saying, I am Christ; and shall deceive many . . .

He and his followers were subjected to intimidation, fines, and arrest. In January 1934 Odongo and several hundred members of Joroho went into meditation and seclusion in a

village in Musanda (then in North Nyanza and now Kakamega district in the Western Region). Cut off from supplies
and means of livelihood a new divine prophecy came to the
sect, that the crops and animals in the vicinity were God's
property, and therefore theirs. When the sect acted on the
prophecy and helped themselves to their needs, the inhabitants of the nearby villages were enraged. One night they
converged on the sect and set the village alight. The followers
of Joroho sang as the flames leapt around them. Alfayo
Odongo and many others were burnt alive. The followers who
escaped kept Odongo's teachings alive and the Church of
Joroho persists in Nyanza to this day. The present leaders
are Barnaba Walhoho, Isaya Goro and ex-Chief Zefania
Abungu.

The African Israel Church was founded in 1942 in Nyangori location near Kisumu. Initially the founder, Kivuli,
called his sect Israel Uhuru Church, meaning the Israel
Independence Church. The British Government officials
were against the word 'Independence' and instructed Kivuli
not to use it, so the Church became known as the African
Israel Church. Kivuli had broken away with Buluku and
Sande from the American Friends African Mission at Kaimosi but, frightened by the ensuing persecution unleashed
by the mother church run by the missionaries, he joined the
Canadian Pentacostal Assembly (Nyangori Mission). In
1942 he broke from the Pentecostal Assembly and preached
the expulsion of foreign missionaries, advocating leadership
of the churches by African Christians.

Dini Ya Msambwa means the Church adapted to African
tradition, or the religion of the Old Customs. The founder
was Elijah Masinde who, like Buluku and Sande, had broken
in 1927 from the American Friends African Mission. In fact,
Masinde started as a political organizer, not a religionist.
His sermons have always been more like those of a politician
than a priest, and his 'amens' alone are a national anthem.

An early confrontation with the authorities was when he took a deputation of four to the District Commissioner at Kakamega to tell him the time had come for the Africans to rule themselves. Masinde played football in the team of the Friends African Mission and during a visit to Kakamega with the team he came across the North Kavirondo Central Association founded by Chief Mulama who was unseated by government for his political activities at the head of the Association. When the discovery of gold at Kakamega brought a threat of land alienation, Mulama's NKCA made contact with the leadership of the Kikuyu Central Association. 'We have to fight,' Chief Mulama said, and Masinde began, in his own way. During the war the government made extensive use of forced labour. One morning Masinde armed himself with a whip and blocked the road to forty men who had been conscripted from their villages for a labour camp. 'If people have to work on the roads they must be paid,' he insisted. 'These men have paid their poll tax and must not be forced to work.' Masinde's revelation that the time had come for the Whites to leave the country to make room for a black government came to him after the end of the war when he climbed to the top of Mount Elgon.

Wherever he appeared there began a popular movement of non-cooperation with the recognized church and the administration. He served a succession of jail sentences and periods of restriction. On one occasion when he defied the attempt of the District Commissioner to allocate land for the chief's camp a large armed group was dispatched to arrest him. He met the police party with his Bible in his hand. Fighting broke out nevertheless. Several spells of hard labour did not change Masinde, nor his confinement in a mental institution in Nairobi for two years. When he began to preach in earnest, after the revelation on Mount Elgon when a voice said 'The Kingdom of Africa has been ruined by the British Empire', people left the other churches in

71

great hordes to join him. He evaded a summons from the District Commissioner and the government instituted a large-scale search for him. Masinde was underground—hiding in an excavated ant hole on which potatoes had been planted as camouflage. He surrendered himself after police had opened fire on a large body of his supporters at Malakisi killing eleven. Three months in jail were followed by eleven years in restriction, at Marsabit and Mandera. His only company were lions and elephants, his only food a meagre daily ration. He was a modern-day martyr in the wilderness.

Elijah Masinde's Dini Ya Msambwa spread all over the Western Province, and among the Kalenjin of the Rift Valley and into parts of Eastern Uganda. The Suk of Pokot in Baringo District of the Rift Valley became converts and like Masinde's converts everywhere, were very militant. The leader of this Church among the Suk was Luka Kepturit who, it is claimed, was among the dead when police fired on Suk converts and elders at Kolloa. The Suk for their part killed the District Commissioner and one police officer during the Kolloa incident, which occurred when the Suk refused to welcome and listen to a new District Commissioner who had come to a *baraza* among the Suk people for the first time.

Yet another Church was started by Joshua arap Chuma as an independent sect among the Kalenjin of the Rift Valley in 1959, the year that arap Chuma broke from the foreign Church in similar mood from that of other African independent Church leaders when they founded their own Churches.

The founder of yet another independent African Church was Bildad Kaggia of Central Province who came back from military service in the Middle East, England, and Europe in the Second World War embittered by racial discrimination and inequality between Europeans and Africans in the British forces. He came back convinced that the greatest bondage on Africans was the foreign religion. He had made up his mind to liberate Africans from foreign religious teachings. Formerly an ardent follower of the Church Missionary Society he had been dissatisfied with his former religion which discriminated against converts of African origin. His new Church was against denominations and aimed at bringing together people from all denominations, and non-church people. On this principle he did not like to give it a label but nevertheless his followers came to be known as 'Dini Ya Kaggia'. The Church spread like wildfire in the whole of Central Province and Ukambani. Some of the Luo workers on the Sisal Estates near Kandara were converted and later when they returned home they spread the church in Nyanza.

The tenets of the Church were:

1. to establish a purely African Church completely independent of European domination;
2. to sanctify the Church from European abominations which had been offered to Africans as part of religious teachings;
3. to establish a reformed catechism to suit the African, incorporating useful African customs and culture:

   (a) all new converts had to be baptized or re-baptized in their mother names, erasing all foreign names;
   (b) matrimonial ceremony had to be done in a new African fashion.

After a short time the Church became very strong in Central Province, Ukambani, and Nyanza. Kaggia managed to convert many foreign Church followers so much that many foreign churches in Central Province had to be closed down. The European Church felt the strength of the new Church, so sought peace between all the Protestant Churches and the Dini Ya Kaggia. They convened a peace meeting at a place

73

called Ndugamano in Muranga. But after three days of serious discussion the talks broke down. The missionaries were trying to win the new Church back to the former denominations but Kaggia and his followers resisted and maintained that the time for religious independence had come and Africans must lead.

After the breakdown of peace talks the missionaries met separately to consider ways and means of suppressing the new Church which was becoming too forceful for them. They came to the conclusion that the new Church was too powerful and they had no alternative but to call upon the government to suppress it by force. This they did and the government started to persecute Kaggia and his followers. At first they thought to isolate Kaggia by singling him out for imprisonment hoping that his followers would be discouraged. He was sent to prison four times but this did not deter him or his followers from their activities, and the movement continued to grow.

Then the government resorted to mass arrests and imprisonment of men and women who were adherents of the new Church. Hundreds and hundreds of people were imprisoned in various districts in the Central Province and Ukambani. This action also acted as fuel to the fire of the movement which was spreading every day.

Roughly speaking there are today in Kenya well over thirty independent Churches. They were obviously a retaliation to the war of the Christian missions against African tradition and African independence. Africans wanted a form of worship which would accommodate their way of life. Africans from time immemorial knew God—Nyasaye Nyakalaga (the God Who is everywhere). They were impressed by the superior material possessions of the Whites when they came, and attracted by their more elaborate Church organization and ritual, especially in the Catholic Church. But the Church not only demanded that the African

74

reject his traditional marriage custom and much else but, for all the preaching about brotherhood, the African priest was invariably graded inferior in the Church. It dawned that administration and Church were different representations of the same White authority. The policy of the Church was ever in accord with that of the administration. When there was general dissatisfaction among the people it created, inevitably, disaffection with the Church. Mission training stood the breakaway religious leaders in good stead: they had become adept in quoting Bible texts and these could be turned with great facility against the established Church which differentiated between Christian White and Black.

The independent Church movement was not only a religious revolt. It was an aspect of the nascent political struggle. There was no permitted outlet for popular protest against White rule, so protest emerged deviously, in many forms, in the Church, in social organizations, and even, as was my own experience, through business enterprise.

CHAPTER FIVE

Independence through Business?

THE years towards the end of the war were a black period for me. I had been suspended from the Veterinary School and cold-shouldered in an application for a scholarship for further study in Britain. Five of us, including Walter Odede and Argwings-Kodhek, had applied, but though the other four were granted scholarships I did not even receive a reply to my application. I had been the first at Makerere to express an ambition for higher education abroad, I had worked hard in several fields; this neglect, I thought with bitterness, was the thanks of the government of Kenya. I was disenchanted with the teaching profession and my treatment at the hands of missions and government alike. I turned my head from the classroom to face new directions.

I was convinced that to start the battle against White domination we had to assert our economic independence. We had to show what we could do by our own effort. We had had it drummed into us that the Whites had the brains to give the orders and it was for Africans to carry them out. We had to show we were capable of enterprise and development in fields beyond our shambas. It was no good bridling at accusations of our inferiority. We had to prove our mettle to the government, to the Whites. We Luo had also to assert ourselves among the other peoples of Kenya. I was haunted by the view which other Africans had of the Luo people. I had been hurt at Makerere by the accusations of fellow students from other tribes that the Luo were extravagant, self-centred, and exhibitionist; that they used their money for show and not to save to improve themselves. The Luo needed to build a sense of unity, common purpose, and achievement. I hated the idea of our people begging from the government. We had had enough of memoranda which addressed the District Commissioner as our father and the government as our mother and which appealed for schools, hospitals, and roads. Petitioning was accustoming people to ask but not to do anything for themselves. It was time to instil confidence; time to show we could stand on our own feet in the modern world. Economic effort, self help and development would be the hurdle to our advance in Nyanza and in Kenya.

At Maseno in the early forties a small group of us had decided to save to launch a business venture, taking advantage of the sale of cheap trucks released from army stocks. We accumulated 2,000 shillings in a year and purchased an open truck which we put in the charge of a teacher, Omuodo Ayila, whose father was a Church elder and a businessman. We had dreams of making money from the transport of goods to and from Kisumu but the scheme did not appear to work, the books were not well kept and the lorry itself broke down. This was a setback not only to us as individuals but as members of the educated group whose failure, I thought, would be watched with derision by those among us who were uneducated but successful in business. So many business ventures seemed doomed to founder. In the years I taught at the Veterinary School I had joined the Karadha Company, started in Gem—the secretary was B. A. Ohanga—a savings association which loaned money on interest; the rate of interest demanded was high and many people did not honour their loans.

As a counter to this failure I had begun in 1944 to write

77

rules and regulations for a different type of savings association. I had named it the Bondo Thrift Association. A few of us agreed to contribute savings of 11 shillings a month, of which 10 shillings would be accumulated and 1 shilling expended on running expenses. We opened a Kisumu bank account, enrolled many members and made plans for expansion. In the beginning this association was confined to Sakwa people but in 1945 we opened it to people from farther afield. This was the time when many of our people were returning from the war, with demobilization grants and compensation sums. We urged them not to squander their money on buying useless things in the Indian shops but to invest their money in our association. We were trying to instil in our people a spirit of thrift, responsibility and working and saving together.

When I abandoned teaching at Maseno, my family was united in its disappointment. I had become an important source of family revenue. I harvested six bags of *wimbi* and fifteen bags of maize from my garden at the Veterinary School, and I had about thirty-six chickens. When I arrived home I was greeted with criticism and quarrels and my wife joined in the general disapproval. I was biding my time, I explained, there would be a place for me to work but I had to plan my next steps.

I shut myself in a small office in Bondo and I began to write an improved constitution for our cooperative society. The District Commissioner of Kisumu warned me that a cooperative would not be registered and that I would be better advised to launch a company. In fact, though our constitution for a cooperative was modelled on the lines of the Kenya Farmers' Association it was turned down by the Registrar of Cooperatives. When I sought help in forming a company from Indian lawyers in Kisumu they advised a welfare society; companies would be beyond our knowledge and ability, they said. I went to Kisumu to buy books on company law and settled down myself to draft our memorandum and articles of association. We were then ready to decide on a name. We called a meeting for that. Some said it should be called the Bondo Thrift and Trading Corporation. Others were in favour of calling it the Luo Corporation, others the Kenya Thrift and Trading Corporation, and still others the East African Thrift and Trading Corporation. Country-wide nationalism was not yet articulate and well developed at the time; I was afraid that if we called it the Kenya Thrift and Trading Corporation people would feel remote and uninvolved in the company's affairs. If we called it the Luo Thrift and Trading Corporation the Luo people would be proud of it. I plumped for that name and it was accepted.

When it came to registering the company the District Commissioner, C. F. Atkins, had recommended the well-known Nairobi Negro lawyer Mr James Buck. He was surprised we had managed to draft our own constitution and asked 3,000 shillings to have the company registered. We withdrew our savings and sent him the money. Suddenly Mr Buck died intestate. Our money and that attempt to register the company were lost. Nevertheless we struggled on and the company was registered in August 1947.

We had not waited for the official registration but had already launched a programme for development. John Paul Olola who had founded the Kisumu Native Chamber of Commerce as far back as 1927 and who helped me in 1946 with the Bondo Thrift Association worked closely with me. Members flocked to us. Though we called this the Luo Thrift and Trading Corporation, we did not restrict the membership to one tribe but opened it to Africans throughout East Africa. Our first undertaking was to build a shop at Maseno. The second was to launch a press to propagate our aims and objects. Orinda Okun and James Omoga had started the *Nyanza Times* but printing costs were crippling

79

them so it was agreed that we would purchase a press and publish the paper. After that we would build a hotel in Kisumu. Kisumu was our capital yet Africans did not run a single business there. Why leave the field to the immigrant races? We would build our hotel and our members would grow the produce and supply the meat and vegetables for it. Scheme number four was to trade in hides and skins, to market crops and set up a chain of flour mills.

Olola and I journeyed throughout Central and South Nyanza preaching in the market places and at meetings about the aims of our movement. One journey took me from Kisumu to Kericho, then to Lumbwa, and there I met Argwings-Kodhek, Ojal, and Akatsa setting off in the train on their journey to Britain to study. That re-opened an old wound but I wished them luck, told them briefly what I had embarked on, and went on with the work. I travelled to Nairobi, to Nakuru, to Kitale and Eldoret, then to Mombasa.

It was on a journey to Nairobi that I met Achieng Oneko again. In 1940 when I was a teacher at Maseno he had been a student. I became housemaster, he was dormitory prefect. I was athletics master, he was a good sprinter. He had gone to work in Nairobi as a government meteorological observer and clerk. During a 1946 visit to Nairobi to canvass money for Bondo Thrift I had been dressed in shorts, and had talked of thrift and simplicity of living; I was critical of the handsome salaries earned by our educated young men and of their town sophistication. I have the impression that Achieng found my views peculiar. We had talked then about politics but our thinking did not seem to converge. When I was on the carpet in the Central Government Offices for my rebellion as a teacher, Achieng had accompanied me when I argued my case, and this time he was impressed. By the time I was full-time organizer of the Luo Thrift and Trading Corporation, Achieng had started the newspaper *Ramogi* (a secret activity since his government service did not permit involvement in political affairs); he had become Nairobi representative of the Luo Thrift and was giving it publicity in the columns of *Ramogi*; and Achieng and I were beginning to achieve a mutual understanding and reciprocal arrangement for work among our people which was to grow into a decisive political partnership in later years.

In Nyanza the sales of *Ramogi* began to grow. Its readers were my contemporaries who were perhaps for the first time beginning to think about national, as distinct from local, affairs. But when a Kenya African Union mission of Achieng, Jesse Kariuki, Awori, and Mathu (the first African to sit in Kenya's Legislative Assembly) travelled to Nyanza Province to organize for KAU, they held meetings in North Nyanza, round Kakamega, but completely by-passed Central Nyanza. Our people were not free to take part in politics: school-teachers were forbidden to do so, Chiefs were under the thumb of the government; every meeting was reported to the government by Chiefs and informers. Two of us only had independent means and could embark on political activity: Achieng and I.

Eliud Mathu, the first African member of the Legislative Council, visited Kisumu on one occasion and he, Achieng, and I had a discussion in a poky room we had found for use in Kisumu. I remember Mathu looking around him and saying: 'Where are your Luo people? You don't even have a building of your own.' This sparked off something in Achieng and me. Achieng later became a member of the Nairobi Municipal Council; I buckled down anew to the task of building the Luo Thrift and Trading Corporation.

Okuto Bala, who had been expelled as one of the ring-leaders of the student strike at Maseno Veterinary School left a post as hospital dispenser in Nakuru in 1947 to do a course in stenography and book-keeping, and was then installed in our new company office. This was a tiny room in Kisumu's Market Street that had been used formerly by a charcoal dealer. We had searched for and found it despite the advice from the Town Clerk at the municipal offices that we should establish ourselves in the African reserves because all Kisumu town was meant to be exclusively for Europeans and Asians. Our monthly rental was 90 shillings. My salary was 40 shillings a month (I had earned £6 a month as a teacher), and Okuto Bala earned 20 shillings a month.

With the appointment of Okuto Bala I was free to travel widely again to enrol support for the company. I became an itinerant business-preacher, combing Uganda and Tanganyika as well as Kenya for member-investors. I covered anything up to 100 miles by bicycle but resorted to passenger bus and trains for journeys to Nairobi, the coast, and outside Kenya.

By the end of our first year, in 1947, we had purchased and established a press in Nairobi, an old flatbed machine on which we printed *Ramogi*. Soon other African editors were knocking on our doors. We printed the Kikuyu *Mnyenyereri* edited by Mworia and *Agikikuyu*; *Mwiathia* in Akamba; *Mulinavosi* in Maragoli; *Radioposta* in Swahili, published by W. W. Awori; and *Mwalimu* published by Francis Khamisi. The level of politics differed in these papers, but some were quite outspokenly critical of the government; I wondered sometimes whether the government knew what was in these papers. The most radical, hard-hitting paper was *Uhuru Wa'Afrika*, run by Paul Ngei, the young, fiery, and impressive Kamba leader.

We made no profit from printing these African weekly papers, but this was our contribution to the cause of African independence. We took a decision to employ only Africans and from our devoted Zablon Oti our young employees learnt printing techniques and the management of the business. One of our first apprentices who later became the

manager of the press in Kisumu was Atinga Odima, the
present Chief of Alego Location. By the time we had purchased the press we had only 8,000 shillings remaining in our
bank account, but we began to build the Maseno Store. The
building and my collection of contributions went on side
by side. Some people paid accounts of only 10, 20, and 30
shillings and it required tremendous effort to muster the
capital. In 1948 the Maseno Store was officially opened by
the then Governor, Sir Philip Mitchell, while on a visit to
Nyanza. (The District Commissioner Mr C. F. Atkins made
the official opening possible, despite strong objections from
the then Provincial Commissioner.)

Ours was the only shop in Maseno and I must admit we
often let our customers down badly. We learnt about stocking
through our losses. There was depreciation to be taken into
account; and the peoples' needs and tastes in the locality. I
learned to buy tea and sugar, dishes, and cutlery, exercise
books and socks. I bought the goods from the wholesaler,
loaded them into the truck, drove the truck, stacked the
goods on the shelves, counted the cash, did the account
books, and trained and supervised the staff. Those early
days in business are still vivid. I was a company director but
Okuto Bala and I slept on a mat on the floor of our office.
My gumboots went unpolished for days. I wore a long-
sleeved khaki shirt, khaki shorts, and torn socks. I started
work in the office at six o'clock each morning, and stayed
at work during lunch hour ; lunch was a lump of thick
porridge with vegetables, for 50 cents. I was buyer, shop-
keeper, transporter, book-keeper, commercial traveller, all
in one. The finances of the shop were always precarious. We
were under-capitalized and our only chance of survival was
a rapid turn-over: converting goods into cash and into goods
again, and so keeping this cycle of trade moving. We
suffered losses by pilfering and bad buying. But people were
impressed by our efforts and went on investing in the shop

although we were unable to pay dividends. Among our investors were Kikuyu from the Londiani area and Elburgon, Kipsigis, Abaluhya, Kisil, Kuria, and Baganda from across the border.

By 1949 we were ready to embark on our next project, the Ramogi Hotel. A plot was up for auction and we bid 16,500 shillings for it, and got it. But we had only 4,000 shillings in the bank. We paid that amount over and were given seven days to pay the remainder. I can remember no time when I have worked so hard. We sent telegrams to our shareholders all over East Africa and raised 12,000 shillings before the week was past. I was buckling under my load of duties so that year we moved the Ramogi Press from Nairobi to Kisumu (Zablon Oti decided to remain in Nairobi but Achieng Oneko came with it) to concentrate our business in one centre. Achieng became secretary of the company and I became managing director. Okuto Bala moved to Maseno to manage the store. We had only 8,000 shillings in hand when we embarked on a scheme for the erection of the hotel on our Kisumu site. Our directors signed the contract but said they could not imagine how we could raise the contract price of 120,000 shillings. We paid the first instalment and began new journeys throughout East Africa to rally our shareholders. We applied to the government for a loan but a condition of assistance was that we should instal a European director. In the end we raised half the amount and were granted a mortgage by an Ismaili company, the Diamond Jubilee Investment Trust. At last the building, Ramogi House, stood erect, a double-storey structure which housed the Winam Hotel.

The company had shown results. It was one of the first companies founded and run by Africans; it had been subscribed by virtually all the tribes in Kenya, and was, in its own way, a national movement of the people. We asked the Provincial Commissioner to request the Governor to officially open the building. The Commissioner seemed to think the building was too assertive of African rights for those days—he was heard saying that such a move by Africans should have waited a hundred years—and he suppressed the invitation. We turned instead to the High Commissioner for the Government of India, Mr Apasaheb Pant. That day Kisumu was bursting with people. The people from North Nyanza came dancing, and the Luo from many places; the Kalenjin who had joined the Luo Thrift and Trading Corporation came dancing. Apasaheb Pant delivered a memorable speech. We called the building Ramogi House. The people celebrated with joy the first African-owned building in Kisumu. It delighted them that it was double-storey, a double proof that Africans had entered a field pronounced beyond their powers for as long as they could remember.

A European missionary whom I had known at Maseno thought our building an ominous sign. Nationalism, he commented at this time, can begin in any quarter. Sometimes it begins with business ventures, or in the church, sometimes directly through politics. This was not simply a business, he said, it was a national movement which the government should watch. 'This man', he said, referring to me, 'must be closely watched.'

The Corporation next operated as building contractors. We formed a team of bricklayers and supervisors and undertook building commissions in Central and South Nyanza. By 1953 we had also put up three posho mills, one in Bondo, one in Ng'iya, and the third at Dudi, which not only ground the peoples' corn but also marketed crops and supplied grain to the schools. We were not reluctant to launch ourselves in new fields, but our attempt to market fish from the lake was a financial disaster and had to be abandoned, and the man put in charge of the hides and skins section misappropriated our funds.

My years spent at the feet of the elders, learning the Luo idiom, helped me to speak to the people in examples they understood. Visiting one village after another I made untold numbers of speeches, stressing the message of cooperation, unity, and economic independence by our own effort, varying my words for the audience I faced. When we built our hotel we had to break the resistance of the Luo to eating away from their homes: eating houses were unknown in our country. Every Luo believed that the place to eat your own food, cooked by the women of your family, was in your home. I promised that in our hotel the people would be served not bread and butter and tea but *nyuka mbudwe* (porridge made from brewed wimbi flour), *mito* and *alot bo* (a local vegetable), and *nyoyo* (maize and beans). When we set up posho mills I said 'Carry your own maize to the mill and in a matter of minutes you'll be carrying your own flour back home'. Our building contractors put homes up in a month or a fortnight: 'Place your order today and tomorrow we bring you the key,' I said. I tried to inculcate responsibility and vision. 'Think for the future,' I urged. In life we planted crops that could be reaped after a short season, crops to ameliorate hunger. We also had trees that took seven or ten years to bear fruit, and so we learned to plan ahead. In life too we had to plan for short- and long-term needs. In forging not a narrow tribal pride but a broader unity we had to learn how to approach people and work with them. All humanity was equal and important, I told my listeners. The miserable man you see today might previously have been an important and responsible member of the community; some misfortune might have reduced him to wretchedness. No man should presume to judge another by his appearance, but men should be approached with the idea that all men are equal. People should be respected as individuals, not as members of a particular tribe.

Side by side with the Luo Thrift and Trading Corporation

we built the Luo Union, to unite our people throughout East Africa. When I had been a schoolboy the Luo Union was mainly an organization in Nairobi of our people working in and around that city. We teachers at Maseno were conceited: we thought of ourselves as the educated élite and Maseno as the centre of learning. Richard Arina, Walter Odede, and I hatched ambitions of starting a Luo organization that would envelop not only Nairobi but the whole country. We organized a meeting in 1946 and invited the participation of the Luos in Nairobi but they rejected the invitation with the retort that anyone who wanted to join a Luo Union could do so in Nairobi and they could not conceive why Luo Union headquarters should be moved from the capital. We held a discussion with leading Luo from all parts of the country and I made an earnest appeal which brought agreement that the national union should be started with headquarters in Kisumu. Temporary office-bearers were elected. I was to be treasurer. Our efforts that year were largely abortive though, because the Nairobi organization refused to join in. But in later years, as the company grew, and I was constantly on the move among Luo living in all parts of East Africa, the Luo Union welded our people together. It raised funds for classrooms and books for our children, sent students to study abroad on scholarships, organized traditional dances and gave a new life to Luo communal activity, linking villagers with townsmen. In those years we built an unprecedented national consciousness and unity.

Evaluated as a business, though, the Luo Thrift and Trading Corporation did not bring impressive returns. We must admit that our balance sheets have more often showed losses than profit. We were inexperienced. We had to learn the hard way that under-capitalized small businesses like ours live ever on the edge of bankruptcy. We were unable to pay dividends until the mid-fifties, largely because we were bonded to pay interest as high as ten per cent on the loan we had raised from an Asian trading company to complete the hotel. We found, as the years went by, that we had more to contend with than just routine business difficulties. Far from encouraging African economic ventures, the government seemed set on producing obstacles. The British Labour Government, in power after the end of the war, encouraged cooperative societies, but only those run under government supervision, and ringed round with restrictions and control. When groups of Africans began individually to try to run cooperatives the authorities worked to undermine confidence in their ability. 'Don't deposit with new companies run by inexperienced Africans' their Commissioner and agents said. And added 'Like Odinga and company. If he dies tomorrow where will your money be?' When we began to build our posho mill at the market at Dudu the District Commissioner stirred up trouble for us, urging the people not to permit us to establish a mill in their area, and later pressing for our eviction on the Central Nyanza African District Council, on the grounds that we were building without the consent of the Council and the Commissioner. A narrow majority of two on the Council defeated the Commissioner on this issue. When we were found guilty of offences like driving our lorries without a licence or overcharging a penny or two above the pegged price control, or even with a delay in filing returns to the Registrar of Companies, the fines were disproportionately heavy. In the years when we were on the verge of transforming our losses into a small profit, government campaigns were mounted against cooperatives that were not government-approved or supervised, and we had to counter the resistance to our ventures stirred up among the people.

We had hindrance on all sides, and little assistance. Invariably when we applied for loans we were turned down. A condition generally attached to a loan was that we should accept a European general manager; African effort was clearly not acceptable. We could raise no loans from banks because in the African areas communal land ownership prevented individual land title which could be offered as security, and the banks would accept no other security. There was a network of trade regulations and restrictions designed to 'protect' Africans but which merely served to militate against their economic initiative and to leave the monopoly of trade in the hands of the Asians and the Whites. Grants of licence were entirely at the discretion of government officials; there was no appeal against their decision. The government argued that it protected Africans from getting into debt by making it difficult for them to borrow money; this put the African trade at a constant disadvantage. We could not buy stock on the basis of ordinary commercial credit. We could not raise loans in the normal course of business because the government decreed that loans above a certain amount were not recoverable by the lender unless he had previously obtained official permission to advance the money; wholesale businesses that might have been inclined to extend credit to us were dissuaded from doing so. The authorities had decided that trade was not to be an African preserve, and where he did venture into commerce, this was to be in the bush, in the reserves, not in a trading centre like Kisumu. (Even there trading was largely in the hands of Asians, working with and through the chiefs.) Our economic effort was frowned upon not only because it was competition against established trading preserves, but also because it was a demonstration of African initiative and independence.

At every twist and turn I came up against the stone wall of government policy that decreed against African advance. I tried taking part in politics in the only sphere approved by the government, the local African councils. The year that I left teaching and went back to my village there were elections to the Central Nyanza African District Council and the people urged me to contest. I was intent on building a business, and I knew that if elected I would unseat a senior tribesman of veteran experience in the council who was reluctant to make way for me, but I could not resist the urgings of the people; I agreed to be a candidate. I took part in an election for the first time in my life. The voting procedure was for the candidates to be ranged alongside one another and for their supporters to line up behind them. A long line of people stretched behind me and I defeated my opponent by over 50 votes. This pleased me but I had to think seriously of the duties involved in being a representative of voters. When Joel Omino had been a member of the District Council and we had been together at Maseno Veterinary School he had brought sets of the council minutes to the school and we had helped him translate them into good English. This was the sum total of my knowledge about the council system. I took my new duties earnestly and asked for information and advice about how to conduct myself in the council. It did not take me long to reach the conclusion that the councils were used by the Commissioners as a post box to carry their orders to the people. Matters already decided and finalised by government were brought to the councils for confirmation and acceptance. Council members were powerless to change anything or make suggestions contrary to the decisions already reached. (In 1950 the local councils gave way to the African District Councils which were supposed to be more representative organs of local government: instead of merely advising they were supposed to run some of their own services, but they were crippled by lack of funds.) The council chairman was the District Commissioner who held complete veto power.

It was not possible, under this system, to be a true representative of the people. On our council we submitted a proposal for the division of the council into two sides:

government officials and nominees on the one side, elected members on the other. The chairman ruled that this was not possible: our council was purely advisory and its structure and methods of work derived from this advisory function. At one session we had estimates of expenditure placed before us. At the time the issue of land preservation dominated the countryside, and the council was being asked to pass a specially large vote for land preservation. I stood up to say that while we appreciated the seriousness of soil erosion we should not concentrate on land preservation schemes at the expense of other equally important projects; land preservation was a long-term undertaking and other allocations should not be neglected. This annoyed the Commissioner and he interrupted me while I was talking. I did not know what I was talking about, he said, I had best sit down. At that I, too, lost my temper. 'I'm not going to sit down,' I said. 'You must sit down,' he shouted. Then: 'If you don't sit down, get out of the room,' and 'If you don't leave this room I'll get you out of it.' Council members appealed to me to give way, but I strode angrily from the council chamber. The Commissioner scolded the chief of my area telling him he was a fool to have an elected member from his area who could not behave properly. The Commissioner reported me to the Provincial Commissioner who called me to his office. If I continued to be rude to the District Commissioner I would be removed from the council, I was told. I tried to explain the incident and how the District Commissioner ran the council proceedings by trying to bludgeon us into agreement, but the Provincial Commissioner insisted that my only course of action was to apologize to the District Commissioner. If there was anyone who warranted an apology it was myself and I told the Provincial Commissioner I would rather be out of the council than treated like that inside it. I went back to Sakwa location to explain that my treatment had done dishonour to the people I represented.

To my delight the *baraza* and even the Chief approved my action.

The councils were the shield with which government protected itself from the people: measures which were unpopular were imposed through the councils, punishments for infringements of unpopular measures were meted out through us, and the government told the people: 'You elected your representatives on to the District Council, this is their decision.' It was not difficult to get the councils to see eye to eye with government. Outnumbering the elected members on the councils were the chiefs, the centres of power in all the constituences; there were also nominated members who owed their presence on the council to a policy of courting favour with the government: and even the elected members had to be confirmed in office by the Provincial Commissioner and could be unseated by his decision.

On the Central Nyanza Council our Commissioner, a liberal and reasonable man, was replaced by another official, who returned to Nyanza after an absence of many years in government service in other regions, and who lost no time in expressing his disappointment in Nyanza, and admonishing us, on the council and in public, for what he called our 'slackness and laziness'. When the Governor, Sir Philip Mitchell, opened the new council hall in Kisumu the address of the Provincial Commissioner took up this theme, that the Luo were slack and lazy, and the same insulting speech was published in *Baraza*. I protested against the public shaming of the Luo, and I was suspended from several council meetings as punishment. At meetings of the council we were constantly admonished, and preached the virtues of sobriety, hard work, and obedience. The atmosphere was one of condescension and patronage towards us; we found the Commissioner difficult as chairman of the council because he never allowed a member to speak his mind. If a councillor rose to speak in language the Commissioner did not understand, or to express an opinion contrary to his, the chairman would interrupt us. When we protested the Commissioner, as president of the council, ordered our names to be recorded in the minutes as a mark of censure. We were back in the classroom again. The Commissioner recorded in his reports that while one or two of the councillors were 'sensible', I was 'tendentious and over-talkative'. Production records were low, the government officials accused, because the Luo were a lazy people. In the council Zablon Aduwo pointed out that the reason for the non-production of rice and cotton was the low price that the African was paid for his produce. This was ignored. The province was encouraged to cultivate sisal. Then the price paid for sisal dropped. We protested in the council. The Commissioner replied: 'The price paid for sisal is no concern of the local native authority. No one is compelled to sell sisal if they don't like the price offered which, as a matter of fact, will probably be reduced as it is proving uneconomic.'[1] And the Commissioner added: 'I have read these minutes (of our council meeting) with considerable dissatisfaction as they reveal that members have a lamentably poor understanding of how the problems of local government must be dealt with. It must be remembered that such powers and authority as the local native council possesses have been delegated to it by the central government which remains the ultimate arbiter in all matters of government.'

The government and their appointed chiefs were the final arbiter. On the council we could talk and pass resolutions but we had no power to enforce our decisions. I was outspoken because I believed I was expressing the needs of the people, but the government did not seem to accept that this was the function of a member of a council. I noticed that my assertion of independence brought reprisals against the Luo Thrift and Trading Corporation. I was summoned to court to face several prosecutions, seemingly routine, but, I was

[1] Minutes of the Central Nyanza Local Native Council, 1949.

convinced, largely intimidatory. The District Commissioner who had been present when I was locked in battle over a local issue with one of the chiefs sat on the bench in a case in which I was charged with overcharging two cents on empty beer bottles, and he levied a fine of 600 shillings. It seemed that even in business I could not be independent if I fell out with government. I was growing increasingly sceptical of the advice we heard from the government that we had to seek economic advance before political power could be given to us: wherever we turned government-made obstacles seemed to loom in the way of our economic advance.

I was being forced to the conclusion that the admonitions to us to seek economic power before political rights were not genuine advice from the colonial government; these were devices by the authorities to mislead us, and gain time for the administration. I was becoming more and more convinced that political power had to be struggled for and achieved as a stepping-stone to any advance at all.

94

CHAPTER SIX

Peasants in Revolt

PERHAPS the government believed that the people would indefinitely accept powerless local councils as the channel through which to make representations. This miscalculation was carried to its most absurd extreme on the return to Kenya of Jomo Kenyatta who had grown into a world-famous African figure since the days when the KCA had sent him, as its secretary, to England to present evidence to the Carter Commission on the theft of Kikuyu lands. Gigantic meetings greeted Kenyatta in 1946. When the co-sponsor of the Fifth Pan-African Congress (held in Manchester in 1945) suggested to the Governor that he take an active part in political affairs, he was told that he should start first in local government, on the native council of his area!

By the end of the war and Kenyatta's return, large parts of the country were in a state of ferment. Land was still the burning issue. The KCA had never died. On and off in the span of thirty years political organization had been allowed to come to the surface. Though the KCA was restricted by the Government to represent only the Kikuyu, it was forging common cause, through struggle, with other associations. In 1938 the government ordered the Wakamba to de-stock as an anti-erosion measure and Kamba cattle were pushed on to the market at rock-bottom prices. A huge demonstration marched on Nairobi in protest. The Taita Hills Association grew out of the loss of land in the heart of Taita country to European-owned coffee and sisal estates. The KCA, the Kamba Members' Association and the Taita Hills Association joined together in protest action; their leaders—twelve Kikuyu, eight Wakamba, and two Wataita—were jailed together.[1] A secret inquiry was held at Naivasha into charges that the twenty-two arrested men were in touch with German-Italian-Japanese enemy agents. This spurious charge was never proved, but the leaders were restricted at Kapenguria for the duration of the war. The banning of the KCA as an illegal organization sent Kikuyu political organization underground once more; it had been said that if there is any one event which ignited the fuse which led to the armed revolt of the Emergency period, it was this banning of the KCA, that a state of emergency can be said to have begun not in 1952 but in 1940. KCA fires never went out; the organization of the people round land grievances never stopped; there was a general training in agitation and in secrecy lest the movement be betrayed to the government. Land was the one burning issue; female circumcision was another. In 1929 the Church of Scotland had refused to admit circumcised girls to its schools; Kikuyu independent schools, which numbered about 300, educating something like 60,000 children by 1946, were the answer to this attack on a custom central to Kikuyu culture and an assertion of Kikuyu loyalties and nationalism.

KCA membership was bound by oath-taking, the traditional sanction of African society; it bound members to allegiance of their cause. The membership fee for taking the KCA oath was as high as 62 shillings 30 cents, so that young

[1] These men included: Githae Kariri, Paul Njuguna, Nehemiah Mwangi, Wanyeri Karumbi, Gichuki Kiahi, Marius Karatu, John Muchuchu, Jesse Kariuki, John Mbugwa, George K. Ndegwa, Zakaria Musia, Peter Maingi, Jacob Mutiso, Charles Wambaa, Shem Muthuwa, Elijah Kavulu, Isaac Mivalonzi, John Kavula, Woresha Mengo Kamundi (now Senator for Taita), Jimmy Mwambichi.

Kenya police search Kikuyu villagers whose homes have been demolished by bulldozers.

Arrested Africans being led away to detention camps.

A detention camp seen from a watchtower where a guard is posted with an automatic weapon.

A gallows is erected in a camp for the hanging of members of the Land Freedom Army.

The longer the emergency the poorer the country becomes both Kenya and England and the

more the enemity and hatred grow strong, and worse still the British Empire will be blamed by the world for its injustice.

In Kenya there has been an average death rate of a hundred persons daily since the declaration of the emergency, the death has been due to weapons, starvation, & treatment which are organised by the Kenya Government.

Who will pay all this cost? Definitely the British Empire which has appointed and supervised the Kenya Government is responsible for the cost.

There is no other peace or settlement of Kenya troubles except:- WIYATHI, UHURU, FREEDOM, of Self-Government to the Kenya Africans.

Extracts from a letter from the Forests, written from the Land Freedom Army.

Dedan Kimathi, one of the leaders of the forest fighters, being brought to court on a stretcher after his capture. He was subsequently executed.

The African elected members to the Legislative Council holding a meeting in Nairobi in 1958.

people without land or earnings were disqualified for the most part, and KCA membership was generally found among the older men of the clans. Oaths had begun to have political significance in the twenties when the land agitation started in force, but a new type of oath—the administration of a mass oath to a whole community—emerged in 1947-48 when the crisis of the Olengurone squatters came to a head. Eleven thousand Kikuyu were faced with forcible eviction from their lands; the oath taken on that occasion was not the entry to a secret society of the select, but a community pledge—a commitment to a kind of verbal constitution—to resist removal and agricultural restrictions.

In 1944 the Legislative Council was opened to one African member—a government appointee. Eliud Mathu was selected. On the advice of the Governor the Kenya African Study Union was formed as a colony-wide African body with which the lone African member could consult. I had joined KASU at its formation while a teacher at Maseno. Study? Africans asked one another, what have we to study about our grievances? It was not a matter of study but of organization. The s was dropped from the name and we had KAU, the Kenya African Union. The adoption of not only a new name but also a more outspoken constitution meant that civil servants were prohibited from becoming members of KAU, though some wriggled round the prohibition and remained members by using their wives' names.

Within KAU there was a constant tussle between the moderate and the more militant elements. The days had passed when an organization was needed solely to support one elected member, the people said. They were critical of leaders to whom compromise with the authorities seemed easier and safer than action. At times internal disputes paralysed the organization, as in the argument about White Papers 191 and 210 on the racial proportions of representation on the East African Central Legislative Assembly when

97

Mathu was in favour of accepting the settler formula for representation, and he was defeated by the more militant trends in KAU. The people were demanding a more dynamic leadership. Never in the history of Kenya was there a more crucial period for the freedom struggle in the years from 1946 to 1952; the great upsurge of support for KAU when Kenyatta returned in 1946 was the overt expression of the tumult among the people.

I had met Kenyatta for the first time in 1948. He visited Kisumu with Ambrose Ofafa (who was then treasurer of Luo Union in Nairobi and a leading figure in KAU), but though Ofafa came into our office, Kenyatta remained in the car. I went to shake him by the hand and welcomed him back to Kenya, but for some years nothing came of the hope I expressed that afternoon that we might one day have discussions.

In my blood I think I had been a politician all along. There was not a school where I did not form or lead an organization of one kind or another. Carey Francis had asked me: 'Why this need to organize, organize, organize all the time?' During the early years of the Luo Thrift I believed that our people would shoulder political responsibilities more ably when they had furthered themselves economically. When Achieng Oneko returned from Nairobi to work with me in Nyanza we constantly argued priorities. I said self-improvement came first; Achieng was in favour of more direct political action. 'Look ahead,' I said, 'if we both enter politics at this stage when the people are not politically alive to the issues, they will not be ready to support us in case of our arrest or persecution.' The old Nyanza generation of political leaders had been tamed or absorbed into missions, chieftainship or administration; the times needed new leaders, men who did not depend on the colonial administration for their livelihood or approval. Our people had to look beyond district boundaries and district issues to be fired by the national interests, but this would not be achieved over-night. At times I thought of transferring Luo Thrift business to other shoulders to free myself for direct political action, but I could not forget that I was the repository of the peoples' savings; I could not shirk my responsibilities.

For the time being Achieng and I would work side by side to complement one another. We were obsessed by the same problems; our stress on priorities would be different. I con-centrated on Luo Thrift business ventures, on organizing the Luo Union and cementing the unity of our people; Achieng edited *Ramogi* and *Nyanza Times*, mincing no words in criticism of government, and he plunged into political organizing in Nyanza. He had been involved in the direction of the KAU branch in Nairobi, but in Kisumu he started not a KAU branch but the Kisumu Residents' Association. KAU, he judged, would gather little support in Nyanza because by government and newspapers it had been dubbed a Kikuyu organization led, this propaganda said, by 'men like Kenyatta, who have failed in life, demagogues'. The Resi-dents' Association worked at removing the smear for about six months and then converted itself into a branch of KAU.

In 1950 the Kisumu branch of KAU sent a letter to Kenyatta inviting him to address a public meeting; the letter was blocked from reaching Kenyatta but Tom Mbotela, KAU assistant secretary and Ambrose Ofafa, then KAU treasurer, came instead. A great meeting was held. The Nairobi and Kisumu branches became among the most influential in the country. Here was the renewed Kikuyu-Luo-Abaluhya partnership in politics.

In November 1951 Achieng and Mbiyu Koinange had been sent to London as a delegation on the land question. Monies to pay for the delegation were collected throughout the country, and at many Nyanza meetings. When Achieng returned (Mbiyu remained in London) the public meetings

99

were bigger than ever. The land delegation had been cold-shouldered in British official circles, but in Paris the United Nations was in session and lobbying was highly successful; the Colonial Office had to sit up and take notice of the reception given the two Africans from Kenya. By coincidence the plane bringing Oneko home also carried the Governor. Kenyatta was waiting at the airport for an immediate report. The public meeting held at Kaloleni mustered a crowd of 60,000 and 20,000 shillings were collected on the spot for the then initiated Freedom Fund. KAU was reaching a new peak.

It was in 1952 that Kenyatta came to Kisumu again. Achieng introduced me to him and for several hours before the big Kisumu public meeting we had close talks at the Maseno Store. I talked of my conviction that Africans had to attain economic independence for themselves. 'That will come when we have political power,' said Kenyatta. Until we had snatched the reins of government we would not control the products of our efforts, he argued. I had heard this before but not put as emphatically. How could we take over the government? By unity and sacrifice in struggle, preparing even to die for our case, said Kenyatta. He added: 'We must get to know one another. The Kikuyu must know the Luo thoroughly.' Kenyatta's plan was that the Luo should select twelve influential elders to tour Kikuyu country, to travel as far as Mombasa, and that twelve influential Kikuyu would tour Luo country. The conclusion of the two delegations would be inevitable: that we are Africans one and the same. United we would be formidable. 'I have lived with these people in Great Britain,' said Kenyatta, 'I know they fear unity.' I agreed to the plan for the exchange of emissaries and representatives. From then on Achieng Oneko, my indispensable colleague, would be free to work wherever he was needed in the political movement. I would need time to free myself from my business and other commitments, but he could depend on my complete political support. I wrote this in a letter to Jomo Kenyatta, dated 27 June 1952.

You can't imagine the happiness I derive from your one-day visit to Maseno on Tuesday. I really enjoyed your company heartily and hope we will have many more moments like that in the coming days of our self-government. In this I am your disciple to the hilt. You were so much at home and felt so very much native to the house as if Maseno had been your home Kikuyuni. I will never forget that memorable day . . . When you return again to us in August as you have promised to do, I hope to attend many meetings with you and to give you as much assistance as will be possible from a nationalist businessman.

I remain, always,
Your Disciple in Nationalism.

There was a postscript to the letter:

One minute again, Jomo,
Achieng Oneko had been my right hand man and I could have lost all the world but Achieng. But for the sake of KAU and our freedom, I had persuaded, I have persuaded, I am persuading and will insist that Achieng must remain with KAU Executives. No Business will ever prosper, nor schools, nor other freedom-loving African enterprises, unless and until they have *strong political backings*. May the Almighty and the Holy Ghost of our Forefathers initiate you the more to be the first witness and champion of our long awaited-for Freedom. I know I shall be there with you.

Kenyatta's speeches in Kisumu had moved me deeply. 'The tree of freedom is planted,' he told the people. 'For it to grow it needs the water of human blood.' Many in Nyanza had not expected such strong talk and in some areas his hot language frightened the people. But for me this was a turning point: I threw myself into the work and spirit of the Kenya African Union.

We continued to plan a series of meetings for KAU and Kenyatta throughout Nyanza but they were banned by the government. Opposition to Kenyatta meetings in South Nyanza came from supporters of Paul Mboya, the first African to sit on the Central Legislative Assembly. Members of this and other advisory bodies, Kenyatta had once told the Governor, were no more effective than 'pictures on the wall' and Mboya's supporters had taken this as a reference to him personally and smarted for a lifetime under this taunt.[1]

But there was more to the banning of meetings than the opposition of local moderates. By now the atmosphere throughout Kenya was taut to breaking point. KAU's central committee was summoned to an urgent meeting in Nairobi. This was the first KAU central committee meeting that I attended. During the meeting Kenyatta and Achieng were summoned for questioning by the government Attorney-General and the police; they were warned that their speeches were inflammatory. In Kenyatta's absence I was chosen to chair the meeting. All at the meeting spoke against the Whites and the government with great bitterness. We felt that a crisis was approaching. We warned one another that

[1] Paul Mboya commanded great influence among the Luo people. His own life illustrated growing African protest against foreign domination. Mboya had been converted to the Seventh Day Adventist Mission Church where he played a prominent part in church affairs, but then he found race discrimination making inroads into the Church, African ways being ridiculed, and African education suppressed, so he broke with the Church and became the Chief of Karachuonyo Location, founding the first schools to be run not by the missions but by an African District Council. He wrote a book on Luo custom; married a second wife, according to Luo though not mission practice; and as a chief asserted his authority according to Luo traditional ways, thus winning admiration and popularity all over Nyanza. Mboya was also the first chief to build a Council hall for the Location assemblies. In his own way Paul Mboya encouraged the development of the African personality as opposed to the imitation of foreign ways, and he thus helped in the awakening to national consciousness and the freedom struggle. There were others like him in the service of the foreign government who contributed directly or indirectly to our advance to ultimate independence.

ruthless action was being planned against the political leaders and we has to face whatever the future would bring. Among those at the meeting were Bildad Kaggia, Fred Kubai of Nairobi branch, Dedan Kimathi, the secretary of KAU's Thomsons Falls branch, and Stanley Mathenge, leader of KAU Youth in Nairobi. I had no idea of the important part Kimathi and Mathenge would play in the future struggle, but they were angry and impatient. I made a warning summing-up speech: 'We can all see that the government is out for trouble, and we must be prepared to face it. There will be arrests and torture . . . many of us might not stand up to this . . . will we betray others?' Achieng was elected KAU secretary-general at that meeting.

A few days later I was in Nairobi again. Achieng's wife came to tell me: 'Achieng was collected this morning.' There had been a swoop on the political leaders. I thought the police might be looking for me in Kisumu, not knowing that I was on a visit to the capital. I packed my bag to return to Kisumu wondering if I would reach that town or a jail. Seventy miles out of Nairobi, at Gilgil, the busload of passengers was ordered into a detention centre. We spent the night in the open squatting on our haunches under police guard. It turned out to be a routine check. The following day we were told to go home. An African policeman, Zackaria Aseda, who had been a student of mine at Maseno, drove me in a landrover to catch a train to Kisumu. The settlers in the streets were all armed. The Emergency was ruling Kenya.

In the years between the war and the Emergency the government was not unaware that trouble was brewing. Unrest had been deeply aggravated in the overcrowded reserves, and had spread to the African squatters on White farms and into Nairobi, where unemployment was swelling. By the time the government realized that something had to be done, and acted, it was too late. In addition, the action was disastrous.

Changes had begun to work during the war when the British Government pressed for greatly increased crop production in the reserves. Kenya had to produce enough food to be self-sufficient, and also to carry garrisons of troops; throughout Africa there was a demand for increased food production and the strategic raw materials that the continent could supply. Immediately after the war there was renewed pressure from the Colonial Office for the colonies to meet acute shortages in food and raw materials for the reconstruction of the metropolitan economy. The war had brought about a decisive change in the balance of power between Britain and the United States. Britain was losing export markets to the States and her capital investments abroad were shrinking. Sterling was under fierce pressure from the dollar. Britain turned to her colonies to meet her economic deficit. Between 1945 and 1951 the sterling balances of her colonies doubled. Intensified production in the colonies helped restore Britain's balance of payment position but it placed a severe strain on African resources.

Pressure for increased production was a sharp reversal of policy. Given a deliberate policy from the early years of African development, and a planned allocation of national resources, the African reserves might well have been helped to make a shift from subsistence farming to cash crop production, at least until the increase in population overcrowded the land allotted for African cultivation and occupation. But this would not have been in the interests of settlers, and what was not good for the settlers' interests was not considered good government in Kenya. From the first days of White settlement there had been strict priorities for development: the interests of the settlers were paramount. The key resources of the country were allocated not to make the African areas economically viable, but to enhance the prosperity of the settler sector. Land reserved for White occupation was grossly disproportionate in area to the size of the settler community; it was among the most productive land in the country. Settler production could be sustained only by a plentiful supply of cheap African labour, so land hunger and tax collections created a constant flow of migrant African labour to the settler labour market. Railway and road development favoured the settler areas and neglected the African areas. Railway rating policies gave the settlers preferential treatment (there were actually country produce rates that discriminated against the African producer) and marketing boards likewise discriminated against the African farmers. In a blatant move to preserve the market for the settlers there were restrictions against Africans growing and selling certain crops, like coffee.

When the colonies suddenly acquired great economic importance, agricultural officers lectured the local councils and the people in the villages that there was a grave food shortage in many countries and it was essential for the war effort and post-war recovery that all should work hard to increase production. But far from being in a position to provide surplus food for export, African agriculture was by this time in need of reclamation to increase African food production. Production increases were forced through without any long term agricultural planning and this increased the pressure on the already overcrowded and exhausted soil. Erosion was menacing in many areas. African land was seriously overtaxed but there could be no expansion: land reserved for the settlers had seen to that.

A ten-year development plan for African agriculture was launched in 1946. In 1948 the Governor, Sir Philip Mitchell, wrote a paper on 'The Agrarian Problem in Kenya'. He put his finger on the issue: African unrest was not just a political and a security question, but an economic one. Mitchell asked for a commission of investigation into the economic conditions of the three East African territories. His pressure resulted in the appointment of the East African Royal Commission of 1953–55, which announced, when it reported, that something in the nature of an agrarian revolution was essential. The Swynnerton Plan for intensified African agriculture made recommendations along these same lines.

It was an economic solution that was needed but it was already too late and priorities were wrong. In the drive for increased production the interests of the people of Kenya were subordinate to Britain's needs, and so the schemes were not devised to change the basic dependency of Africans in the settler economy, and they did not thus go far enough to meet African needs and demands.

After decades of neglect it was said suddenly to be the official concern to raise the standard of living of the people, to safeguard the land, the source of wealth, and to force a transition to a modern economy. Small-scale family cultivated land under tribal conditions of tenure—after settler encroachment and the destruction of the subsistence economy —was unable to provide even minimum support. The agricultural system in the reserves had become untenable, the government decided. The extension of government control to force a process of agrarian change was needed. Government policy was not to extend African land holdings, but to devise new systems of land usage and control to make more productive the land on which Africans were already overcrowded. A system of individual land tenure was to be imposed. Land consolidation would be the first step towards the registration of individual ownership.

The Governor had gone on record that the most urgent problem was not the question of the alienated land but 'the need to discover and apply systems of land usage'. It was obvious that the purpose of intensifying land use in the African reserves was to block African demands for the return of their stolen lands. There was another motive behind the new land policy. The Royal Commission stated that it aimed at achieving 'economic mobility designed to ensure that the land finds its way into the hands of those best able to use it in the interests of the community as a whole'. In other words, a stable middle class would be created to serve as a buffer between the government and the mass of the people, and to absorb political resistance among the people as mission education and plums of minor office had done in a previous generation.

The government put its new policies into effect as it had always done in the past, by imposing them on the people without consultation. If the people would not cooperate, out of deep distrust of all government policy, then the government would order the chiefs and the headmen to push its policies through by force. This added fuel to an already fiercely burning fire. Resistance to government soil conservation measures and land consolidation gave the mass backing to the political movement that had searched for peaceful solutions and, when it found none, was forced by the pressure of events to embark on altogether new forms of struggle.

From the time of its formation, KAU was a legal political body, expressing and trying to convey to government the grievances of the people. Its strength lay chiefly among the Kikuyu where, when Kenyatta returned, he concentrated his activities, but it was extending its organization throughout the country, including Nyanza, as I have described. Much of the political ferment at times was not visible; lulls in political activity were highly deceptive. For, all the while that KAU was organizing, the KCA was still there. Other movements, too, were working under cover. A network of Land Committees for the protection and return of clan lands had started up, largely spontaneously, at village level, owing their inspiration to the Kikuyu Land Board founded in the thirties by Koinange wa Mbiyu, of persons whose land had been alienated. The Land Committees took on a variety of forms, and had many different names, and some were even registered with the government. The KCA oath was used and developed. The KCA deputed clan elders to organize the Land Committees in the villages; their leaders and their membership were secret. As the committees grew in the villages their work resulted in the adherence of new members to the branches of KAU, especially in Central Province. Between KAU, KCA, and the Land Committees there was an overlap in both leadership and rank and file.

The years after the war were also the heyday of the trade union movement. The spiralling cost of living sparked off spontaneous workers' strikes. There was the shooting during the Uplands Bacon Factory strike and the imprisonment of Chege Kibachia who had led the African Workers' Federation. Its successor, the East African Trades Union Congress was led by Makhan Singh and Fred Kubai, but the government refused it registration. There was the great Mombasa dock strike of 1947, which won its demands, and a strike of transport workers. In 1950 after the arrest of Makhan Singh and Fred Kubai on charges of being officers of an unregistered trade union organization, there was a general strike in protest. Fred Kubai was not only president of the Trade Union Congress but he was also chairman of KAU Nairobi Branch. An influx of trade union strength into KAU revived the Nairobi Branch and greatly increased KAU's membership and militancy. By 1951 the government could no longer withstand the pressure for the recognition of the growing trade union movement. It refused to recognize the East African Trade Union Congress because its leadership was too militant, and because it associated with KAU. The government began to encourage a rival trade union organization. This was the Kenya Federation of Registered Trade

Unions. The KFRTU leader at the time was Aggrey Minya. He was soon replaced by Tom Mboya whom the British Government nurtured as the rising star of Kenya's trade union movement. Mboya was given a scholarship to Ruskin College, Oxford. The KFRTU later changed its name to the Kenya Federation of Labour and Mboya became general-secretary. The KFL lost the support of many nationalists when it chose to affiliate to the American-dominated ICFTU, but also because it was suspect as a trade union federation heavily promoted and financed from outside Kenya, and because it was never a rank and file movement built and supported from below. This is without doubt also the reason why of all the attempts to organize trade unions in Kenya, the KFL alone was never suppressed by the colonial government.

Working closely with the East African Trade Union Congress and giving publicity to it and to KAU in their independent newspaper the *Daily Chronicle* was a small group of young Indian militants, led by Pio Gama Pinto, then on the office staff of the Kenya Indian Congress. In 1923 Indian opposition had blocked a settler declaration of self rule and while on this issue Indian self-interest coincided with African interests, this was incidental; though Indian representatives in the Legislative Council occasionally pointed to injustices affecting Africans, the Indian organizations on the whole concentrated on their own battle against settler domination. With the rise of KAU the Asian community was confronted with the need to define its position towards African nationalism. The pressure of the radical young men in the Indian Congress, like Pinto and his associates on the staff of the *Daily Chronicle*, was directed at reversing the timid trend of the more conservative elements in the leadership of the Indian Congress and in getting the Indian community to cooperate with KAU in a working front against the settlers. With Pinto were the late D. K. Sharda, Haroun

Ahmed, who was imprisoned for his support of the Mombasa general strike, and Pranlal Sheth, now the Kisumu barrister. The *Daily Chronicle* was the first and the only English language newspaper in Kenya to advocate a militant nationalist policy, and to issue a call for total independence of the colony under majority African rule. There were continuous police raids on the offices of the newspaper and a succession of prosecutions for sedition against the paper, its editors and publishers. It was the *Daily Chronicle* group that had sold us the flatbed printing machine on which the Luo Thrift and Trading Corporation ran off the first African language newspapers in Nairobi and later in Kisumu. Pio Pinto helped, too, with the preparation of KAU memoranda, leading up to KAU's representations to the East Africa Royal Commission in 1951, but by then the period of petitioning to commissions was being overtaken by a far more inflammable method of struggle in which Pinto was to play an invaluable role, working closely together with the leaders of KAU, the KCA and the trade union movement, men like Kenyatta, James Beuttah, Mbiyu Koinange, Bildad Kaggia, Fred Kubai, Jesse Kariuki, and others.

After the war yet another stream flowed into the struggle. Militant African ex-servicemen like Bildad Kaggia, J. D. Kali, Dedan Kimathi, P. J. Ngei, and others returned from serving with the British army in India, Burma, Ceylon, Middle East and Europe. They found the Land Committees and the KCA already at work in secret in a field fertile with grievances. KAU had its moments of strength but also its periods of lapse; the moderates in the leadership were losing KAU the confidence of the people. In any case what could KAU achieve from a government that championed the cause of the settlers and automatically rejected African representations? The ex-servicemen played an important part in events. Here were men who had overcome their fear of the power of the White man; they were trained soldiers who had fought in his war, with his weapons, and who could put their fighting experience to use in the freedom struggle. KAU committees went on functioning augmented by the new militants thrown up by trade union struggles and from the ranks of returning ex-servicemen, but, most important, an inner core of the leadership began to prepare for a new type of struggle. The younger men said: 'We need immediate independence' and they set to work to prepare.

The 1951 elections in KAU threw out some of the moderates, the 'good boys'. The constitution was changed to include, for the first time, the demand for independence. The land delegation of Koinange and Oneko to Britain, the militants decided, would be the last deputation. If the British Government took no notice of it, the people would be led to new forms of struggle. First, though, there had to be preparations. Outside of the formal KAU structure, two 'chambers' of leadership were set up: Parliament and the Thirty Group. Twelve members sat in the Parliament and decided policy; they passed orders down to the Thirty Group which relayed them to the districts and the district committees to the local committees below them. Shadow Parliaments and shadow Groups of Thirty were readied to take over the reins should the first rank of leaders be arrested. Special groups were ordered to acquire arms, by illegal purchase or by stealing. Stolen guns and home-made guns of iron piping were stored away; returned ex-servicemen gave shooting instruction under cover of dynamiting at stone quarries; a counter-intelligence organization followed the moves of government security. In Nairobi the taxi-drivers, the black marketeers, the gangs were enlisted, a network of local committees was set up, later to be the vital supply and contact lines with the fighters in the forests. These plans and preparations were not revealed to the official committees of leadership of KAU. The secret committees, like KCA and the Land Committees before them, used oaths to bind members in allegiance to the movement. The preparations were not to be limited to the Kikuyu. There was strong support among the Wakamba, some Nyanza men working as labourers in nearby farms were recruited, there were contacts at the coast with some of the Masai at Narok; there were plans for coordinating with the Dini ya Msambwa sect. The people were told that the crisis was rising. Speakers at meetings warned that there could be no struggle without blood being shed, that the young men had to prepare, that they would face prison and death.

There came the time when the secret preparations of KCA, the Land Committees and of the work of Parliament and the Thirty Group began to leak out. The people's impatience could no longer be contained. Feeling was so strong that there were sporadic acts of violence in several parts of the country. In October 1952 the killing in broad daylight, near Nairobi, of the loyalist senior Chief Waruhiu of Kiambu shocked the government into a realization of the strength of the freedom struggle and its support among the people.

The settlers demanded an undertaking from the government that 'African nationalism on the lines of West Africa' would be dealt with as sedition. If the undertaking was not forthcoming the settlers would 'take matters into their own hands'. Their Electors' Union called for the 'neutralizing' or liquidation of African leaders. 'It is not necessary to mention names,' they said. The Governor's telegram to Britain said: 'The movement has many heads; we are dealing with a hydra.' A state of emergency was declared on 21 October 1952. The first police swoop was called Operation Jock Scott, and 183 KAU leaders were arrested. Kenyatta, Paul Ngei, Achieng Oneko, Bildad Kaggia, Fred Kubai and Kung'u Karumba were the six leaders charged in the notorious Kapenguria trial with managing, or assisting to manage, the proscribed society of Mau Mau. Pio Pinto, Walter Odede, and W. W. Awori were the key persons involved in collecting funds for the defence in this trial. Achieng was the only one of the trialists who won on appeal, but he spent the rest of the Emergency under restriction.

The first arrests were followed by waves of others. Almost overnight Kenya's African political leadership was put behind bars. Of course, we had all expected police action. It was known from the movement's intelligence sources that lists of political leaders had been compiled and that arrests were imminent. No one expected that the Emergency would last much longer than six weeks. Instead it was the beginning of a prolonged revolution. Kenyatta's arrest inflamed the people like few single steps could have done. The day after the Emergency started there was a wave of indiscriminate arrests of Kikuyu by Whites in the streets throughout Central Province; those who had not taken the oath did so that night, in mounting anger. There were insufficient arms, there was a limited force of trained men, active support from the other tribes had still to be consolidated, and plans were in only their early stages, but the preparations for a rising had leaked out, the government had cracked down with unparalleled severity, and there was no turning back.

People disappeared from their homes into prison, but many young Kikuyu nationalists rushed into the forests and disappeared. After the swoop on the leaders and as the Kapenguria trial began, people took the attitude: 'Let the war start, for better or for worse. There is no solution with this government.'

Secret organization and oath-taking can be divided into two main stages: between 1947 and 1952; and from the declaration of the Emergency onwards. This fact comes out clearly in the difference in oathing undertakings in both periods.

In the first period 1947-52 an oath-taker had to undertake to do the following: to be a hero in struggle and battle; to fight for land stolen by British settlers until its return to its rightful owners; to oppose the Beecher report in fighting for the education of Africans; not to reveal any secret to anybody who had not taken the oath; to acquire and hide rifles and ammunition; to kill if ordered to do so anyone who opposed these oathing undertakings, even if the victim was one's own relative; to go to any place ordered for duty. Naturally this oathing started in a small way among tested and trusted nationalists but it spread until it reached a peak by 1952. After the Emergency was declared, top ranking KAU leaders arrested and KAU banned, a new type of oathing emerged. It was simpler. One merely undertook to fight British imperialists until the arrested leaders were released.

Oathing fees of both periods reflected the relative seriousness of the situation at each time. While fees during the 1947–52 period were consolidated at 62 shillings, 50 cents for each oath-taker, the fees during the Emergency period were very high, ranging between 1000 shillings for rich oath-takers and 10 and 5 shillings for poor men and women oath-takers respectively. The fees collected in this second stage were used to purchase rifles, ammunition, clothes, food, and also for assisting arrested leaders. As much as 300 shillings was paid for a rifle at this time.

Secret organization came about because the young militant nationalists noticed and feared a tendency to compromise with the British among certain ranks of KAU leadership. Foremost among these militants within the KAU executive were Fred Kubai (chairman of Nairobi Branch), Bildad Kaggia (secretary of Nairobi Branch), James Beuttah (chairman of Murang'a Branch and vice-president of the Central Province KAU Council), Harrison Wamuthenya (chairman of Nyeri Branch), Henry Wambogo (vice-chairman of Nyeri Branch), Kiragu Kagotho (secretary of Nyeri Branch), Pratt Njogu (chairman of Embu Branch), Romano Jamumo

Gikunju (secretary of Embu Branch), John Mbiyu Koinange (chairman of KAU Kiambu), Kung'u Karumba (chairman of Limuru Branch), Charles Munyua Wambaa (chairman of KAU Kikuyu), J. D. Kali (assistant secretary of Nairobi KAU), P. J. Ngei (KAU assistant secretary). These were the men who took the 1947–52 type of oath. After regular KAU executive meetings, they and other people who had taken the oath secretly (Kamau Gichohi Githua, Stanley Mathenge, Waigwa Kamurwa and others) held closed consultations at KAU Nairobi Branch office at Kiburi House. Kaggia and Kubai who worked at Kiburi House acted as the head-quarters of the secret organization within KAU and the secret officials in the branches formed the basis of the secret organization in the districts. With the arrests at the beginning of the Emergency the head of the secret organization within KAU was decapitated. The arrest of leaders created fright among the people, even those who had taken the oath. It was some time before people found their nerve again and central secret organization could be revived. It was Lawrence Karugo Kihuria, Kubai's successor as chairman of KAU's Nairobi Branch, who, on 15 January 1953, summoned all key secret organizers and a meeting was held at KAU headquarters. This was the meeting that decided to have a fresh oath and a fresh undertaking: to wage war against the imperialists until they released all the arrested leaders. This meeting was attended by Kamau Gichohi Githua, Stanley Mathenge, Isaac Gathanju, Arthur Wanyoike Thungu, Andrew Kamau Gatama, Ndirangu Kabebe, Kanguku Mwanura Gatundu, Mbugua Kaniu, Lawrence Karugo Kihuria. As the decision of the meeting was to fight, the meeting delegated special responsibilities to those present. Arthur Wanyoike was put in charge of finance. Kamau Gichohi Githua was put in charge of the fighting and Isaac Gathanju of adminis-tration, which included planning and controlling contact machinery. The remaining members were put in charge of information, recruitment and so on. This secret War Council had its first headquarters at Mathari in Nairobi in the mud and thatch huts among the trees. It remained the head-quarters until security forces destroyed it in April 1953. Recruits were brought there and trained, and then sent mainly to Nyandarua and Kirinyaga forests. In the districts each KAU branch in the Central Province was required to prepare one thousand recruits. These recruits reached the forest areas with the help of guides sent by the fighters in Nairobi already encamped in the forests. Preference in recruitment was given to tested people, especially if they had served in the army, police or prison service. Between January and February 1953 Stanley Mathenge, Kiego Mboko, and Gitau Matenju received as many as 500 recruits from Nairobi into the forests; they were equipped with 36 rifles, 45 pistols (almost all the pistols were acquired through Pio Pinto), 4 sten guns, over 500 simis, and about 20,000 shillings. In 1953 and 1954 there were, it is recorded, 13 pitched battles with British forces.

It was leaders from Nyeri like Dedan Kimathi, Stanley Mathenge, and Paulo Njeru, a KAU official from Nyeri, who, even before the declaration of the Emergency, had advocated fighting from the forests, and who had begun tentatively to survey the forest areas, to store arms, and to make plans for supply lines.

About 15,000 people entered the Aberdare Forests after October 1952 when the Emergency was declared; others retreated into the forests of Mount Kenya. Two kinds of people went into the forests. Leaders like Dedan Kimathi and Stanley Mathenge escaped the police net and retired to the forests with prices on their heads, there to make a military stand. Round them they rallied the men who had taken not only the unity oath of the KCA but also the later fighting oath. Like their leaders these men had become targets for the police; they retreated to the forests for their safety from arrest and turned to full-time guerilla activity. When the Emergency began, the indiscriminate arrest and beating of every Kikuyu tribesman seemed to augur the elimination of the whole tribe; large numbers of people fled to the forests out of fear of the forces of the Emergency; they, too, formed gangs for survival, raiding for food and clothes and guns.

At the height of the military struggle the freedom forces of the forests were estimated to number 30,000. The widespread arrests of the Emergency had decimated centralized political leaderships, and wiped out links between the town and rural areas. At the height of the struggle there were several relatively autonomous zones of resistance and fighting: Nairobi, which was the vital supply centre, the Kikuyu reserves, Mount Kenya, and the Aberdare Forests and the settler farms of the Rift Valley. In the forests the fighters set up permanent headquarters, which not only resisted government attack, but also launched offensives, like the famous raid on Naivasha police station of March 1953 when 173 prisoners were released and much ammunition seized. The forests were virtually impregnable to the army for about eighteen months. Unable to come to grips with the nationalist forces the army and the police concentrated on destroying their support in the reserves and the towns, establishing prohibited areas along the fringes of the forests, breaking down the traditional dispersed villages and ordering the concentration of villages under army and home guard control. The aim was to cut the forests off from supply lines and starve the nationalist forces into the open.

Inside the forests there were attempts to set up the Kikuyu Defence Council for overall military planning. In August 1953 Kimathi organized a five-day meeting in the forests of fighting men. Lines of general strategy were laid down. Direct clashes with government forces would be avoided and attacks would be aimed at the weak points of the enemy. Areas of operation were assigned to divisions of the freedom-fighters' army. Six months later the Kenya Parliament was formed when 40 leaders and some 800 fighters met to act as a central political authority in the absence—in prison and in detention camps—of the former political leaders. That first meeting decided among other things that emissaries would be sent to neighbouring tribes to enlist their help and to disprove the settler claim that the struggle was a strictly Kikuyu tribal affair.

In the same month that the Kenya Parliament met in the Aberdare Forests to plan an overall strategy that reflected not a narrow tribalism but the aim of a united independent African Kenya, the offensive of the government security forces began to achieve results. The capture of General China, leader of the Mount Kenya freedom-fighters, and his ultimate confession gave the army the leads it needed to cut vital supply lines and to formulate new tactics against the nationalists.

In Operation Anvil 25,000 soldiers and police rounded up the entire African population of Nairobi—just over 100,000 —and screened and dispatched to specially prepared detention camps all men between the ages of sixteen and thirty-five—the warrior age—from the so-called 'affected tribes'. The effect of Operation Anvil was the effective disruption of the last resistance groups in Nairobi and the severing of the supply of arms, ammunition, money, clothing, and medical supplies to the freedom-fighters. A three-month army operation was launched to bring about the surrender of freedom-fighters through negotiation. The Kenya Parliament rejected the surrender offer placed before it, and demanded the return of alienated land to its rightful owners and the formation of an independent government under African leadership. Before negotiations could begin, the Kenya Parliament said, the army would have to be withdrawn and the government would have to agree to participation of African political leaders in the talks.

In the Aberdare Forests Kimathi's army was trying to send a mission to Ethiopa to arrange arms deliveries; contact had been made with some outside districts; and a Masai delegation had been received. But the bombings of the forest, security raids, and supply difficulties were making the nationalists less and less mobile; contact between sections became sporadic and an effective over-all chain of military command ceased to function. The Kenya Parliament was unable to meet after 1955. There were leadership conflicts within the Kenya Parliament and the freedom-fighters' army. The British improvised a devastating new tactic in the formation of pseudo-gangs of captured and surrendered fighters under the control of police, which penetrated forests to track down the fighters' groups. Their greatest success was the capture of Dedan Kimathi and his subsequent execution. Where bombing of the forests had not destroyed the guerilla bands this infiltration did. The war lasted three years. Towards the end the freedom-fighters were reduced to small isolated poorly armed bands using their forest skill to survive, and being hunted like animals by the imperialist army and its pseudo-gangs.

The Kenya Parliament and its army represented an all-Kenya nationalism with advanced and clearly stated political aims. After the capture of General China, surrender talks were mooted and the Kenya Parliament was asked: 'Why are you fighting? What must be done to get the freedom-fighters to come out of the forest peacefully with their arms?' The reply was: 'We are fighting for all land stolen from us by the Crown through its Orders in Council of 1915, according to which Africans have been evicted from the Kenya Highlands. . . . The British Government must grant Kenya full independence under African leadership, and hand over all land previously alienated for distribution to the landless. We will fight until we achieve freedom or until the last of our warriors has shed his last drop of blood.'

Of the battles or encounters with the British army and police during the Emergency special mention must be made of the heroic military leadership of Mbaria Kaniu and Muraya Mbuthia on Naivasha police post and at Lari; Stanley Mathenge on Othaya (Nyeri) police post and Kairuthi (Nyeri) home guard post; Kago Mboko on Kinyona (Muranga) home guard post; Waruhiu Itote on Kiamachimbi (Nyeri) chiefs' camp, and the greatest of all battles of the Emergency at Roiboiro (Nyeri); Ihura Kareri on a British army camp at Muranga and the very successful Kiriya (Murang'a) ambush; Kago Mboko and Ihura Kareri jointly at Mihute (Murang'a) battle; Nyoro Kiragu at Kamacharia; Manyeki Wangombe at Gaturi (outside Murang'a township); and Kariuki Chotara at the Lukenya Detention Camp in Nairobi suburbs. The results of these battles or encounters proved the heroism and determination of these young Kenyan fighters because invariably their objectives, whether defensive or offensive, were achieved.

This struggle has been distorted as the savage activities of primitive murdering gangs, the Mau Mau. Persons better qualified than I have argued that this word is unknown in the Kikuyu language, that those who participated in the struggle never called themselves 'Mau Mau', that this became a term of abuse against every Kikuyu who did not volunteer for the government's security forces and give proof of his loyalty to the government. A year after the Emergency was declared Dedan Kimathi wrote a letter from his headquarters in Mount Aberdare to the Nairobi newspaper *Habari za Dunia*. There was no such thing as Mau Mau, he said. The poor were the Mau Mau. Poverty could be stopped, but not by bombs and weapons.

The sensational anti-Mau Mau propaganda of the

period is a gross insult to the leadership of Dedan Kimathi and the brave men he led who defied death in a guerilla army for the freedom cause in Kenya.

There were brutalities and massacres on both sides. One day there will be a proper investigation of such incidents as the Lari massacre. Much of the government information about oath-taking was obtained through forced confessions in the detention camps and was unreliable. But there were perversions and abuses of the unity and fighting oaths. In the latter part of the struggle an overall military and political direction was defeated—there had also always been forest groups that did not fall under this direction—and hard-pressed persecuted groups were forced into a desperate struggle for survival. Reversions to rites and superstition took the place of political and military aims and organization. The nationalist resistance was distorted into tribal frustration when the leadership was destroyed and a people despaired, fearing they were facing total obliteration.

The propaganda against the Mau Mau as a 'savage atavistic movement'—from sensational press reports, to government and army handouts and the British Government Corfield Commission (which Kenyatta dismissed in 1960, the year of its publication, as 'a pack of lies collected from needy informers')—was so fierce that it infected even Africans. Only now in Kenya is it becoming possible to present a truer version of the events of this time. The Emergency was a time of revolutionary war in Kenya. For almost a decade in the fifties only one side in this battle was able to present its case and its account of events. Our political leaders were locked away in the camps and prisons, or fighting for survival in the forests. The restriction and silencing of our leaders continued long after the worst physical combat of the Emergency had ended, into the period when we were negotiating for constitutional progress for Kenya; at this time it was difficult to set the record straight because our veteran leaders were not free, yet, to talk, and the official propaganda had been so powerful that it built a resistance, especially in Britain, to any new version of events. We in Kenya have still to write our history of these years. For this the men who founded and led KAU and other patriotic and political organizations, those who organized the trade unions and led the first strikes, who spent the Emergency years in the detention camps and, above all, the fighters in the forests, will have to combine. The story is far more complex than the official versions make out. Many streams flowed into the movement, some converging on one another and joining up, others flowing along their own courses till they were joined in the final flood of revolt. Until Kenya sets this record straight our people will not fully understand how we are today on the road to full independence.

CHAPTER SEVEN

From Battalions to Polling Booths

KENYA nationalism turned violent because for thirty years it was treated as seditious and denied all legitimate outlet. KAU spokesmen were dismissed as agitators instead of being recognized as the vocal chord of a whole people.

The irony was that the preparations for an uprising were not only not initiated by KAU, but were deliberately kept away from it, and yet when the government cracked down, it was KAU that was made the scapegoat and Kenyatta the evil genius. To explain the revolt as the organized plot of KAU was to totally distort the facts and misunderstand the nature of the struggle in Kenya. The date and place of birth of the revolt cannot be clearly pointed out; there were many beginnings and many origins. There was seething revolt among the people, on numerous levels, some national, some tribal, some clan, some of a sophisticated political nature, some expressive of the simplest form of anti-White hostility. There was a labyrinth of clandestine committees and organizations of one kind or another.

Even in the late forties a government that faced up to the seriousness of the discontent might have altered the course of events. Bloodshed might have been averted. The crisis came because the most reasoned demands had been brushed aside, and government had not budged an inch, even in the face of explosive unrest. The countryside was erupting. If the political leadership devised no overall strategy for struggle, violence would break out anyway—this was the logic of the Kenya situation. Even while plans for struggle were still in the making, isolated attacks on settler homesteads and the maiming of cattle were pointers that the peoples' patience had run out. They were going into action before the starter's signal.

What sort of struggle? This was pre-occupying leaders on many levels. Mass civil disobedience, a war on settler property and nerves, these could be a beginning, but to sustain itself the struggle needed a co-ordinated, overall strategy, far greater reserves of leading and trained personnel, and, a vital aspect, the broadening of the basis of the struggle to include other African tribes so that the Kikuyu could not be isolated. Preparations for a struggle that had grown inevitable by the fifties were not yet complete and the exact form of struggle had by no means been decided when the government cracked down to order reprisals the severity of which had never been seen in a British colony. It was the strong-arm measures of the government ultimately that decided the military form of the struggle.

Casualties inflicted by the so-called 'Mau Mau' were about 2,000, of whom only 30 were White. By contrast government forces killed over 11,000 Africans and detained 90,000 in detention camps. Here they were subjected to indescribable brutalities. No detainee was released until he had been passed along a security clearance channel known as the 'Pipe Line'; among the Emergency casualties not recorded are the victims of the Pipe Line who were injured and permanently disabled by torture to extract confessions.

This was no war against combatants. Hostilities were declared against the entire Kikuyu tribe. Heavy bombers blasted the slopes of the Aberdare and Mount Kenya forests, but soldiers went into action, too, against women and children. Whole villages were evacuated and the people grouped in large villagization schemes, behind barbed wire, for security and punitive reasons. Agriculture was ruined and children starved. More than this. The government's handling of the Emergency forced a state of civil war on the Kikuyu people. In the beginning the government had virtually no support among the people; from Chiefs, wealthy landholders, tribal police, shop-keepers, government employees, people who ate crumbs from the settler table, perhaps, but from no significant cross-section of the people. The government realized it could never defeat the people until it divided them. The Home Guard movement was begun to turn men into collaborators, to turn father against son, and to enlist brother to betray brother. Men who did not volunteer for the Home Guard were immediately suspect to the security forces. Men joined to protect members of their immediate family and found themselves helping to betray and kill their own people. The Home Guard gave information which resulted in the arrest, detention, and even death of many freedom-fighters; their information helped to cut the vital supply lines to the fighters in the forest. The Emergency thus produced courageous martyrs and heroes but also despicable collaborators.

Treachery was well rewarded. The government used the Emergency years to force land consolidation in the Kikuyu reserves. With one and the same re-allocation of land holdings the government bought collaborators and wreaked vengeance on the leaders and patriots who were fighting in the forests or detained in the camps. Agricultural policy was made to serve the political ends of the government and the punishment doled out to the men forcibly absent from the reserves during the Emergency continued to be exacted in the period after that. The government's agricultural officers who worked the land consolidation programme managed to put it through only because the leaders were locked up and the people were unable to resist it. The government ignored the blatant fact that if land consolidation were done at a time when great numbers of the people were forcibly absent, many would be permanently dispossessed or, at best, allocated the worst land even when the country returned to normal. This is exactly what happened. The men in the prisons and detention camps were unable to present their cases before the land consolidation committees. These committees were composed of loyalists and home guards who were bitter enemies of the detainees and took advantage of their absence. When the doors of the prisons and the camps were opened seven, eight, and nine years after the imposition of Emergency rule, men who had once owned land and been prosperous farmers were destitute. Freedom-fighters had lost their land to collaborators and 'good boys'. The acute division running through the Kikuyu, Meru and Embu tribes was thus carried through to the time of peace. Reprisals did not end with the men and women in the camps, but their children suffered too. It was the children of detainees or dead freedom-fighters who could not pay school fees and were excluded from the classrooms; it was the sons of the loyalists not the freedom-fighters who got employment, or were taken into the administration, the army or the police force, and had opportunities for higher education. The two sides of the Emergency persisted into later years; freedom-fighters were unemployed and landless; and the loyalists had entrenched themselves and had become the dependable middle group that government had aimed to create. Those who had sacrificed most in the struggle had lost out to the people who had played safe. Political divisions had been given concrete economic shape, and so would persist into the post-Emergency period. This, as much as the toll of dead, injured, and detained, was the harvest that government policy reaped: the creation of a group that had vested interests to defend would, it was hoped, block the struggle rising again in open revolt and would capture not only the military but the political victory of the years to come.

Throughout the Emergency years the nightmare of the government was that the revolt would spread to the other tribes. Immediate steps were taken to seal off the Kikuyu reserves and to subject the rest of the country to a continuous barrage of propaganda to inflame anti-Kikuyu feeling. Government and settler tactics seemed designed at little less than the extinction of the Kikuyu (for the accusation 'Mau Mau' was interchangeable with 'Kikuyu') and to win over the Luo, the second largest tribe in Kenya, as an army of loyalists. My primary objective was to block this government offensive to enrol the Luo as pro-government belligerents, and thus fatally to divide the African people of our country.

Political activity was virtually outlawed. Meetings were banned throughout and no more than five persons could gather for any purpose. Our only channel of expression was the Luo Union. We used it well. Everywhere we spoke government agents followed us and recorded our speeches, but we were not deterred. We advocated thrift and self-help, community effort and unity, but under cover of seemingly innocuous speeches we were keeping close to the people and damping down tribalism and the propaganda blared out by the loudspeakers on the touring government vans trying to recruit for the Home Guard and the police force.

Throughout the Emergency there were hints of my own impending arrest. I did not think I would survive the first month after October 1952 without joining Achieng and the others in detention. Somehow I was not included in the round-ups. I felt, nevertheless, that my arrest was imminent. It had been planned with the Indian High Commissioner before the declaration of the state of Emergency that I would visit India as a guest of the Indian Government to assimilate new ideas for Luo Thrift expansion. This seemed an opportunity to let the dust settle round the first period of the Emergency and to conserve effort for days beyond the immediate crisis. I left Kenya for India in February 1953, surprised that I was allowed to leave the country, for I felt sure I was black-listed. The Kenyatta trial was then in progress at Kapenguria. Pio Pinto and others had done a sterling job in helping assemble an international defence team led by Britain's D. N. Pritt, Q.C., and Chaman Lall, a distinguished lawyer from India who had been his country's ambassador to Turkey, and composed of Advocate Kapila and Jaswant Singh from Nairobi, Dudley Thompson from Tanganyika, and H. O. Davies from Nigeria. The Luo Union amongst others had helped to raise funds towards the Kapenguria defence.

I travelled via Aden and Karachi to Bombay. During my tour of India I met the great Jawarharlal Nehru. We talked of the effects of the Emergency in immobilizing all political advance and of the directions in which nationalist expression could nevertheless break through.

When I returned to Kenya two months later I traced the whereabouts of a few KAU members (namely Muinga Chokwe and Stephen Ngombe) who had not been arrested and they gave me a briefing of the situation in the country. No sooner had I left Mombasa than the people in whose homes I had stayed were taken into custody. In Nairobi Pinto was an invaluable supply man, working with the Nairobi War Council that siphoned food, money, arms, and intelligence information through to the forests, and smuggling out of Kenya and into the world's press reports and photographs of atrocities by the security forces, until his activities were discovered and he, too, was detained.

When I got to Kisumu there were many gaps among our people. Walter Odede who had become KAU president on Kenyatta's arrest was in detention; Oluoch Okello was arrested soon after my arrival and sent to MacKinnon Road Camp (he was later removed to Lodwar, Manyani, and Hola among other camps), Oloo Otaya who had welcomed me back with a slaughtered ram, was accused of organizing an oathing ceremony and was arrested, brutally beaten and taken to Manyani Camp.

One night after midnight I was taken from my bed by the security forces. I was driven into the bush in the hills round Kisumu where four armed men questioned me about what I had discussed with Nehru in India. It was said that I was hiding arms, they said, I should show them the hiding places. 'The truth, we want the truth,' they shouted. 'You know you must talk!' I knew this was sheer intimidation. After some hours I was taken back to my house. If I reported them, they said, I would be found dead.

I refused to be cowed. Not long after this incident teachers and prominent members of the Church were called to a meeting in Kisumu in the hall of the government Indian school where the District Commissioner and a leading settler businessman who was a member of the Legislative Council presented to us a professor of history from London. The professor talked of the glories of the British Empire. Once again I heard how this was the empire on which the sun never sets. This was because the British, when they judged that peoples in their charge had developed and were ready for independence, gave it to you, the speaker said. We were asked to consider the cases of the United States, Canada, Australia, South Africa, and India. People were developed when they no longer listened to demagogues trying to confuse the country. When the people of Kenya were more mature British fair play would grant them independence. The people from Nyanza should be realistic, diligent, ready to labour on the farms and in the civil service. They should turn away from confusion and cooperate with Britain.

The chairman said the professor would answer questions

for clarification, but no one came forward. I thought that if we kept quiet they would leave with the impression that everyone agreed with this version of history.

'Question, sir,' I said, and stood up.

'Yes, Mr Odinga,' said the Commissioner. 'What sort of question?'

'The Professor,' I said, 'has propounded to us the idea of fair play: that Britain has given independence to so many countries. But as far as I knew the United States of America had fought for independence . . .'

The Commissioner tried to stop me.

'No,' I said. 'You asked for questions.'

'Go on, then,' said the Commissioner, 'but be brief.'

'I do not count the United States,' I said, 'because they struggled. As for Canada, they were White people like you. In Australia and New Zealand the Whites got independence but they are suppressing the aborigines. And in South Africa it was only the Whites you gave independence. . . .'

'Be brief,' said the District Commissioner.

'I must be given fair play to finish,' I said. I agreed that India had got independence, but only after she had struggled and had called on the British to quit India. 'And if it were not straight after the war when you were weakened you would never have given way. We in Kenya want independence now. We are a Black race but we do not agree that we are not fit to rule.'

'That,' said the Professor, in reply, 'is the type of person who is confusing Kenya.'

Questions now shot up from all sides of the hall.

The next day Kisumu was buzzing with talk of the meeting. 'He will be arrested,' some said. 'He will not be here tomorrow.' But others said: 'That is the man, this is what we want.'

The arrest of Achieng had made our Luo people specially angry. The government was intent on rounding up every possible KAU supporter in Nyanza, but it was conscious that if it did not tread warily, the Luo might be provoked, as a result of the arrest of their most prominent leaders, into direct involvement on the side of the freedom-fighters. I think it was to this need to step warily that I owe the fact that I was not detained, though there were times when I thought I had narrowly missed being arrested. The detention of Achieng Oneko had been a calculated risk by the government, but he, after all, had been deeply involved at the centre of KAU politics in Nairobi. My arrest, the government must have known, might have meant the incitement to rebellion of Luo: it would have been stupid tactics to open a new front of struggle in Nyanza.

We continued to use the Luo Union as our sole channel of expression. In August 1953 we held a conference to establish ourselves on an inter-territorial basis, and delegates came from all over East Africa. I was elected the first president or *Ker*, Mzee Joel Omer was elected vice-president and Adala Otuko (now Kenya's Ambassador to the Soviet Union) general secretary of the Luo Union (East Africa). We inaugurated traditional dances, wrestling, and games; twice a year we held meetings for members from all over East Africa to discuss community affairs; we instituted scholarships and assisted students to enrol in universities abroad. We wanted our people throughout East Africa to be united and as one, but we did not want a narrow-minded tribal organization. We told our people they had a role to play to free Kenya from imperialist and settler domination. We told them that the struggle raging during the Emergency years was their struggle too; we had to maintain a national, not a tribal spirit. We travelled throughout East Africa opening one branch after another until there were ninety in all. Once again I was constantly on the move. Next door to the shop of the man who headed the Luo Union in Dar es Salaam was Julius Nyerere who had left teaching to organize TANU and was trying to make ends meet with a small shop. His political influence was beginning to be felt then. We talked exhaustively. He described how TANU was working and I met many of his colleagues. I thought Nyerere a gentle and retiring man, too mild, I thought in my error, to survive a heated political temperature, but I was soon to discover that his appealing modesty was equalled by great stores of determination and vision.

In November 1954 there was a crisis for the Luo when the fatal shooting occurred in Nairobi of Ambrose Ofafa, the treasurer of our Luo Union and a member of the Nairobi City Council. Ofafa was one of several Africans who took over shops previously tenanted by Kikuyu in the Kaloleni location, when the policy of deporting the Kikuyu from Nairobi was put into effect. It was never established who the murderers of Ofafa were, but the newspapers pounced on his death to incite Luo feeling against the Kikuyu. There was a Mau Mau plot against the Luo, these newspaper reports alleged. There was talk of the government issuing arms to the Luo to defend themselves from attack. The week of Ofafa's murder numbers of Luo came forward to be enrolled in the Home Guard and the Government seemed on the point of a successful incitement of an inter-tribal clash. I travelled speedily from Nyanza to Nairobi to investigate the circumstances of Ofafa's death and to judge the feelings of the people. I held a large public meeting in Nairobi and told the people that there should be no question of them taking up arms in the thought that this would avenge Ofafa's death: he had called for unity, not inter-tribal strife, and the people had to unite. When I got back to Kisumu we started a collection to build a constructive memorial to Ofafa. This is the origin of the Ofafa Memorial Hall in Kisumu which was conceived as a Luo centre for stimulating Luo traditions, not for tribal ends, but for national unity for Kenya's freedom.

It was at this time that the people began to call me Jaramogi. Ramogi is the legendary ancestor of the Luo and because I encouraged the preservation of our customary ways I was given a name symbolizing that I continued in the example of our ancestral fathers.

With the deflection into constructive channels of the peoples' anger against the death of Ofafa we passed the danger-point in the recruitment of the Luo on the side of the government's security forces. So-called 'hard-core' detainees were held on Mageta Island and Sayusi islands in Lake Nyanza and some among the working party brought to the mainland to clear the bush under armed guard managed to escape. Members of the Luo Union sheltered these freedom-fighters, fed them, gave them the clothes from their own backs and, camouflaging them by having them carry bundles of grass on their heads as is our custom when we are gathering grass for thatching, guided them away from Nyanza and back to the forests. During the latter years of the Emergency I managed to get in contact with detainees in some of the camps and by letters smuggled in and out we planned to further inter-tribal unity at all costs.

It was during the Emergency that the independent African churches grew enormously in influence in Nyanza, chief among them Elijah Masinde's Dini Ya Msambwa. Masinde himself endured a bitter martyrdom in exile, prison, and then in exile. The Churches, as all bodies, could not function without registration under the Societies Ordinance. I spent a considerable portion of my time writing constitutions and helping the Churches to lodge applications for registration.

Meanwhile the government was proceeding with the Swynnerton plan for more intensive agriculture but was handicapped by the shortage of manpower. There were more calls than ever on Nyanza labour. The government was expelling the Kikuyu from the cities and employment and pursuing a deliberate policy of filling the labour corps with Nyanza tribes. As Kikuyu workers were displaced from employment Nyanza tribes were sent in to fill the vacuum. Nyanza people went into the civil service in greater numbers than ever before and at this time the status of the civil servants was raised to benefit its newest, Nyanza, members. The government was thinking ahead to the time when, the Nyanza people having filled the employment vacuum created by the displacement of Kikuyu workers, the latter would direct their wrath against the Nyanza people and not against the government. Inevitably, though, the more rapid absorption of our people in the labour market accelerated the process of their urbanization and the quickening of their political consciousness.

With labour drained from the land for other parts of the country women were called out on soil conservation projects. This inflamed the villages. We were not opposed to communal labour as such, but only if it were a voluntary system. The outcry against the commandeering of labour reached such heights that it proved virtually impossible to organize. Instead, in many districts the government had to use prison labour from the detention camps. Land consolidation raised opposition too, and *barazas* to discuss schemes ended in disorder. Pilot schemes started in some areas had to be abandoned for some years. It was not that the Luo people set their faces against agricultural improvement—though the Luo are proud, even conceited about their agricultural prowess and they doubt that after countless generations working the land they have much to learn from outsiders, least of all a hostile government—but land consolidation had to be carried out with the consent of, and after close consultation with, the elders and the people. The traditional system of land tenure and the functions of the land elders had to be taken into account in a new arrangement; forcing the pace simply aroused opposition. Negotiation, persuasion, and education could have done more than any degree of compulsion.

The sharpest confrontation with the government was over the Kisiani Hills Afforestation scheme. When first the scheme was broached in 1953 the affected landowners had declared their total opposition and a public *baraza* had rejected the scheme. The Kisumu Council accepted the scheme on the condition laid down by the then District Commissioner that the location would have control and on the understanding that the money for the scheme would be a free grant from the Swynnerton Plan, but the landowners were never notified of this acceptance and their own consent was never obtained. Four years later the Kisumu Location Council did not recognize this as the same scheme; there had been a complete departure from the original conditions laid down. Far from the location authority having control over the land it was under the management of the forestry authorities, and boundaries were being demarcated without any consultation with the landholders. As for the financing of the scheme, this was not in the form of a free government grant as first offered, but the African District Council was obliged to contribute half the sum of £10,000 as a loan. In 1958 the District Council voted by 30 votes to 16 that 'The Kisiani Afforestation scheme be abandoned'. £13,000 had already been spent on the scheme but the council adamantly refused to make provision in the estimates for higher rates to repay the amount.

The government instituted an inquiry which glossed over what it called 'some misunderstanding . . . in the early days . . .' when it was at first stated that the finances would be put up by government, and it attacked 'the immaturity of the average councillor'. When we refused to do what government wanted, or we caught it out breaking an undertaking, we were 'immature'! After the council's decision to repudiate the scheme the government refused to give financial assistance for any development projects, and councillors were not slow to understand that they were being punished. There had been a threatening note in the government statement after the inquiry: 'The council has inevitably prolonged the time when the District Commissioner must remain as their chairman,' and the council was reminded 'that the Governor could by proclamation dissolve any council'. The following year the council was dissolved, on the orders of the Minister. A commission of two government officers was set up to run the Central Nyanza Council pending new elections. The system of dummy representation had ended in complete stalemate.

The army fought the African nationalists in the forests and in the detention camps and the settlers fought on their farms and through their powerful pressure groups and in the Legislative Council. Settler thinking, for all the shocks of the Emergency, was never shaken out of its state of chronic reaction. White members, White views, White policies dominated the Legislative Council. The settlers would not entertain any notion of Africans having a share in government. They were living in the past. (In 1956, only seven years before Kenya was to become an independent state, a motion—hardly very revolutionary—by Eliud Mathu in the Legislative Council that an African should be made chairman of the Central Nyanza District Council was roundly defeated, with the admonition by a settler speaker: 'The District Commissioner . . . instead of sitting in the chair will sit on the right-hand of the chair to advise how local government should be run. The District Commissioner has not the time, and will not be out making the Honourable Member for the Coast's roads.' The African members, Mathu and Ohanga said, would not be disappointed that the government had turned down the proposal; they were so used to disappointment and frustration that they were almost immune to it.)

However, by the latter half of the Emergency the British

136

Government realized that some move had to be made in the direction of political concessions for Africans. Settler intransigence had produced a state of Emergency in Kenya. It took battalions of British troops and something in the neighbourhood of £60 million to put down the African national rising. Continued rule by force and violence not only bottled up even more explosive situations but cost vast sums of money. A military solution was not only a burden on Britain, but it was coming to be realized that it would not work. First steps in a new direction were very tentative. Britain's Colonial Secretary, Sir Oliver Lyttelton—who was imposing Central African Federation on the people of Malawi and Zambia (then Nyasaland and Northern Rhodesia) and calling this 'trusteeship'—opened talks with the settlers on a new constitution.

'Multi-racialism' was the theme of the day and under this deceptive formula one Ministry was allocated to an African, two to Asians and three to Whites: three non-Europeans balanced by three Europeans, in a country where Africans outnumbered Whites by one hundred to one. The African members of Legco could not agree to boycott and when B. A. Ohanga was offered it he took the ministerial portfolio for community development in the face of African opposition to a concession they considered valueless. Up to this time the African members of the Legislative Council had been nominated by the Governor from names sent forward from the African District Councils. The Lyttelton constitution of 1957 was a half-hearted attempt to regain African confidence. The Coutts Report of 1956 established voting qualifications as income qualification of £120 a year (nearly double the average African income, so it is not surprising that only about one in twenty Africans qualified for the vote). The Kikuyu, Embu, and Meru had to acquire a certificate of loyalty to vote. In the Legislative Council the African and Asian seats taken together equalled the White seats, but there were also twenty-three non-elected White members as against two Africans and five Asians, giving the Whites an overall majority of sixteen.

I had on many occasions been approached to accept nomination to the Legislative Council but I had always rejected the suggestion. Now, though the representation for Africans was far from adequate, we would at least have elections. Ohanga, who had beaten Mathu to the acceptance of the only African ministerial portfolio, called himself the Luo Minister and was influential in Nyanza. We had been together on the teaching staff at Maseno and at first I was loth to stand against him. But when he defied the African rejection of the ministerial portfolio and I heard him talk about the great influence of the settlers and how anyone who attempted to challenge them would do so at great risk to his own position, I decided he had long given up the fight and could not represent the people. His apologetic, conciliatory approach was alien to the political awakening of Nyanza and while there was now an opportunity to set a new pace for advance, the former members of the Legislative Council would not dare, and did not want, to do this. Masinde Muliro, who had just returned from studying in South Africa and had taught for one year at the Alliance Girls' High School and then, as a student at a South African university, had a baptism of fire of White domination politics, was emphatic that men like Ohanga would better serve us in other quarters. Muliro and I had talks at Maseno and Kisumu about using the elections to sharpen the struggle. We agreed to go to the country together. I would fight Ohanga and he would stand for the North Nyanza seat against W. W. Awori.

Before I could accept nomination as a candidate I had to be released from my duties by the Luo Union executive council and the directors of the Luo Thrift and Trading Corporation. They were not easily convinced. At the Luo

Union general meeting the majority of members were reluctant to agree, but a subsequent committee meeting thought the matter over deeply and consented to my plan to stand for election. I developed a simple allegory. 'I see from afar,' I told them, 'a fierce fire burning the fields of Kenya. The winds are blowing the flames hard towards our houses. Let me go and put the fire out before it reaches our villages.' Joel Omer took office as president of the Luo Union and although I was not altogether released from the Luo Thrift and Trading Corporation, Okuto Bala was promoted assistant to the managing directorship, and I was therefore relieved of much of the work. I had won over the elders and officials of the two bodies I headed (and they gave me invaluable support in the elections) but a larger task was to win the confidence of the voters. Public representatives up to this time had been like civil servants; nominated representatives had not dared to strike out against the government or the settlers in public speeches, let alone in action. The people were disappointed in their old-type representatives and conscious of many injustices, but they did not know how to get rid of representatives who were chosen for their subservience to authority or who were no sooner in office than they were cowed. The people were bitter about the imprisonment of Kenyatta and other leaders, and about the treatment of ordinary people at the hands of the army and the police.

When I appeared before the people at election meetings I talked again of the raging fire. If we did not put out the fire we would not solve the grievances of forced labour on the roads and government land policies. As for the Luo Union and the Luo Thrift, which were the organizations which the people had supported under my leadership up to the time of this election, I said that these two bodies were like heifers: they needed a bull to produce calves and milk. The bull was political power and a say in the government.

My election manifesto was written jointly with Masinde Muliro. He called his manifesto a *national* policy for Kenya. I changed mine to a *nationalist* policy for Kenya. We pledged our total rejection of the Lyttelton Plan. The so-called parity or 'multi-racialism' on which it was based was a means of concentrating power in the hands of the Whites and was fatally dangerous to African interests. I stood for adult franchise, the abolition of discrimination in the legal code, the revision of labour laws to give Africans access to apprenticeship, free medical treatment for the poor, and compulsory education for all children up to the age of fifteen. I advocated complete independence for Kenya, which seemed a far cry in those days. 'Kenya,' my manifesto said, 'must be led from the status of a colony to that of a nation.' I demanded equal pay for equal work, for the opening of the White Highlands to Africans, and agricultural loans for African farmers.

In the field I stressed the need for African self-help and initiative to win our objectives, and I campaigned chiefly on local issues, against the marketing boards and trading regulations which discriminated in favour of the settlers and the Indian commercial community. 'Closer administration' had been introduced in Nyanza during the Emergency years and there were more district officers, more government officials, all White, sons of settlers, in our midst and running our lives than ever before. My opposition came from members of the educated community and the Church who labelled me a rebel because I had left the teaching profession and government service because I would not accept that my role was not to think for myself but to carry out orders. Despite this opposition and the difficulties of covering a vast constituency I won twice as many votes as my opponent.

CHAPTER EIGHT

Council Chambers and Constitutions

I HAD a problem to solve before I entered the Legislative Council chamber for the first time in 1957. This was the kind of dress I would wear for my entry into the political arena dominated by settler politicians. I looked at it this way. I was going into battle, a battle against White domination and against British imperialism. I had to rally support from my own side and get the African mood adjusted to battle conditions. I had to revolutionize the minds of Africans who had taken it for granted that no African challenge against entrenched Kenya settlers' policies could succeed. We were working to get the African to reject European domination of our lives and this involved throwing off all his influences and the inhibition of his supposedly superior way of life. We had to attune the outlook of our people to our ways and customs. Why take for granted the European mode of dress? By discarding this convention I would make an assertion of African standards and values. So I entered the Legislative Council chamber wearing a skin round my waist, a coat of long tails, beaded stockings, sea-shell sandals, a beaded collar and cap, and carrying a whisk of a cow's tail. The settler press called my dress disrespectful of a civilized legislature, and that merely illustrated the approach I was trying to demolish—that civilized meant European and that anything traditional was inferior. Later, when African representation in the Legislative Council was augmented by additional members many of my colleagues —Towett first, then Mboya, Tipis, Moi, Kiano, Muimi, Muliro, and Oguda followed my example. Ngala has stuck to his beaded cap up to today. We wore traditional dress to the first Lancaster House constitutional conference but as we had not agreed on a uniform national dress, everyone wore his own variation. Today our women are leading the way towards the adoption of a national dress for the country. I made a demonstration of my adherence to African standards by wearing traditional dress on public occasions; I also modified my usual form of dress, designing utility suits which I had made by a tailor in Kisumu. Suit, collar and tie are both too elaborate a dress for our hot climate and too expensive for the African pocket. The tunics which I wear today are the result of several experiments in design and though it has been said that the Chinese influenced me, I was wearing my collarless cotton suit with large pockets long before I went to China or met any Chinese, and when I visited that country I wore the suit of my own design. My adoption of simple dress adapted to African conditions dated, as did my use of traditional ceremonial dress, from my entry into the Legislative Council.

Eight African members—Mboya, Ngala, Mate, Oguda, Muliro, Arap Moi, Muimi and I—took the oath of allegiance in March 1957. I had been into the Legislative Council building once before, but only as far as the lobby. My experience in the Central Nyanza District Council at the hands of the District Commissioner chairman came back to me and I fully expected to be ejected from the debate and this citadel of White settler politics, especially as the atmosphere towards the African members created by the local settler press was anything but friendly. But then I recalled that this time we were elected members put in office not at the pleasure of the administration but by our own constituencies, and I resolved to acquire a close working knowledge of the rules of procedure and to be as critical and outspoken as the needs of my constituents demanded. This, I found, was possible in the Legislative Council—as long as we could take the fire of the settlers.

We eight African representatives were for the most part strangers to one another. Muimi from Ukambani had been my school friend at Makerere. He was a teacher of long standing and a mature man, able to take decisions for himself. But he was a member of the educated élite and found difficulty in mixing with ordinary people. Oguda from South Nyanza had already decided in those days that the road to power was the road of African nationalism, and though he appeared to be quiet and slow, when he made a decision he stood firmly by it. Not long after his entry into the Legislative Council he was imprisoned for a year on a charge of sedition and this put him out of the political running. Oguda was critical of Tom Mboya, whom I had met previously, but only casually, during visits to Nairobi. Mboya was said by the newspapers, especially the British and American press, to be the African rising star. He had formed the Kenya Federation of Registered Trade Unions, which stepped into the vacuum created by the banning of the militant trade union movement of Fred Kubai and Makhan Singh (the latter was held in exile for eleven years), and was making a name for himself as an outstanding negotiator. Arap Moi, the Kalenjin representative, was, like Muimi and Ngala, a school teacher; he was influenced by the missions, overawed by settler power and making a slow adjustment to political trends and the need to make independent judgement. Ngala, too, seemed unable to get over his mission background: in the presence of White society and White officialdom he was meek, humble, and malleable.

Soon after our election Mboya convened a meeting of the eight of us in his trade union office in Nairobi. From this

meeting grew the African Elected Members' Organization
—AEMO. We were to achieve team spirit and cohesion, to
co-ordinate our work in the council with African political
activity in the country, to keep the people informed of
political developments, to work for democratic government
for Kenya in the shortest possible time. I was elected AEMO
chairman, with Mboya secretary.

We were faced with an issue of crucial importance, our
stand on the Lyttelton Constitution. We had been elected
under the Lyttelton Plan but even during the election had
declared it null and void. The Colonial Secretary, Lennox
Boyd, retorted that we had thrown down a sterile challenge.
That we were still to see.

The Legislative Council was discussing a five-year development plan for Kenya when I made my maiden speech. I got
the opposite of the traditionally courteous considerate
treatment accorded maiden speakers. A previous speaker,
I said, had been paying tribute to the Development Programme for 1957 'but with me, Sir, I will say that the whole
plan is most unsatisfactory in so far as the African is concerned'. I discussed the place of the African in agriculture.
I attacked the working of the ministries, especially the
Ministry of African Affairs, and the work of the Chief Native
Commissioner. I was ordered to sit down more than once,
but I finished the speech. The Minister of African Affairs
whose salary I had suggested should be cut, rose to say that
he had always been a firm supporter of the tradition that
one should, where possible, deal sympathetically with
maiden speeches. But in the case of my speech, he said, 'I can
see not little but absolutely nothing to praise in his speech'.
Perhaps those members thought that after such blistering
criticism I would not dare to speak again.

It was Tom Mboya, in his maiden speech, who gave the
settlers a taste of their medicine. 'I detect a certain hidden
... resentment ... of statements ... made by my colleagues

144

The author in national dress (first Lancaster House Conference, 1960).

The author carried by cheering supporters after the KANU Governing Council motion of suspension is overruled in 1961.

The author leading the Kenya delegation to the Afro-Asian Solidarity Conference, Conakry, 1960 (*left*)

The author and Achieng Oneko after the latter's release from detention, 1961. (*right*)

KANU leaders after the 'Kenyatta Election', at the opening of the Legislative Council, 11 May 1962: (*left to right*) Tom Mboya, T. M. Chokwe, James Gichuru, Mwanyimba, the author, Mathenge.

in their maiden speeches. The eight African members sitting in this council today are the first batch of African elected members . . . elected according to a franchise that the government itself expressed as the very best, that would return the safest possible person to the council. If they are not the type the government expected, I do not think that we are to blame.'

After the first Legislative Council session I held a huge meeting at Kisumu to report back to my constituency. I invited Mboya, Muliro, and Oguda to attend and speak, also Argwings-Kodhek who, though he was a defeated Legislative Council candidate was the president of the Nairobi District African Congress. We talked to the people of our first experiences in the Legislative Council as their representatives. I said that the council was a huge forest with deep-rooted trees; we had tried to shake the trees but they were firmly rooted. We needed unity and the whole-hearted backing of the people to pull them out. I painted a word picture of each of my colleagues in the council. Muliro, I said, was a sailing boat whose next direction it was difficult for the settlers to assess. Ngala was a young hippo who hid from his father but went secretly to measure his footprint in that of his father, and on the day that he was satisfied that his footprint was equal in size to his parent's, he challenged his father to a duel. Mboya, I said, was a rabid black dog that barked furiously and bit all in his path, while Oguda was a black dog that barked seldom but bit dangerously. Mate was a philosopher, Moi was a giraffe with a long neck that saw from afar. I myself was called Mzee, the elder one.

Our speeches inside the Legislative Council and outside were rousing the ire of the settlers. They castigated us as young men in a hurry, trying to upset everything stable in Kenya. The Nyanza meeting in particular roused the temper of the settler community and questions were asked about it in the Legislative Council. Sir Charles Markham moved a motion against what he termed the 'Nyanza clique', and the Europeans began to try to work on the non-Nyanza members—Bernard Mate, Ngala, Moi, and Muimi—to tell them that they were being misled by the clique of Nyanza radicals.

From the time of that memorable meeting in Kisumu the government restricted our movement and our meetings in our constituencies, alleging that we were using meetings to conspire against the good government of Kenya. We had to apply for a licence and permission from the police to convene a meeting, the police recorded our speeches, and could even restrict the numbers of attendance.

From 1953 to 1956 there had been a total ban on African political organization. When the Lyttelton Constitution with increased African representation was in the offing, the government decided to permit the formation of district political associations (except in the Central Province still heavily under the Emergency where the government would permit nothing more than an advisory council of loyalists) but no national political movement under any circumstances. This was the start of a policy that for the next years prohibited the formation of supra-tribal political bodies and fostered every kind of local separatism. When, as a result, a profusion of parties and leaders developed, all with district and not national loyalties, the African people were blamed for tribalism and disunity! This was the policy of divide and rule at its most obvious and Kenya paid the penalty for many years after the Emergency. Indeed, up to the present day, the remnants of this pattern of splintered political development play havoc with Kenya national unity.

From the first days of AEMO and our entry into the Legislative Council, we grappled to build a national unity though political organizations were allowed to function on only a district basis. Argwings-Kodhek had formed the

Kenya African National Congress to cut across district and tribal affiliations, but the government would not register the organization or the name, and it had become the Nairobi District African Congress which put Argwings-Kodhek up for the election. He was defeated by Mboya and his Nairobi People's Convention Party (the P.C.P. was actually a splinter from Argwings-Kodhek's Congress). In Nyanza Ohanga's Central Nyanza District Association was converted to our needs, and chaired by D. O. Makasembo. Muliro had an association centred in the Kakamega district, Francis Khamisi was the head of Mombasa's Democratic Union, and so on, until in each constituency there was yet another organization imposing pressures and counter-pressures, local rivalries, and endless strain on the over-riding need to build national unity. The government was removing the restriction on African political activity reluctantly, inch by inch; giving way to the pressure for organization, yet at the same time trying to keep movements well under control.

By the time of our second session in the Legislative Council we were well into the swing of council procedure. We placed a spate of questions on the order paper, we argued motions of no confidence in the government's African agricultural policy. The settlers appeared to be hostile in principle to everything I said. Some tried to avoid us and others met us at occasional social gatherings and seemed surprised that face up to me I was not an ogre, but a person like themselves. On one occasion I invited the present Speaker of the House, Humphrey Slade, then a member of the council, to my constituency and he spent the night in my village. This staunch champion of the settler cause advocated policies of segregation. 'When you're in Kenya,' I told him, 'you are in Africa. There is no part of the soil specially reserved for the White man.' Humphrey seemed impressed by the ways of the Nyanza people and to me he seemed a changed man after that, his attacks on us abating in ferocity. But for all that now and then we were able to meet Europeans on a man-to-man basis, we were not allowed to forget that Africans occupied a subservient position in the life of Kenya. I recall the time when I went to the Central Government building to see the Chief Secretary. I was seeking permission for a visit to Walter Odede in restriction by myself and his wife. The European caretaker of the building came up to me and said: 'Are you a hospital worker?' (my cotton tunic might have given him that impression) and he ordered me to leave the government building.

From time to time messages filtered out of the detention camps. We pressed in the Legislative Council for news of the health of the men in Kapenguria, for the release of the detainees. I told the House I was not convinced that the Emergency should be kept going because the government claimed there were still fifty 'terrorists' at large. 'The people whom you call the hard core Mau Mau are the most genuine people, the people who hold sharply to their views . . . their grievances must be faced and we must try to settle them. . . .'

Sir Charles Markham interrupted me: 'Is this the way to get votes?' he cried.

'The Kikuyu are not actually in my constituency, so I am sorry, I will not get votes,' I retorted.

'I do not know how I shall make the government here understand that the African is not a child,' I continued. 'The man who produces children cannot be a child. . . . When I hear the words "backward nation" it cuts me to the quick . . . People think that this is a multi-racial country. We Africans . . . believe that this is Africa and Kenya is an African country.'

An Indian member of the House, Mr Mangat, Q.C., voiced the general disquiet at our speeches. He said our tactics were 'hell-raising' and 'not the right way to proceed about evolving a new constitution or building a nation. At this point of the journey the brakes of the train are more important than the engine,' he said.

We did not agree. We had gone into the Legislative Council with a clear set of aims. These were to make the council a platform from which settlers and the governments of Kenya and Britain could hear African opinion. We were pledged to campaign for more African representation, to use this, in turn, to remove the political, economic, and social restrictions on our people. National political organizations were prohibited; above all we would use the Legislative Council as a national forum to build national unity. Our Legislative Council was a parrot-house of Westminster. There was the same parliamentary procedure, the debates, the motions, the bills, the divisions, the passing of statutes. But this was a parliament presiding over minority domination; our presence as an African group achieved nothing for our people but gave the settler minority a basis of recognition and their rule an authorisation. African representation could change nothing. We could make brave speeches but the solid benches of White members brushed aside our motions. The constitution had been deliberately and carefully loaded against us. Our most urgent immediate need was to win increased African representation. Our eight representatives had a toe in the door; we had now to exert pressure and fling it open.

AEMO'S first press release was brief. It declared that the constitution which gave Africans eight elected members was already void; we would be the last eight to be elected under this arrangement. Not one of us would accept a ministerial post, or the position of parliamentary under-secretary which had been opened to an African member. We were against any arrangement that would secure White domination over other sections of the community.

The statement said:

We, the eight elected African members, wish to make it publicly known that we do not consider ourselves nor those we represent a party to the Lyttelton Plan nor the standstill agreement contained therein. We declare

The Lyttelton Plan and Agreement null and void.

That none of the undersigned shall accept a ministerial post or the position of parliamentary under-secretary.

That the most urgent and immediate need is to secure constitutional reforms in the Legislature giving everyone effective and real representation, to which end it is our intention to direct all our efforts and energies.

We are firmly and unequivocally opposed to any system which serves as a device to secure for certain people permanent political and economic domination of other sections of our community, which end the Lyttelton Plan is promoting to the advantage of the European community in Kenya. We shall fight to build a government and society in which all enjoy equal rights and opportunities and no one enjoys privileges or a privileged position.

The government suggested to us, in its reply, that the matter of increased African representation should be negotiated with all the racial groups, and the onus would be on them to reach agreement. We had never accepted that changes in the constitution had to take place only with the agreement of the three racial groups. We would put our case to the government (which could consult the other communities if it wished) but we held government ultimately responsible for the inadequacy of African representation, and we demanded official recognition of the justice of the African claim for more seats. We announced that we would campaign for fifteen more African seats.

We were determined to show that the constitution was unworkable. AEMO decided to send Ngala and Mboya as a delegation to London to press for a new constitution. Each of us went back to our constituencies to collect funds for the trip, and at a send-off meeting in Kisumu we gave Mboya and Ngala beaded goat-skin coats and caps to show London that they were the real representatives of the people.

The European members had proposed conditions before any consideration of our claim for increased African representation, and one of the conditions was for a period of standstill during which no constitutional reform would take place. We could not commit our successors to future policies, we said. When the Lyttelton Constitution had been adopted the Africans had not been consulted, so we could not be a party to it. We would not accept Ministries; we wanted to negotiate an entirely new Constitution. The Lyttelton Constitution had been intended to last until 1960 but it could not work as long as the African members consistently refused government office. Our London delegation persuaded the Colonial Secretary, Mr Lennox-Boyd, that when we had declared the constitution unworkable we had issued no sterile challenge. He agreed to come to Kenya to negotiate on the spot.

By the time he arrived the settlers had laid their plans carefully. Their leaders—Havelock, Alexander, and Blundell—were proposing a multi-racial society on the lines of the Central African Federation, with provision for electoral colleges to choose specially elected members, and a council of state to stop the enactment of racially discriminatory provisions. Plans for the Colonial Secretary's mission were suspiciously cut and dried. At the airport where we had gone to greet him on arrival, the African elected members were not allowed to meet him on the tarmac, where the settler and government representatives were gathered; we were left in the midst of the crowd. We couldn't get close enough to shake his hand. He stayed at Government House which was virtually inaccessible to us, unless we were invited, but Blundell and company saw him frequently. There was no round-table negotiation. The African group was interviewed separately, then the settler group, then the Asian group. We discussed the matter on settler terms throughout, but without being able to confront them and their arguments. On the one occasion we all met together, Sir Alfred Vincent, the settler spokesman, put forward what the settler group would accept and we were virtually told to take it or leave it.

The Colonial Secretary admitted to us that he and the Governor were trying to sell to us the European point of view. We publicly criticised the breaking of the promise of a round-table conference. I was elected the spokesman of the African members. At one meeting I bluntly told the Governor, Sir Evelyn Baring, who was leaning heavily throughout the talks on the diehard stand of the settlers, that KAU had denounced him when he came to Kenya and that having come from South Africa he had nothing good to offer us. At that Lennox-Boyd closed the meeting with the words: 'Your Excellency, I think this meeting will serve no useful purpose.' In the AEMO group members thought my language had been too strong and urged me to apologise which I did, without retracting the contents of my statement. We were demanding fifteen more seats, to bring the total of African seats to twenty-three, three more than the Whi and Asian seats taken together. The new Lennox-Boyd constitution increased African seats by only six members, to give us fourteen elected members altogether. There were fourteen European seats and six elected Asians. Our objection to specially elected members was over-ruled and there was provision for twelve such members (four each of Whites, Africans, and Asians) who would not be elected but chosen by the Legislative Council. In effect this meant that the special Members would be chosen by the Whites, for they had an absolute majority as a result of their twenty-four non-elected members. There was provision for a Council of State (eight Whites, four Africans, and four Asians) nominated by the Governor. This council was to have reserved powers on all legislation which discriminated against any racial community. The only discrimination exercised was that of Whites against Africans, but this is *not* what the constitution-framers had in mind!

The settlers liked the new constitution. This, they said, would prevent Kenya turning into a Ghana. What they were offering us was a Central African or South African regime. 'If it is a bus ride we are invited to join let us have in clear and definite terms the destination,' we said, 'for unless we are agreed on this we shall not agree on the route.' Within a month we had rejected the constitution. It had allowed some limited African advance but once again the Constitution restricted any real inroads into White power. Our objective was democracy based on the principle of one man–one vote; this constitution, like the previous one, was not leading us in that direction. We agreed in AEMO not to accept the special seats or recognize any African who was elected to a special seat, and we agreed not to accept positions as Ministers.

We were divided in AEMO on the six new elected seats. I was in favour of a boycott of the six seats as a protest against the unsatisfactory new constitution. My main reason was that it simply did not accommodate our demands. I also saw an ominous significance in the constituencies allocated to the six new seats. Mate's constituency of Meru and Nanyuki was allocated an additional seat, also the Kikuyu district of Fort Hall, Nyeri, and Kiambu, as well as Embuland, Machakos, Mombasa Island, and the Kericho and Masai area together in the Rift Valley. No extra seat was allocated to Nyanza Province because the settlers were afraid of the influence of the so-called 'Nyanza clique'. I was not concerned with this as a Nyanza representative as such, but I was troubled that the new representation was being deliberately weighted against the areas from which the most radical and outspoken policies were coming at this time, and at the evidence that the government was devising new ways of dividing us and undermining our militancy. At the AEMO meeting members agreed that we should boycott the six seats. The boycott campaign was already beginning to be carried throughout the country when Dr Julius Kiano, then a lecturer in the Royal College in Nairobi, announced in the press that he would stand for election. AEMO decided that it had no option but to review its stand as the boycott had already been broken, but we suspected strongly that the settlers' scheme to divide us had prevailed upon one or two of us who had inspired Kiano to stand, and the undermining of our decision caused serious tension within AEMO.

Our rejection of the special seats and African Ministries was in anticipation of the search by government and settlers for Africans who would try to deflect our people from our struggle. Plums of office might tempt men to accept the continuance of White domination if there was a comfortable seat somewhere in government for themselves. We had to take a firm stand of principle. Settler sniping at our stand was never-ceasing, often malicious. At a Caledonian Society dinner a member of the Legislative Council suggested that our refusal of ministerial appointment was not principled opposition to the constitution but a realization that if we took office our 'real worth would soon be found out'.

At the beginning of 1958 AEMO was asked to elect one of its number to attend a course run by the Commonwealth Parliamentary Association in London. I was chosen to go. Before I left I travelled through many parts of Kenya—the Coast, Taita, Kabarnet, and the Rift Valley—to judge the mood of the African people. It was clear to me that Kenyatta and the leaders in the prisons and camps were the central thought and concern of the people, who believed that the struggle so condemned and misrepresented by the settler community was a heroic resistance by the Africans to the evils of settler rule. In London I was met at the airport by our Kenya students who similarly felt that our main task was to win the release of our veteran political leaders. The African voices—our voices—in the Legislative Council were heard by the grace of the settlers in Kenya and the British Government. We had stepped into a vacuum created by the state of Emergency when the true organizations and spokesmen of the people were imprisoned. Until they were reinstated in their positions of leadership we would lose not only the military battle of the Emergency but the political one too; the achievement of the political aims of KAU and allied movements was what we were fighting for, and nothing should deflect us from this. This had to be said in Britain, especially in London, the heart of the colonial empire which also during the Emergency, had been the focal point of vigorous solidarity action with the people of Kenya led by the Kenya Campaign Committee. African students from all over the continent gathered at the West African Student Union Centre—the student bodies that convened this meeting were later to make up the Council of African Organizations (CAO) in Britain—and I told them that the central issue for Kenya was the release of Kenyatta and his colleagues. I was invited to address Conservative Members of Parliament in a committee room at Westminster, and there, bearding the lion in his den, I said Dedan Kimathi was a hero of Kenya, that Kenyatta and the leaders with him in restriction could lead Kenya to independence, and that there would be no real independence as long as the leaders of the people were locked up. I was challenged from the floor. An M.P. shouted: 'Will you repeat that in Kenya?' I replied that I would. So, before members of the British Parliament, I pledged to pursue the issue of the release of Kenyatta on my return to Kenya's Legislative Council.

CHAPTER NINE

Bombshell in the House

By 1958 and the time I resumed my seat in the Legislative
Council I was less popular than ever with the settler members
and the government. Reports of some of my London statements had seeped back into Kenya. My opportunity to raise
the Kenyatta issue came soon. The British *Observer* carried
a letter from Kenyatta and the other four prisoners at
Lokitaung complaining about the conditions under which
they were detained. The government replied: 'Lengthy and
careful inquiries have been carried out and no evidence of
any irregularities has come to light.' We discussed this
question in AEMO and agreed that Mboya would move a
motion for an inquiry into the prisons and detention camps.
The letter from Lokitaung had begun: 'We Political
Prisoners . . .' The government objected that these men were
not political prisoners, but, said the Minister for Legal
Affairs, 'convicted and disbelieved by the court'. The debate
was being diverted with a red-herring argument about
whether prisoners were 'political', or 'convicted' and 'proved
liars'.

'These people,' I told the council, 'before they were
arrested were the political leaders of the Africans in the
country, and the Africans respected them as their political
leaders, and even at this moment, in the heart of hearts of
the Africans, they are still the political leaders. . . .'

Sir Charles Markham shouted: 'You are going . . .' but in the ensuing uproar I could not hear the end of his sentence.

'This has got to be known,' I continued above the shouting, 'because it is right deeply rooted in the African heart. . . .'

The uproar and shouts rose again. I had been given the floor at the end of the day and the council adjourned in the middle of my speech. I resumed the following day.

'These people are the leaders of the people. Just as when Archbishop Makarios was arrested by the British Government, he was taken to the Seychelles and he was put in the Governor's lodge there. Nearly every day there was a report of his health, of his activities, in the press. The same thing should be done with Mr Kenyatta. . . .'

I was interrupted by shouts, and the Speaker struggled to call the House to order.

One of the members shouted: 'Mau Mau!'

'Well,' I said, 'maybe you take them to be Mau Mau or you take them to be any other thing, but I am giving you what you should know about our feelings towards them as the African people, and before you realize that, you can never get the cooperation of the African people.' I was ordered to stop speaking.

Mate and Mboya spoke after I had resumed my seat. Mate said: 'None of us sympathized with the kind of thing that took place at Lari . . . Genuine political activity must be clearly distinguished from criminal activity.'

Mboya said: 'Some unfortunate statements made in the course of the debate might create a wrong impression as to the reason for the motion.' (For an investigation into the conditions of political prisoners.)

The press had a field day. They reported gasps in the House when I made my speech and the comment of the chief secretary 'almost incredible!' The East African Standard editorialized: 'Mr Mboya's motion was put down from irreproachable concern for his fellow men. He and his colleagues will be quick to realize how their case has been weakened . . . by Mr Odinga's outburst.' One paper said, 'Let the people come forward now and hound Odinga out of political life forever.'

My enemies in Nyanza said I represented not Central Nyanza, but also the Mau Mau. The Whites in Maseno boycotted the Luo Thrift shop there and we had to close our doors and rent the shop to an Indian, and a portion to a bank.

My fellow members in AEMO said that I had slipped up badly. When we met the air was heated and I, as chairman, was in an awkward position. The AEMO meeting suggested that I should apologize for my stand. I asked for time to consider that. I sent an urgent wire to D. O. Makasembo, chairman of the Central Nyanza District Association, to convene a meeting in Kisumu that weekend. Under a heavy cordon of police armed with tape recorders I addressed an audience of over 6,000 people. I repeated what I said in the Legislative Council chamber and asked for their opinion. The people stood as one body to support me; I had said exactly what they felt about Jomo Kenyatta, they said.

That same weekend Kiano told a *baraza* at Fort Hall that he disagreed with my statement that Kenyatta and the others were still our real political leaders. He said the statement had been made in a fit of anger, and the only leaders of the African people were 'those of us whom you elected and the chiefs'.

Fortunately the press carried reports of the reaction of the Kisumu meeting, and not long after that the Nairobi District African Congress led by Argwings-Kodhek passed a resolution supporting my stand, as did the Mombasa African Democratic Union, and the people of Eldoret.

The resolution of the Nairobi meeting said:

We solemnly re-affirm our confidence in the leadership of Jomo Kenyatta and other political prisoners now languishing in

158

imperialist jails for relentlessly fighting against injustice, settler domination and its sister the colour-bar. We unreservedly condemn all those self-seeking African Elected Members who have paraded themselves with the settler in denouncing imprisoned political leaders as 'criminals' and wish to express Congress' full concurrence with the statement made by Mr Oginga Odinga in the Legislative Council . . . and unanimously supported by his constituents at a public meeting in Kisumu . . .

But within AEMO there was still strong opposition. A resolution passed at a meeting and recorded in the minutes stated

The general feeling was that the statement with all its merits and demerits was inopportune and would retard other efforts which aimed to seek cooperation from the Government and particularly in connection with the lifting of Emergency regulations and restrictions.

I told AEMO I was not convinced by the argument, and I would make the same statement again. I was urged to issue a statement that my stand was my own, not AEMO's, but I refused, telling other members that they could issue their own disclaimers if they so decided. I was sticking to my guns. Inside AEMO we had reached deadlock, and throughout the country the argument went on.

Central Province loyalists put pressure on Mr Nyagah, the member for Embu who told a public meeting:

My colleagues and I are of the opinion that Mr Odinga's statement was unfortunate and harmful to the progress of the people of Central Province.

When I replied, through a press statement, to Mr Nyagah's charge that my Kenyatta speech was harmful, the *Kenya Weekly News* published my reply, under the headline 'Oginga Odinga Brays Again'. Once again I said that my statement about Kenyatta should be put to the test of popular opinion in Kenya. Nyagah's statement was due to pressure from the settler caucus.

This is an ill omen for the African masses who must rely on their courageous political resilience. I pity Mr Nyagah and his revered colleagues. They have proved that they do not know the mind of the people they represent. . . . Just as the Irish did not forget De Valera, and India Gandhi and America George Washington, the English Oliver Cromwell, the Africans shall not deny their leaders simply because an imperialist group has branded them this or that. To urge us to forget our leaders is to undermine our nationalism in a fundamental way. We shall not have it. . . . On an issue like this I will not flinch, I will not be moderate, and I will not withdraw.

I issued a challenge to Nyagah and those of our colleagues who supported him to ask their constituents to endorse their stand, and to share a platform with me, in their and my constituencies, to ask for a vote of confidence on this issue.

The settler press was in full cry. They sensed that the Emergency was in its last days and they could not for ever cling to Emergency powers under a state of martial rule. They could see that the African members in the Legislative Council had got their teeth into the struggle to make government fully representative of the African people, and in their cries of protest they used insults, ridicule, and threats. Kenyatta, said the *Kenya Weekly News*, was not merely the leader of a violent movement . . . he was 'stained with the Mark of the Beast'. The columnist of the *Kenya Weekly News* wrote:

In my view Mr Oginga Odinga should be put in his place—I need not stipulate the place I have in mind—for starting this accursed cult of Kenyatta. Not so long ago, as usual at the expense of others, he was stalking about the Parliament of Westminster arrayed in a robe of duck-egg blue, ostensibly to learn the ways of parliamentary democracy. Clearly he learnt nothing and is probably quite unteachable in any case.

The abuse slid off like water from a duck's back. I did not care what they said about me. I did care that the settlers were trying to provoke a split in our ranks by playing on the susceptibilities of those who took fright at allegations of violence and subversion. The editorials played again and again on the same theme that we had 'divided councils', and pressed the other African representatives to say whether they agreed with 'the awful nonsense to which Oginga Odinga stands committed'.

Things were not easy inside AEMO in those days but we denied that the elected members were about to split. In the interests of unity I withdrew some of the allegations I had made about Nyagah's speech.

After the first open denunciations of my call for Kenyatta's release those African representatives not in agreement resorted to equivocal statements (Kiano: 'a lot of people are opposed to subversion while at the same time revering Kenyatta as a man whose name will occupy a prominent place in Kenya's history') but when Mboya and Kiano returned to Kenya from attending the All African Peoples' Conference in Ghana they had spirit for the fight to have Kenyatta released.

AEMO as a whole eventually resolved that as a body we would press for Kenyatta's release and his return to normal life, together with all those imprisoned, detained, or restricted under the Emergency. At all meetings after that we called for this policy. In Nairobi the slogan of Mboya's P.C.P. was 'Uhuru na Kenyatta' but in Nyanza we reversed the order and cried 'Kenyatta na Uhuru', to stress that only with the release of the Kenyatta generation of leaders could we have true independence.

All through 1958 and 1959 we struggled to have the Emergency lifted. This was the time of the brief experience of KKM—Kiama Kia Muingi, a local organization of men who had been in the detention camps and who were organizing oath-taking. As long as there are detainees to be released, said the Chief Secretary Coutts, as long as KKM flourished, and people are either 'so foolish or so wilfully abandoned as to promote the Jomo Cult, then the lifting of the Emergency in Kenya must inevitably be delayed'.

News was leaked to the world of the Hola Camp killings in which eleven prisoners died at the hands of warders. More and more information was filtering out about the conditions of the detainees. I found my meetings in Central Nyanza banned on the grounds that I was glorifying Mau Mau. Allegations against me were irrelevant, I said. The root causes of revolt—landlessness, the frustration of the peasants and an unjust administration—had to be removed before there could be hope of a contented African population.

We continued to struggle against the Lennox-Boyd Constitution. We attacked the principle of the special seats, which undermined the principle of a common roll, and we attacked the Africans who announced they would stand for these seats: Wanyutu Waweru (who during my days at the Alliance High School had been expelled during the food strike) and Musa Amalemba who went so far as to accept a seat in the Council of Ministers. We called these men 'stooges, quislings, and black Europeans . . . traitors to the African cause'. Seven of us were sued for criminal libel. Half the African members of the Legislative Council found themselves standing in the dock charged with 'using undue influence to incite Africans to refrain from becoming candidates for the specially elected seats'. Once again D. N. Pritt, Q.C., came to Kenya and after his defence in our trial we were fined £75 each—quite unimportant to us because the people supported our stand.

By the end of 1958 we had decided that the time had come for sharper opposition to the Lennox-Boyd Constitution. All fourteen elected African members walked out of the Council Chamber when the Governor, Sir Evelyn Baring, said that the Constitution was going to stay, regardless of what we African members wanted. By the end of the year we were not taking part in council proceedings. Our demand was for new constitutional talks, a round-table conference, and effective constitutional changes.

Settlers and government stood united on the Lennox-Boyd Constitution and we found we could make no dent in this block. We decided to enlist the support of Asian members of the Legco and we even had one White member of the council join us. This was Mr S. V. Cooke. In this way we formed the Constituency Elected Members Organization (CEMO) and decided on a multi-racial—though I prefer the word national—delegation to London to break the constitutional deadlock. The delegation was unique, including members of all race groups for the first time in Kenya's history, and was composed of Muliro, Moi, Kiano, and myself as leader of the group from among the African members, Nazareth, Pandya, and Deen among the Asian members, and S. V. Cooke and a second European who was not a member of Legco, also Sheik Mackawi (representing the Arabs). We put our case forcefully to the Colonial Secretary.

We were promised that a constitutional conference would be held. There would be preliminary discussions and work by 'experts' on proposals for a new constitution. Our delegation raised the question of the Emergency, pressing that it should be ended. The British Government was still taking an intransigent stand, refusing to be committed to a date for the relaxation of restrictions and insisting that there was no possibility of relaxing or ending Kenyatta's restriction order. At a meeting at the Colonial Office with the Minister and the Secretary of State we were told that we should keep distinct the questions of constitutional progress and the need to maintain order. We could only see how inter-related these two questions were. I stressed that if the Emergency were not lifted by the time the new constitutional conference opened, the Africans of Kenya would feel there was no prospect of cooperation. A bold step was needed to improve the political atmosphere and to get rid of the widespread suspicion that the Emergency was being used as a political weapon, to stop the Africans uniting on a national scale, and to prevent their elected representatives from campaigning freely. We were promised a constitutional conference later in 1959. This was a great victory for us. We ended our boycott of the Legislative Council.

The prospects of new constitutional proposals caused a flurry of activity in the settler camp, the guiding hand of the Colonial Office clearly visible. The month after our delegation's return from London Michael Blundell, the leader of the settlers, resigned his Ministry of Agriculture to form the New Kenya Party. Forty-six members of the Legislative Council backed him, twenty-one of them government nominees and all the specially elected men. The 'multi-racialism' of the new group was deceptive. The purpose of the NKP was to take the bite out of African policy for a common electoral roll and unrestricted adult franchise. The manoeuvre was to win time for an 'orderly transfer of responsibility' to an educated and 'responsible' leadership. We scorned the new Blundell policy as one not genuinely interested in inter-racial cooperation. Blundell said in a speech for unity that Kenya needed 'the ability and integrity of the Europeans, the adaptability of the African, the thrift and industry of the Muslim and Indian and the tolerance and experience of the Arab'. In other words, I said in a statement, 'Mr Blundell wants a Kenya where Europeans govern, Africans follow, Asians supply the wealth and Arabs sit musing with tolerance'. We were sure the Blundell policy was government sponsored and we said so. The government, we said, should have been spending its time negotiating a new constitution with the representatives of the people of Kenya instead of

164

trying to devise an evasive policy through Mr Blundell and the nominated members. We were genuinely looking for a way out of the then political deadlock but manoeuvres like these would spread confusion, not bring solutions. I invited Mr Blundell to share a platform with me, or any of the African elected members both in the African areas and before meetings of Whites. He did not accept the challenge.

The Blundell middle-of-the-road policy was not acceptable to us. Nor did it rally the majority of the settlers. Group Captain Briggs' United Party won support by preaching a far more reactionary policy. This was the beginning of a scheme for regionalism. Briggs' group wanted the abolition of the Legislative Council and the establishment of regional assemblies instead, illustrating that after their struggle for self-rule since the twenties the settlers were prepared to forego this in the face of the African challenge.

In the face of tactics to split our ranks and confuse us with promises of a transfer of power if only we would be moderate enough to come to terms with settler pressure groups, African unity was the key to our advance.

My conviction that African unity had to be unbreakable had been reinforced by my talks with Kwame Nkrumah. After reporting to AEMO on the success of our London talks I had visited Ghana in response to an invitation by Nkrumah. This was my first visit to an independent African state. Nkrumah felt about Kenyatta's release the same way as I did: that the government was keeping the genuine leadership of the Kenya African struggle in indefinite detention until it had found a substitute leadership of men who would gently, flatteringly, be given a modicum of participation in government but only as much, and at the pace, as government decreed. Nkrumah talked of the problems of emancipating other African colonies, of the inspiration of Pan-Africanism and his conviction of Pan-African government. I found that Mboya, when he had attended the All African Peoples' Conference in Accra, had disagreements on African trade union affiliation to the All African Trade Union Federation; his Kenya Federation of Labour was already committed to affiliation of the American-dominated International Confederation of Free Trade Unions.

I had also made the first plans and business contacts for the founding of an independent African press in Kenya. I talked to Nkrumah of our need for a press that would break the monopoly of the government and settler press. During my earlier visit to London I had talked with Othigo Othieno, Ngumbu Njururi, Mbiyu Koinange and Joseph Murumbi (the latter two had been KAU's representatives in exile since the Emergency) and we had agreed that a London office for the Kenya struggle was indispensable to project our cause on an international scale.

International support and Pan-African unity would be indispensable, but their promise would be unfulfilled without African unity within Kenya. The government knew what it was doing when it prohibited the formation of national political bodies and left us to organize our people in district associations. We tried through the Convention of African Associations, to unite the district associations but the government refused the convention registration. Much was achieved by the district associations in bringing political questions to the fore after years during which martial rule had silenced the people. But inevitably local bodies developed rivalries and jealousies, encouraged petty political ambitions and were used by ambitious men not to advance the national cause but to build themselves as career politicians. This canker began to eat away at our political life in the late fifties, and, I regret to say, sometimes swelled to epidemic proportions in the battles of the years to come. Men adopted policies and political manoeuvres not to build Kenya's greater national unity but to further their pursuit of personal power. As far as the settlers and the government were concerned, this was all to the good. The more disunited and quarrelsome we Africans showed ourselves, the less energy we would have for a concerted attack for our demands. We knew, and the settler government knew too, that this was the vital period when a new political leadership for Kenya would take shape. There was a vacuum in the national political leadership created by years of Emergency rule, and the settlers were asking themselves: 'Who can we groom to take over the leadership so that our influence is not broken?'

It was against this background that the disputes, some major, but most of them minor, that occurred in the ranks of AEMO were so unfortunate. In AEMO and later in CEMO I found myself mediator between Mboya and Muliro. Muliro won the support of other members of the group on the grounds that Mboya was trying to steal what was a group show, and he criticized me, as chairman, for not controlling Mboya. In the second year of AEMO when we held elections for officials, Mboya was on a visit to Ghana and he was displaced as secretary and Ngala elected in his place. Mboya was bitter against me, as elections had been held in his absence, but I pointed out that the result of the election was the concensus of group opinion. Much of the difficulty of our work in AEMO, and in later years, especially in 1960, was caused by the concerted world press campaign to elevate Tom Mboya to the unchallenged leadership of Kenya Africans. The Kenya and world newspapers and politicians who referred to him in this way did not know, perhaps, what harm they were doing Mboya. In the early days he was as much victim as culprit, in the interests of a British–United States strategy to build a leader who would overshadow and make the people forget Kenyatta. His political colleagues resented this imposed promotion, and held against him the honours which outsiders seemed ready to bestow on him, and the alacrity with which

167

credit for leadership was given him instead of the group. Early strains developed in our relations when he showed he resented my being appointed AEMO chairman (I sensed that he felt I might be senior in age but I was his inferior in political experience and shrewdness). Later loggerheads had beginnings in individualistic and ambitious motives and other incidents. Our unity was often elusive under the tensions.

In the middle of 1959 we were deep in discussion of our tactics for the next constitutional fight when an irreparable split occurred in AEMO. I was unexpectedly admitted to hospital in Kisumu after a sudden collapse in my health. I wrote to CEMO, which was meeting in Nairobi, to urge that it depart not one iota from our basic policy of universal adult franchise on a common voter's roll, but that we could not leave long in abeyance the hammering out of detailed policy matters, lest this affect our preparations for the forthcoming constitutional conference. At the time of the discussions tension between Mboya and Muliro was rising to a head. Muliro had declared that there was no room in one party for himself and Mboya; he had had enough of Mboya's habit of over-ruling our decisions. Moi, Mate, Muliro, Towett, Nyagah, and Ngala wrote to me, as chairman of AEMO, to say that they resigned: 'You will be hearing about the reasons why we have taken the step we have adopted, and what our next move will be.' The next move was the launching of a new organization, the Kenya National Party. Muliro announced that CEMO had out-lived its usefulness and should be dissolved and he wrote the constitution for the new party. It was joined by all but four AEMO members—Mboya, Kiano, Oguda, and myself.

Behind this move there was more than the rivalry of political leaders and disgruntlement at the behaviour of some of our members. The new group led by Muliro had decided to cash in on the government's refusal to register any national body except a multi-racial one (though of course exclusively White bodies were permitted and had been all along). All the Asian and Arab members of the Legislative Council joined the KNP, as well as one White member. The new party stood for independence in 1958, but said it would accept the continuance of nominated and special seats. It wanted African majorities in the Legislative Council and the Council of Ministers, but two houses, an Upper and a Lower.

I issued a public statement expressing surprise at the announcement of the party. We had agreed, at the last meeting of CEMO that I had attended, that CEMO had coordinated our policy in general terms, but that we had to reach agreement on detailed constitutional proposals. All the African elected members had been of one policy, which our White member Mr Cooke and an Indian member Mr Travadi shared, but other Asian members were wavering and, it seemed to me, using CEMO to disrupt the unity of the African members. I was convinced that we could still achieve unity . . . and I thought the announcement of the new party a rash decision. It surrendered the African demand of the right to organize a national political organization.

AEMO, we realized, reluctantly, had been split apart. The four of us left in the body—Mboya, Kiano, Oguda, and I—decided on a last unity effort and plan for the formation of a united national African political movement. We convened an urgent meeting of all political leaders and associations in Nairobi, including the new KNP. The conference broke up over an argument on delegates' credentials. The AEMO members who had formed the KNP announced that they had expelled me from AEMO because I had not been impartial in the chair. The expulsion was meaningless, of course.

The danger of a multi-racial party at this time was of adulterating the demands of the African people in a bid to form an alliance with immigrant groups whose only interest was to use the African majority to achieve their own aspirations. Africans wanted a universal franchise; the Asian members of the Legislative Council wanted a qualitative franchise. 'African freedom', we said, 'will be achieved only through African nationalism.' We refused to sacrifice our nationalism for vague and deceptive phrases of non-racialism and multi-racialism. I do not think that the non-African members of the Legislative Council were genuine in supporting and cooperating with the national struggle and I said so. We launched the Kenya Independence Movement. Mboya was elected secretary of KIM, Kiano, chairman, and I, president.

KIM, of course, was refused registration by the government. But it was never doubted that it mustered far and away a majority African support. The difference between the approach of the KNP and KIM was vital in those days and for years afterward. There were three major areas of disagreement. Firstly, our attitude in the Kenya Independence Movement was that Africans had to spearhead the struggle for a democratic and independent Kenya. We were not against allies from the other racial groups joining us, and we welcomed their cooperation and worked for it, but Africans had to lead, and be alert against compromises which would undermine our claim for majority government, for we were the majority that had been dominated by minority groups throughout our history. So we had fought the principle of 'parity' in the Lyttelton Constitution, the reservation of seats for special members, and any constitutional formula which descrted the stand of one man—one vote, on a common roll. Secondly, our strength at constitutional talks and all negotiations with Britain lay in our strength of organization among the African people. It was their national struggle that was winning their demands, and they had to be convinced it was a national struggle, with a national African leadership dedicated to their aims. KNP, as it turned out, had great difficulty persuading the African masses that it was dancing to their tune and not to the tunes played by the minority groups that tried to climb on the African band-wagon when it looked as though things would go our way. (In fact only a few months after it was founded KNP threw out its Asian officials and declared that its leadership was all-African.)

Finally, KNP's strategy for the constitutional talks was vague and unsatisfactory, and this meant that the Africans were divided on the timing of independence and in the strategy we would adopt in the tussle with Britain. The nearer the round-table talks came, the more important it was to try to put a divided African house in order. With the constitutional conference almost upon us by a miracle of effort we achieved a joint conference of leaders at Kiambu, and here it was agreed that we would take to London a joint delegation led by Ngala for the KNP and Mboya for KIM as delegation secretary. Muliro and I who were the presidents of the two bodies ceded the leadership to Ngala and Mboya in the interests of a joint delegation.

We had cemented a rather precarious unity, but a unity all the same, and we set off for London to speak with one African voice for a new constitution.

CHAPTER TEN

Winds of Change

By 1960 and the opening of the first of Kenya's Lancaster House constitutional conferences, great changes had swept through Africa and were blowing into the Colonial Office. The winds had begun to change with the end of the Second World War and the loss to the British Empire of India in 1947. When India went there had to be a complete re-assessment of Empire. The loss of the brightest jewel in the British Crown, together with the crisis created by the pressure of the dollar on the pound, made Africa very important in the years immediately after the end of the war. Kenya in particular was marked out to replace India as a key military base (Kahawa, Mombasa, and the RAF station in Nairobi). But Britain emerged from the war a weakened imperial power and although in the immediate post-war years she needed to develop new wealth in her colonies to make up for shortages at home, and her dollar deficit, she could no longer afford to maintain extensive colonial garrisons nor did she relish the prospect of colonial wars. A burden of £60 million to put down the so-called 'Mau Mau' rebellion was not blithely to be assumed again in Kenya or elsewhere. The national rising in Kenya and the need to govern by emergency law taught a lesson that was driven home in West Africa by post-war restlessness there: that rigid methods of political control and a refusal by the colonial power to give ground placed the grip of administration in serious jeopardy. In West Africa the end of the war brought bright talk of the new future and the Atlantic Charter, but also rising economic and social tensions. Previously Britain had believed that she could control the timing of African advance, and that provided she supervised a gradual (and in some cases barely noticeable) evolution in representative institutions, she was firmly in control. This illusion was shattered by the changing face of Africa. The riots of 1948 in the Gold Coast precipitated the granting of a new constitution for the colony that was a short step to the founding of Ghana as an independent African state. Once the dam broke in Ghana, the waters began to seep over the rest of West Africa and even further afield on the continent. Britain began to build dykes to try to stop the floodwaters of African liberation. She devised a policy to cut her losses, and make a new start, on a changing continent, to entrench her influence.

Constitutional advance was granted to forestall victorious national revolt. Former subjects were enlisted as allies, agents, and friends, were even told they were equals. A process of decolonization was set afoot that would obscure the political controls, yet guarantee the retention of economic influence. The refurbishing of the colonial image had a three-fold purpose. It was necessary to blunt the edge of African independence. It was a strategy to prevent Britain being eclipsed in competition with the United States of America for spheres of control and influence. Finally it was to repel the attraction of socialism and the socialist countries, especially the Soviet Union, to African nationalists. All these three forces acted as a catalyst on British policy in Africa. In his book, *British Policy in Changing Africa*, published in 1959, Sir Andrew Cohen, a former Governor of Uganda and head of the African division of the Colonial Office, gave advice on an adapted colonial policy for Britain. This, he wrote, was to recognize that nationalist movements were bound to grow steadily more powerful, and that the intelligent thing for Britain was to 'recognize this early and by skilful anticipation to try and guide the energies of nationalists into constructive channels'. The West, he said, set out in Africa to achieve three purposes: the moral and humanitarian, the economic interest, namely the need for raw materials and trade and thirdly, the political interest to 'help them (African nationalists) to remain stable and friendly to the western world'.

The changed strategy was to ensure the survival of Britain as a world power, to avoid open clashes in colonial areas, to modify colonial relationships to make them more enduring. There was still another factor at work. Throughout the fifties there had been falls in the world price of raw materials. This deterioration in the terms of trade of the colonial countries, or former colonial areas, was disastrous for us: earnings from raw materials remained stationary, or slumped, while prices for the manufactured and machine goods we needed continued to rise. An unfavourable trade balance reaped for Africa and Asia rebounded to the advantage of Britain and the metropolitan countries, where mechanized agriculture, as part of the technological revolution of the highly industrialized states, made many colonial territories and their agricultural exports expendable. The changed economic relationship between Britain and her colonies coincided with the politically induced changes.

In different parts of the continent British colonial policy adapted itself variously to economic and political changes. But even as the forces of colonialism improvised ways to tame the forces of independence and bring compromising sections of Africa's political leadership into association with imperialism, the establishment of independent states brought a dynamic new momentum into African liberation. The

Egyptian Revolution of 23 July 1952 gave Egypt independence. It was the abortive Suez adventure of 1956, the twentieth-century exercise in gunboat diplomacy that failed, that united all Africa, and Africa with Asia and the Arab world, to give a great spurt forward to national independence. An African state, backed by the socialist world, repulsed with ignominy the concerted attack of several of the world's leading powers of which even the United States was critical. Africa was never the same after Suez and the coming into play on the continent and in the world of the forces of Pan-Africanism. Ghana became independent in 1957 (a year after Suez). Britain's policies could not be the same either. Her paced scheme for decolonization had to be speeded up; it was no longer the planners in the Colonial Office who set the tempo, but Accra and Cairo, the All-African Peoples' Conferences, Algeria's war of liberation and Sekou Toure's challenge to France.

Kenya, of course, was not West or North Africa. Settler domination and settler pressure saw to that. But if the national rising of 1952 and the prolonged Emergency had not won the fighting they had caused a re-thinking. British policy that rested squarely on the retention of White privilege in Kenya would clearly have no room to manoeuvre in a rapidly changing continent. There had to be a departure from the support of settler claims at all costs, and a gradual shift in the balance of political power in our country. Britain was preparing to play the rope out gradually to the forces of African nationalism. It would be for us to get a grip on one end of the rope and tug it sharply to our side.

By the late fifties the White-dominated Central African Federation—launched as a 'great experiment in multi-racial partnership'—had blown up in Britain's face and had to be abandoned. Between them the civil disobedience in Malawi (then Nyasaland), the political opposition in Zambia led by Kenneth Kaunda and his party, and the findings of the

Devlin Commission, later followed by the Monckton Commission, condemned federation as a colossal failure in British colonial policy. When the Conservative Government was returned in the election at the end of 1959 some colonial re-thinking on the subject of Kenya could be tried out in the field. It was on the eve of our Lancaster House conference that Macmillan set out on his African tour and made his 'wind of change' speech. This was the high watermark of the new British colonial policy.

By the time our constitutional conference opened Colonial Secretary Lennox-Boyd had been replaced by Iain Macleod. For the first time the Colonial Office was about to concede Kenya an African majority—though a narrow one—in the Legislative Council, and to begin a delicate manoeuvre to shift the balance between settler control and African nationalist pressure. Not that precautions had not been built into the conference to guard against too sharp a shift in Kenyan political positions. Blundell's New Kenya Group was represented out of all proportion to its support, and held the key to the conference. Its role was transparent. We could not but agree with Briggs' angry charges that government plotting to use the New Kenya Group had gone back a full year before the Lancaster House conference, and that the British Government in Lennox Boyd's day had backed the formation of the new party. It was to be a counter-weight, not as Briggs thought to his right wing forces, but to our forces of African nationalism.

In the conference room the whole Legislative Council sat, transplanted from Nairobi to London. It was a strange meeting place with new umpires but old forces, armed with most of the old arguments. The Briggs group of four members wanted a return to Colonial Office rule, and a reversion to an advisory council. Our demands were responsible government in 1960, a common roll with universal adult suffrage, the

A press conference after a visit to Kenyatta at Maralal in 1961. (*left to right*) Ronald Ngala, leader of KADU, the author, Lawrence Sagini, a press reporter, Tom Mboya.

KANU celebrations at Gatundu after Kenyatta's release, 1961. (*left to right*) the author, Gichuru, Mboya, Ochwada, Ngala (giving the KADU salute).

The author meeting Dr Nkrumah, Ghana 1963. Luke Obok, MP, is second from left; Mbiyu Koinange is behind Nkrumah.

The author as Minister for Home Affairs addressing Chiefs and Regional Assembly members in 1964.

right of the majority party to form the new government, the abolition of nominated and specially elected members, the release of Kenyatta and the opening of the White Highlands to landless Africans. The Blundell group had a half-way scheme for communal and common roll elections.

The conference could not get its teeth into negotiation until the matter of our advisers had been settled. Through Mboya we had retained as an adviser Mr Thurgood Marshall, the New York attorney for the National Association for the Advancement of Coloured People. This gave United States' circles a foot in the door of the conference and I was not happy about it. On the eve of the conference we arranged for Peter Mbiyu Koinange to travel from Ghana, where he was then working in the Ghana Government's African Affairs Bureau, to act as additional adviser to us. This caused a storm. Macleod vetoed Koinange's entry because of his 'special responsibility for the unhappy events which led to the Emergency'. Ngala replied for us: the decision as to the person suitable as adviser should be made by the African elected members themselves, and by no one else. We wanted Koinange. In protest against his exclusion we boycotted the opening day of the talks. Macleod found a compromise solution for the admission of Koinange not to the conference itself but to the offices set aside for our use in Lancaster House, but by then the settlers had dug in their heels. The talks were deadlocked for five full days. Eventually Macleod devised a compromise. Each group, it was agreed, would be entitled to have one special adviser, but also one 'extra adviser'. The name of the 'extra advisers' did not have to be notified to the Colonial Secretary. So the African group was given a blank pass to Lancaster House, and we filled in the name 'Peter Mbiyu Koinange'. The Colonial Office was spared the embarrassment of having to write his name on an official card, and this face-saving device enabled us to admit the man we had selected as adviser. The Briggs group threatened, at even this compromise stage: 'If Koinange is in, we are out!' but later it was seen that Briggs had found a way to reconcile the presence of his group with that of Koinange.

The conference started a week later. We held a week of plenary sessions with speeches on general questions and the admission in the Macleod approach that 'the African voice must *in time* predominate'. The question was: how long a time? When the details of the Macleod constitutional proposals were made known the African group expressed its bitter disappointment. Though the new constitution made a start in reversing settler-African proportions of representation it did not go nearly far enough in eliminating the communal and racial basis of representation. The Macleod plan provided for a total of sixty-five members in the Legco. Of these fifty-three would be elected on a common roll, but twenty of them would be reserved seats (ten for Whites, eight for Asians and two for Arabs). The remaining twelve would be 'national' members (four each for Africans and Whites, three Asians and one Arab) chosen by the fifty-three elected members. Under this arrangement African strength in the Legislative Council would be increased threefold and Africans would for the first time have a majority. But there was no universal adult franchise, only a wider franchise on a common roll which would lead to an increase in the African vote.

Of the twelve members of the Council of Ministers, there would be four government officials, four African members, three Whites, and one Asian. The ministers would be appointed by the Governor.

Discussion on a Bill of Rights was turned by the settlers into an opportunity to raise the thorny land question. Blundell insisted that specific guarantees for land ownership should be incorporated in a Bill of Rights, and he wanted us to exclude any future possibility of land expropriation even for compensation. Thus did the settlers demand land guarantees as a price for accepting African advance in the constitutional field. We refused to be tied down in such a way as to restrict the freedom of action of a future government. Macleod's solution was to persuade us to postpone the land rights issue for the time being: a Bill of Rights would be put before the next Legislative Council.

In a private meeting with the African delegates Macleod said the British Government would be prepared to let African political parties function on a national basis, and to relax restrictions on political meetings. But there would be no release of Kenyatta.

Macleod as a spokesman of the British Government to put over its wind of change policies was an excellent choice. While there had been no doubt that Lennox-Boyd's starting point for negotiations was the state of mind of the settlers, Macleod appeared to be concerned with what was acceptable to Africans. He was a skilful psychologist. His direct approach infuriated the settlers, and their fury impressed us that we were winning. In retrospect we were naïve and did not notice how the settler reaction was being played against us. Macleod was patience itself. He called us in one by one, sounded us out, talked to us as man to man. We were at a constitutional disadvantage, he said. We should assist him in dealing with the settlers who were not prepared to give an inch of the way. He conscripted us into looking at the problem from his point of view, caught between the demands of the Africans and the intransigence of the settlers. His threat, by implication, was 'the talks will break down'. When he put forward his final plan it was a matter of take it or leave it. We had talked ourselves out at a prolonged conference during which the African representatives had been made conscious of their minority position. We had been worn down over the weeks of talking and softened up one by one. After all this time we could not go home with empty hands. We would struggle to advance from the new point of departure of the Macleod constitution.

The Briggs group called the proposals 'a death-blow to the European community'. Blundell, who was trying, like the Colonial Office, to adapt to new times, was quoted in the British press as saying that he attached 'much importance to a friendly agreement with Africans' (that earned him thirty pieces of silver thrown at his feet by angry settlers on his return to Nairobi). We went home to hold victory meetings. I told a Kisumu rally that though the constitutional reforms fell far below African demands, they were a great stride ahead of the proposals made only one year before by Lennox-Boyd. We would use the majority gained under the new constitution to steer Kenya to complete independence in the shortest possible time.

Looking back now, much of our time in those years was devoted to constitutions and constitutional negotiation in Nairobi's Government House and in London. Kenyan delegations seemed constantly to be travelling back and forth to London, and the ins and outs of the constitutional manoeuvring make for repetitive recital. I have always believed that what went on among the people outside the conference halls was a great deal more important than the discussions in the legislature and round the tables of the Colonial Office, for in the end our representatives were as strong as their organization and their unity at home made them. This was the reason why, once one set of constitutional negotiations was concluded, we could turn round, and, to the enormous chagrin of the settlers, say 'This constitution is already dead'. Blundell believed that the Lancaster House constitution was designed to last ten years and he accepted it on that understanding. The same assessment had heartened settlers over the Lyttelton Constitution and the Lennox-Boyd one. But no sooner was each of these constitutions achieved than it was swept aside by the pressures of African nationalism. Our work round the table was a formal recognition that African claims were asserting themselves. We used the constitutional conferences like rungs on a ladder, climbing ever higher towards the top step of complete independence. In Kenya settler power blocked legitimate African advance. Our pressure for successive sets of negotiations presided over by Britain was an out-flanking operation against settler power, and we used constitutional conferences with this aim in mind.

We could advance only if we were true to the African people whose strength gave us power, if we were equipped with sound strategy, and if we were united. While still in London we had been troubled about the shape of political organization in Kenya. African unity had forced greater concessions out of the Lancaster House talks than we could possibly have achieved had the African side been divided as KIM and KNP representatives. A united African team would be as essential for the next stage of the struggle. Ngala, Moi, and I lived in the same Bloomsbury Hotel in London and we talked together about this and agreed, on our return to Kenya, to sink differences and set to work to build one united party. We proposed a new party to our delegation and all agreed except Mboya, Muliro, and Onyango Ayodo who said they would consider signing only when they returned to Kenya. Once again there had been trouble in our delegation due to the role in which Mboya was cast by the imperialist press and by Western politicians. One paper called him 'the strong man of the Kenya nationalist movement'—and due to Mboya's ambition, or so it seemed to us, to bring his own party, the People's Convention Party of Nairobi, into the ascendancy, to assert its claim to be the leading party over all the others, and his claim to be the future Prime Minister, our delegation was in danger of splitting more than once as a result of this build-up of Mboya.

It was imperative that we should have a truly representative national party, with a national leadership and clear policy. We needed the reinforcements of some of the older political leaders and above all the men who had worked with and had known Kenyatta, to help fight the battle for his release. It was at this time that Governor Renison called me to Government House for a private talk on our demand for the release of Kenyatta. The Governor said that it was largely due to my stand that there had been opposition to sending African members into the Council of Ministers while Kenyatta was not free. He had access to information which a person like myself clearly did not know, the Governor said. He advised that it would be fruitless to pursue the question of the release of Kenyatta. Britain had taken the firm decision that Kenyatta and his associates would be a danger to peace and good government in Kenya and he would not be released under any circumstances. The Governor added that he was not ashamed to tell me that many prominent Kenya African leaders of standing backed that decision. That gave me thought about the state of our leadership ranks. For my part I told the Governor that he had not convinced me; if that were his attitude he would not help Kenya.

The elected members who had been signatories to the document for a united political movement met at Dr Kiano's house in Riruta to agree on a public declaration to launch a new party. Present with us was James Gichuru, who as President of KAU had stood down for Kenyatta when he returned from Europe in 1946, and who had since been detained and restricted. I had gone to see Gichuru at his home, with Arthur Ochwada who had been in the trade union movement, and we had urged Gichuru to re-enter the political field.

We agreed that we wanted the new movement to be called the Kenya African National Union, as the closest to the name of our old body, Kenya African Union (KAU), but for tactical reasons our first proposal for a name would be the Uhuru Party. We circulated a draft constitution, written by Ojino Okew, my personal secretary, and we set to work to prepare for our first conference in March. Nairobi was the centre of rivalry between Mboya's PCP and Argwings-Kodhek's Nairobi African District Congress and we knew there would be factional troubles if we held the preparatory conference to launch a new movement in the capital. We decided to convene the conference at Kiambu, twelve miles from Nairobi.

All the while we were immersed in preparations for a united political movement, Mboya was extending branches of the PCP from Nairobi to other parts of the country in a bid for power. He had been fêted and sponsored in the United States and with apparently unlimited supplies of foreign money and scholarships and his impressive organizing ability he had made the PCP into the best organized political force in Nairobi. But his organizing efforts were directed less at building a unified political movement than at building his own ascendancy. By the time of the Kiambu conference, however, Mboya's supporters had convinced him that he would lose support if he isolated himself from the national party and so he came to the conference. At this point we dropped the name Uhuru Party of Kenya and used the maximum unity achieved at the conference to launch the Kenya African National Union. Kenyatta was declared first president. Gichuru was elected chairman of the preparatory committee and Dr Mungai, secretary. The preparatory committee was to convene the first national conference at Kiambu in May. Ojino's constitution was, with a few changes, adopted. Tragically that night, as he travelled back to Kisumu from Kiambu, Ojino Okew was killed when the bus in which he travelled was involved in a collision in the Rift Valley. Ojino's death was a heavy loss to our national cause and to me personally. I never knew such a person who fitted all walks of life and all society. When he was with the intellectuals he was considered a mediator between them and the masses. When among the masses he was at home. He was writer, painter, artist, historian, and I must say foremost a dedicated nationalist of the first order.

When we came back from the Lancaster House conference we African elected members had a major disagreement on policy towards the ministries allotted to Africans. My view was that we should reject the offer and tell the Governor that if he wanted African participation he should arrange elections as speedily as possible so that the new constitution could take over from the old one under which we were boycotting the special seats and the ministries for Africans. We had the country behind us in a repudiation of the Lennox-Boyd constitution and to send Africans into ministries at this stage would be to go back on our word and to have our men associated with Amalemba whom we had ostracized. More than this, we would be cooperating in the Government before Jomo Kenyatta and his colleagues were released and I was totally against this. We argued about this for some weeks; some among us were emphatic that we should use the seats in the Council of Ministers. Our group decided eventually that any of our members who took office would do so not under the Lennox-Boyd constitution which we had constantly attacked, but that the executive sections of the Lancaster House agreement should immediately come into force. We would have four Ministers thus, not three, and we refused to count Amalemba as one of the four. Ngala and Muliro, Muimi and Dr Kiano took ministries.

The next stage in the formation of KANU was two months away. I took advantage of the opportunity to visit Ghana a second time to attend the Conference Against Atomic Tests in the Sahara. Arthur Ochwada and Argwings-Kodhek travelled with me. At Accra airport I sensed afresh the spirit of nationalism and African brotherhood abroad in the new Africa. I told the conference of our plans to form one party with Kenyatta as president. When we met again Nkrumah and I embraced. His visions of a union of African states were as vivid as ever. We argued hotly, though, on the organization of African regional groupings. I advocated a regional grouping for East Africa on the grounds that we shared a common history and colonial overlordship, common language, problems, and goals. Nkrumah was apprehensive that a federation with internal difficulties would engross our attention and cause us to neglect the goal of broader African unity.

From Ghana I went to Conakry for the Afro-Asian Solidarity Conference. My speech on the release of Kenyatta had an enthusiastic reception, not least from delegates from socialist countries whom I was meeting for the first time. I met Sekou Toure and watched party organization in action in Guinea, each branch with its own youth and women's section, the power of party organization there for all to see. I was convinced that Guinea, abandoned like a hot brick after her stroke of independence in voting 'no' in the 1958 De Gaulle referendum, would forge ahead because of her determined leadership and organization.

I appreciated with a new urgency the importance of travelling abroad to learn from other peoples and from other struggles for freedom, and to enlist support for our Kenya struggle. Throughout the Emergency years Kenya freedom-fighters had struggled on their own resources, cut off from any help that might have been forthcoming (although it was only towards the sixties that the majority of African states emerged to independence and to Pan-African solidarity), and unable to counter the propaganda against us spread by the hostile settler and imperialist press. We had an unanswerable case. If the world-wide news agencies would not disseminate our material we would have to find other ways of doing so. This is one of the reasons I supported the establishment of the Kenya Office in Cairo. This office was opened at the beginning of 1959 by three young students, Odhiambo Okello, Wera Ambitho, and Abdulla Karungo Kinyariro. Kinyariro was a Kikuyu freedom-fighter from Lari in Kiambu who had escaped arrest. Okello and Ambitho had won scholarships to study in Italy but had their passports impounded by the Kenya Government the day they boarded ship to leave. I pleaded their case before the Chief Secretary, but to no avail. The three young men made their way out of the country illegally, travelling across Uganda and taking three months to reach Khartoum where the students at the university helped them. Othigo Othieno, who had left Kenya to study in Britain, became one of the representatives of the Kenyan students in London. Wera Ambitho and Okello gave up their studies to do a much-needed job of publicizing our cause in Africa and in socialist countries. The Sudan Government agreed to open and finance a Kenya Information Office but before the arrangements could be finalized a *coup d'état* toppled the Khalil Government. President Nasser (who at that time had welcomed three of our students who travelled by the same route to Cairo—namely—Kamwithi Munyi, Rev. James Ochwata, and Okore Seda) offered his country's hospitality and the Kenya office was opened in Cairo, from where it issued the publication 'New Kenya' and, after the formation of KANU, broadcast Kenya news regularly over Cairo Radio, as the Voice of Kenya. The Cairo office was later to play a vital role in helping students to travel out of Kenya to take up scholarships abroad. It was in Cairo that we made our first contact with liberation figures in other parts of the Continent, among them Felix Moumie of the Cameroons, Kenneth Kaunda, Chipembere, Simon Kapepwe, Joshua Nkomo, and the Rev. Sithole. Dr Mohamed Fayek, the UAR

Director-General of African Affairs, gave us invaluable assistance in assembling a press and making pan-African contacts.

A narration of my visits to the socialist countries in 1960 and their positive results cannot be complete without mention of the historic trek of Kenya students to study in these countries. Conscious of our retarded education facilities I had explored the possibility of sending Kenyans to study in the socialist countries. Many scholarships were made available, especially in the Soviet Union, Yugoslavia, North Korea, Bulgaria, Czechoslovakia, Hungary, Yugoslavia, and the German Democratic Republic. As Kenya under British rule was denied direct contact with these countries the Kenya offices in Cairo and London became the centres from which Kenya students were routed to the socialist countries. These countries made air tickets available in Cairo or London. (Some tickets were available in Nairobi too, but for the most part the students had to make their own way to Cairo or London.) Working in the London office were Othigo Othieno, Burudi Nabwera (now Kenya's Ambassador to the United States and Permanent Representative at the United Nations), and Ngumbu Njururi; in the Cairo office were Odhiambo Okello, Wera Ambitho, and Abdulla Karungo. It was not easy for the students to leave Kenya to take up the scholarships because if the authorities had known their destinations were in socialist countries, the students would have had their passports impounded and they might also have faced arrest. Someone had to organize these surreptitious journeys out of the country. James Machyo, my constituency secretary at the time and now a Senator and Assistant Minister, began the work, but later Oluande K'Oduol (the secretary of the Lumumba Trust) shouldered this responsibility from 1960 until we achieved independence. Without the sympathy and cooperation of the independent governments of the United Arab Republic, Sudan, and

Tanzania, this trek of Kenya students would have been extremely difficult to the universities where scholarships awaited them. By the time we achieved independence in 1963 we had sent close to one thousand Kenya students to take up scholarships. Kenya will be ever grateful to all those who made possible this socialist educational breakthrough and the training of future Kenya specialists in a variety of professions. We also sent students, over the years, to Italy, Canada, Cuba, Britain, and the United States.

The Cairo Kenya office was at the cross-roads of contact between the Afro-Asian countries and the work of our office opened a vital diplomatic front for the Kenya freedom struggle. Through Cairo the demand for the release of Kenyatta received an international hearing. Through our publications in Cairo, our radio broadcast and our relations with the representatives of other African states, Kenya took its place in the Pan-African movement. I saw the Kenya office, Cairo, in action on my way home from the 1960 Lancaster House conference when Odhiambo Okello, Wera Ambitho, and Abdulla and I had talks together which helped me clear my mind about Kenya's next steps, our strategy for independence, and our vulnerability to imperialist intrigues.

I had become urgently aware that our future in Kenya was not just a matter of Kenyan and British politicians bargaining over clauses in a constitution. We wanted independence and we would get it. What would we do with it? We had massive problems of poverty, illiteracy, unemployment and landlessness. How had other countries, other systems, tackled these problems? I wanted to know, to see for myself. I was curious, and I was also prejudiced. Prejudiced against the West which had fathered and nurtured the colonial system which kept Kenya backward and deprived. I was suspicious of the claims of the West that she had the interests of a free Africa at heart; that she was helping us advance as fast as was good for us. I had learnt not to take at their face value the protestations that we might not realize it, but Britain had our best interests at heart. The more I heard socialism and socialist countries condemned, the more curious I was to see for myself.

I had had a brief weekend opportunity to do so when the Lancaster House conference had been in recess and I had paid a brief visit to East Germany. This had been my first visit to a socialist country. I made no secret of it, but the London *Daily Mail* carried a picture of me and a headline 'Kenya Leader in Secret Trip to see Reds'. Was I a Communist sympathizer? The general opinion, said the paper, was that I was not. But I had to be watched.

I was in Conakry studying the workings of the Guinea Government and the Democratic Party, when I received President Tito's invitation to visit Yugoslavia. I knew I would provoke a fresh attack on myself from circles in Britain that would try to damn my efforts for Kenya on the grounds that I was a dangerous Communist, but I had already decided that those who had pursued the wrong policies for Kenya should not be the arbiters of my actions. I met President Tito briefly and explained our struggle to him. After Belgrade I went to Cairo, and the staff of the Kenya office arranged for me to see President Nasser. I found this an exciting encounter. Egypt, I told him, was both in the Middle East and in Africa. We looked to Nasser's leadership to build friendship between the Arab and African worlds in a front against imperialism. I appealed to President Nasser to help in the launching of our national press, and he promised financial support for our struggle.

Later in the year the invitations to go abroad came thick and fast. I flew to Stockholm for the conference of the World Peace Council and was astonished at the emphasis, even by delegations from the western countries, on the need for peace, and against systems of domination and exploitation which lead to war. When I was called to the platform I had no speech prepared but I spoke from the bottom of my heart about the Kenya struggle. I warned this conference concerned with peace that in Africa peace could not be the slogan until all colonial oppression was removed from the continent. I made my first contacts at this conference with delegations from China and from Japan. The Japanese pressed me to visit their country, but first I had to return to Kenya. In London, on the way through, I was searched at the airport—for the first time. I realized that the publicity against me and the contacts I was making in all parts of the world were making for a serious situation for me. Nevertheless, when the official invitation to attend the Anti-Atomic Bomb Conference in Tokyo came, I accepted. What I saw in Japan convinced me of the horrors of atomic war, and that we should not permit a bomb to be dropped again in any part of the world. I met Japanese government officials and talked to them about the struggle in Kenya. I was chosen to speak for Africa at a huge public rally, and I found myself among the leaders of the largest and most powerful countries. I spoke not only for Kenya but for the whole of Africa. When the Tokyo conference was over, the delegation from the Chinese People's Republic invited me to their country. For the first time I could ask representatives of a Communist state: 'What is Communism? How does it work? What are the real aims of Communism?' They brought high government officials and university professors to explain to me. They showed me factories, communes, cooperatives; they showed me their plans for housing, for dealing with unemployment, how they organized farming and small industry, how government worked at village level; how plans for factory and agricultural production were worked out. It was impossible not to be impressed with life in China. So many of the problems of poverty and illiteracy were those of our people, and these problems were being overcome at an impressive rate.

I travelled through Mongolia to visit the Soviet Union, where I spent three days and listened to the trial of the American U-2 spy pilot, Francis Powers. I met Mikoyan in the Kremlin and explained to him in detail the situation of the Kenyan people and why the demand for the release of Kenyatta was so central to our country's political future. I travelled to East Germany to pursue the matter of setting up a national press.

From the beginnings of AEMO I had been pressing for the setting up of a press controlled by Africans and the organization had agreed and minuted a decision that I float an African newspaper company. The government had used the Emergency to kill the virile growth of African broadsheets which did not boast handsome formats but made up for their poverty of appearance by their outspokenness. With the death of these papers the press of Kenya was dominated by the diehard settler press which has links with Uganda and Tanganyika, or the monopoly combines of the Thomson Empire, allied with the Aga Khan. Throughout the territories of East Africa daily and weekly papers slanted the news, distorted nationalist policy, and destroyed or boosted African spokesmen by the standards of reactionary White politicians and business interests. At crucial times in the independent fight the press could be relied upon to build up 'moderates' and denigrate 'extremists'. They could eclipse a leader in the public eye by dropping him from the news columns. The freedom of the press was being used to undermine the freedom of decision of the African people; we could not afford to abandon this field to the forces against us. During my visits to Cairo and my talks with President Nasser I pursued this matter.

Finally, my journeys over, I returned to Nairobi. At the airport I got a rude reception. My luggage was combed through by customs officials; I was half stripped as they searched my person. My diaries and all papers were taken from me and stamped and sealed. And my passport was impounded. In time my possessions were returned to me, including a bank slip that indicated that something like £10,000 had been banked in London for our struggle.

When the matter of the search was raised in the Legislative Council I made no secret of the money or my journeyings. The money had been paid by sympathetic countries to assist Kenyan students to study in socialist countries and for a nationalist press. Of course I had been to China. I had been greatly impressed by what I had seen there. I did not see why the government of Britain should try to deny visits to these countries to African nationalists who wanted to learn from their ways. Macmillan, in fact, had himself just visited the Soviet Union. 'I will accept money from anywhere provided I can get it without strings attached to it,' I told the House. I also said emphatically that my visits to these countries abroad was essential to our cause. Many of my colleagues were unhappy at my outspoken remarks and my travels. The *Nation* said I had 'done much to open the door to Communist penetration of East Africa through my Iron Curtain peregrinations and professions of admiration for the Communist regimes', and some of my colleagues found this pro-imperialist newspaper was expressing their views on this occasion. They were easily embarrassed in our struggle by charges that we were acquiring the wrong friends, but the friends who were considered right for us were powers that had years ago rejected the opportunity to espouse our righteous cause.

CHAPTER ELEVEN

Kenyatta na Uhuru

By May 1960 we were ready for the launching of KANU. The elected members of the Legislative Council—we were fourteen in all—had agreed that we would each bring constituency delegations of sixteen elected representatives. The district associations up and down the country were to be converted into branches of KANU. Ngala and Moi were threatening not to participate if Mboya attended and tension was building up from this and many other directions. Perhaps it was fortuitous but on the eve of the conference both Ngala and Moi left the country. This was to have damaging effects on our unity. Moi was attending the course of the Commonwealth Parliamentary Association and Ngala was invited to the United States. Their absence undermined their chances of playing a role in KANU and whatever the reason for the timing of their departure, it gave people the impression that they didn't really want to join and did not have their hearts in unity. Others of our African members did not take the preparations earnestly and they came singly to the conference without the support of their constituencies. Central Province, Nyanza, the Coast, and Nairobi were well represented, but other areas not. Mboya was one of those present in strength. He had decided to bring the PCP into the new party.

Tension over the elections rose to breaking point at this

second Kiambu conference. The suspense could be seen in the milling crowds round the conference hall, in the evidence on all sides of caucusing and lobbying. Until now the order of the day had been a plethora of local and district organizations. The future of the first national movement allowed in Kenya for seven years would depend on our success in reconciling claims of associations, districts, and leaders to representation and influence. It took hours before the problem of office-bearers could be sorted out. For many the outcome of the elections would determine their political allegiance, and in some instances outright rejection of certain leaders switched precipitately to support as soon as it was announced that they were included on the executive! Gichuru was elected KANU president, on the understanding that he was holding the seat for Kenyatta. I was elected vice-president, Mboya, general secretary, and Ochwada, assistant secretary-general. We had agreed beforehand that Ngala was to be secretary and Moi treasurer but in their absence they were elected treasurer and assistant-treasurer respectively. We had assembled, we hoped, a strong team to carry KANU to great heights.

Meanwhile there were moves on other political fronts. These began, suspiciously, when Captain Briggs returned from the Lancaster House talks which he described as calamitous for the Whites. That month and the next he had talks with the leaders of a newly formed body, the Masai United Front whose three spokesmen were John Konchellah, Lemomo, and John Keen. The line of approach was ironically devious and yet made direct impact: the minority all-White United Party was appealing to the minority tribes to combine with it against the 'Luo-Kikuyu combination of politicians'. The smaller tribes and the Whites were in the same predicament, the argument went, they were all minorities! The Masai United Front caught on fast to this theme. It appealed to the British Government to observe pledges made to the White settlers, because there was reason to fear that the two treaties signed by the British and the Masai guaranteeing the tribe's land might not be observed. If the settlers had to abandon the White Highlands the Masai United Front asked that the land should be returned to its rightful owners—the Masai. There was a splintering of unity in other directions, too. The Kalenjin Political Alliance was launched by Taita Arap Towett, embracing the Kipsigis in the Rift Valley, the Suk, Nandi, and other peoples in north-west Kenya; and in Mombasa fifty delegates led by Ngala formed the Coast African Political Union.

These developments suited the settler book far too well for them to have been coincidental. Sir Cavendish-Bentinck had resigned as Speaker of the Legislative Council after the Lancaster House talks to form the Kenya Coalition Party which would stand, it said, for a 'fair deal for all', for 'ordered transition' and to rally the divided Whites and people of all races whose interests were in jeopardy; the same gentleman was invited to lead a delegation to London to plead the cause of the 'Whites and other minority communities'.

Muliro never came into KANU with us. Instead he formed the Kenya African People's Party. When Ngala returned to Kenya he rejected the treasurership of KANU. I did not believe that Muliro was a victim of the emotional appeal of tribalism but he found himself unable to work in the same party as Mboya and he exploited minority feeling to capture support from his home area and use that as a political base. Ngala was a different case. He, though he appeared to be sincere, had always been susceptible to settler propaganda and once captured he could be relied upon to deliver the goods better than even his settler mentors.

Muliro and Ngala joined forces to accuse KANU of dictatorship, and a few days later at a conference at Ngong they launched the Kenya African Democratic Union to federate the Kalenjin Political Alliance, the Masai United Front, the Kenya African People's Party, the Coast African Political Union, and the Somali National Association. Unity in the national cause seemed further from us than ever.

We were passing through a difficult period, a time of waiting, of marking time, until January 1961 when the Macleod constitution would come into play and the elections would determine where political initiative would rest in a vital phase on the road to independence. By some superhuman effort (or so it seemed at this time of splintering and antagonism) we had achieved African unity in time for the Lancaster House conference and that had won us the day. The settlers were determined that it was not too late to undermine African unity, to sap our ability to form a strong government and so to delay further advance. The settlers were grouped in two main wings. The extremists led by Cavendish-Bentinck raged and fulminated about the Lancaster House constitution which, they charged, was a catastrophic product of Whitehall's appeasement policies and which abandoned civilized Whites to Africans who were gratuitously donated premature self-government. The other settler wing—led by Blundell and Havelock—had made a dilatory start in trying to accommodate itself to conditions in an African majority country, but now was setting to work with a good deal of guile. The manipulative skill of this group flowered the following year, on the eve of the next constitutional conference, but even in the early days of the new settler tactics, it played artfully on divisions of tribe and personal ambition. There were men among us eager to hold the reins of power: they had ambitions to head political parties, to enter government, to outshine political rivals. There were those who fell victim to, or used, tribalism: it is difficult to know who genuinely feared the 'domination' of the two largest tribes, the Kikuyu and the Luo, and who capitalized on this theme to rally tribes behind tribally based political groupings. Many of our career politicians were to show themselves to be malleable to settler pressures for regionalism and other policies in the period to come: this sprang, in part, I feel, from a doubt that Africans could run the country on their own. Perhaps these men felt that their own tenure in office would be prolonged if they leant on settler support, and that settler cooperation instead of opposition would make for greater stability in government. Such politicians among us were getting a personal vested interest in authority, and an appetite for power.

KANU's objective was to work for a predominantly African government; we were determined not to dilute our policy. The leaders of KADU hoped to win enough seats to form a multi-racial government together with the small political groupings of settlers and Asians. There is another important factor which I believe led the KADU men to break from KANU. We in KANU said one thing louder than anything else: that we would form no government, even after victory in the elections, unless Kenyatta was released. KADU proclaimed the same policy but events were to show that this plank in its platform was easily surrendered.

I was convinced that the question of Kenyatta remained the central issue. As long as he was still in restriction—and he was important not only because he was Kenya's leader but also because he was symbolic of all the political leaders still in the detention camps and under restriction—we had not fully emerged from the period of the Emergency. Our country could not attain self-government or independence while its foremost political leaders were imprisoned by government decree or Emergency measure. Every clause in a new constitution was mocked by the power of the Governor to hold a man without trial, for purposes of political victimization. Kenyatta was not only the leader, he was the symbol of the peoples' political aspirations; while he was not free the people could not freely express their aspirations

197

or hope to attain them. As long as the Governor and the Colonial Office could decide which of our leaders to keep locked up, so long could it not be said that we had the right to choose our own leaders. During the Emergency the African political movement had been destroyed, the physical removal engineered of all known political leaders and even, among the Kikuyu, the removal of anyone who did not perform a demonstrable act of loyalty to the authorities. In the post-Emergency period the authorities were still hoping that they could place curbs on the political advances of the people. Kenyatta and his associates were being kept beyond reach for as long as possible in the hope that the younger politicians who filled the leadership vacuum would not be influenced by the older, militant policies and the heritage of struggle. Many of the newer leaders who had emerged in the post-1956 period were capable and talented and played a prominent part in winning great gains for the people. It was vital that there should be no friction between this group of younger leaders and the old guards. The two groups of leaders, from two different periods in Kenya's political struggle, had to see one another not as rivals but as joint builders of our country's freedom. The newcomers held the advantage in terms of political following because by the time the camps were opened and detainees released, they had built their parties, whereas the great old organizations of pre-1952 had been smashed in the fighting and the detentions and deportations. Because the men coming out of the camps had been immobilized for years did not mean that their experience in organizing, and their demands, and their sacrifice in the cause of freedom, had to be brushed aside. The new Kenya would be built jointly by the contributions these two groups made. But we could not make a sound start as long as the Kenyatta generation was still restricted. There was also no doubt that no African government of Kenya would be recognized in Africa as truly free and representative as long as Kenyatta was in exile or a prisoner. Finally it has always been my firm conviction that to lead people you must adhere to their will. The release of Kenyatta was the demand of the people of Kenya.

1961 opened with KANU sending delegations to Government House in Nairobi and to the Colonial Office in London demanding the release of Kenyatta in time for the approaching general election. MacLeod had said that he would not receive a deputation but it travelled to London all the same. Speaking for KANU, Gichuru said: 'We want Kenyatta released before the election. He will be able to unite the African parties. We want him to be our first Chief Minister.' We were told that the matter of Kenyatta's release was in the hands of the Governor—we were, of course, in no doubt that we were being fobbed off by the Colonial Office—and Renison made an official statement about having 'nothing to say on this issue at the present time'. British Government tactics were clear. They were at all costs, in this period when full self-government was approaching, to keep Kenyatta out of the political arena while a last-minute search was conducted for more malleable leaders.

I was less worried about the intransigence of the British Government on the Kenyatta issue than about the situation inside KANU, for while the party was publicly committed to the release of Kenyatta before we took any part in a government, subterranean manoeuvres were being conducted to undermine this policy. We were alarmed that both Gichuru and Mboya had discussions with the Colonial Secretary on visits to London and they did not report to KANU Governing Council on what had transpired. The British *Guardian* said that Colonial Secretary Macleod was 'on the best of personal terms with Mr Gichuru'. Rumours of a furtive Gichuru-Mboya deal with Macleod were flying thick and fast and prompted KANU's Governing Council to appoint an investigating group. The signs pointed to Macleod sounding out Mboya and Gichuru on their willingness to take part in the formation of a government without Kenyatta: the reluctance of KANU's chairman and secretary to take the Governing Council into their full confidence did not inspire our trust in their stand.

British and United States strategy seemed to converge on the grooming of Mboya for leadership in the place of Kenyatta, and with the help of Gichuru, Mboya hoped to rally Kikuyu support. In making the return of Kenyatta to political life the touchstone of African demands I was the main stumbling block. So it was that the undercurrents in KANU coincided with pre-election struggles inside the party, and with a campaign against my policies and reputation.

On my return from abroad the press highlighted my visits to socialist countries and the monies I had received. There was no mystery that I had received money or how I spent it. Much of it went to equip offices for KANU. We could not have a party only in name and we wanted no repetition of the old-style political groupings that functioned round the personality in the ascendancy but had no grass-root organization. Vehicles were purchased for the organizers of KANU branches in many parts of the country. Amounts were earmarked for student scholarships. Large sums were used to build our independent press. Pio Pinto had been released from detention on Manda Island and from restriction and he immediately plunged into work for the release and return to political life of the Kenyatta generation of leaders, and was the moving force in the acquisition of a small press and the publishing of our weeply KANU paper *Sauti ya Kanu* and, later, *Sauti Ya Mwafrika*. But factual evidence of how monies were being spent did not still the propaganda to blacken my reputation. Gichuru's speeches while abroad coincided with the line of attack of the settler press: I was branded because of visits to socialist countries to see the difference between their ways and those of western imperialism and to determine how to benefit from their socialist experience.

Inside KANU matters came to a head over an urgent meeting of KANU's executive summoned by the president, James Gichuru. I travelled from Kisumu to be present, and other members also travelled long distances, but when we arrived at KANU headquarters we found that Gichuru and Mboya had decided to go to Dar es Salaam for another conference. Those of us present met nevertheless. We felt that the absence of Mboya and Gichuru was symptomatic of their attitude to the party: increasingly they were by-passing the Governing Council and the executive and short-circuiting our joint leadership. We had to reinstate the principle that leaders were at the service of the organization and not its masters. Accordingly the executive meeting issued a press statement signed by Mwai Kibaki, Argwings-Kodhek, Arthur Ochwada, other members, and myself, criticizing the behaviour of Mboya and Gichuru. The two latter, on their return to Nairobi, called a public meeting to denounce me. Shortly afterwards I read in the press of my suspension from the KANU leadership. The suspension was null and void because under the KANU constitution only the Governing Council could suspend or expel a member. A meeting of the Governing Council was called and the matter aired. By this time the branches of KANU in many parts of the country were shouting 'Without Odinga no KANU'. When the time came to put my case at the meeting of the Governing Council I tried to get nearer the bottom of the trouble in KANU than my detractors were prepared to probe. The attacks on me were deflecting attention from the real issue: the evasion of party machinery and consultation. Gichuru's statement on my suspension that the party had to 'rid itself of destructive elements, and unite under a leadership devoted to Kenya and not, as appeared to be the case with Mr Odinga, influenced by the interests of Russia or

Communist China', was irrelevant to the real issue. This witch-hunting and my suspension from the party were retaliation for my raising criticism of the actions of leaders. My critics were disloyal to KANU and its decisions. This was sharply revealed over the three-day general strike for the release of Kenyatta that had failed. KANU had decided on the strike and had appointed Mboya to negotiate with the trade unions, and even with KADU, for support. We decided that the negotiations should not be revealed to the press until they had been concluded, but the very next day our strike plans had been given in full to the press. As a result the Kenya Federation of Labour did not support the strike and it failed. This kind of conduct had destroyed AEMO and led to an irreparable rift between African elected members; it could break KANU too. After a twelve-hour meeting, KANU's Governing Council resolved unanimously that my suspension from the post of vice-president was unconstitutional, null, and void. The meeting issued a strong rebuke to Gichuru and Mboya and called on them to 'do their jobs more conscientiously'. Personal disagreements between officials should in future not be made public without prior discussion by the Governing Council. The statement added that there was much indiscipline and maladministration at the party's head office. Most important, we placed on record that anyone who had the ambition to be Chief Minister of Kenya in place of Jomo Kenyatta would wreck the unity of the party.

The tussle to assert the control of the Governing Council as against the personal ambitions of party supporters took place on the eve of the elections, and was reflected both in nominations and in election propaganda. Many members stood for election against the party's official nominee. At times there was utter confusion with KANU unable to sort out claimants for seats and more than one candidate presenting himself as the party's choice. At other times KANU head office was dispersed in the constituencies and there was nobody to make decisions about candidates. To my surprise I found my Central Nyanza seat was contested by Walter Odede, my old associate from KAU days. While in detention he had been visited by the chief secretary and then suddenly released. I heard reports that he would stand in the election but when I asked him his reply was evasive. Later I suggested that if he wanted to contest a seat it should be the special seat and we could campaign together. No, Odede said, he had decided to contest my seat. I knew the electorate would not agree to my standing down for Odede, so I referred the selection of a party candidate to KANU headquarters, which upheld my candidature. Without party backing Odede contested as an independent non-party candidate. He seemed to have no shortage of lorries and money to carry voters to the polls and it seemed obvious that there were forces secretly supporting him in order to oust me. Odede lost his deposit in the election, polling 1,770 votes against my total of 46,638.

When it came to the Nairobi contest I supported Dr Waiyaki against Mboya. Waiyaki's candidature challenged Mboya's back-sliding on the Kenyatta issue, and though Mboya won the election in the PCP stronghold by an overwhelming majority, Waiyaki's campaign drove him to a point where he had publicly to pledge that he would refuse to participate in a new government without the unconditional release of Kenyatta. We had this undertaking accepted throughout KANU. Every party candidate had to sign the following pledge:

If elected I promise to abide by the Governing Council decision that (a) Kenyatta, being the leader of our party and the father of our nationalism, must be the first Chief Minister or Prime Minister. No KANU member under pressure direct or indirect shall accept appointment to such a post and (b) in the event of Kenyatta not being released before the elections all KANU candidates individually and collectively undertake to give up any such seat as will be decided and to cause a by-election wherein Kenyatta would be returned to the Legislative Council to lead KANU and head the first government.

Thus, though we fought the election without Kenyatta's presence, he dominated the contest throughout. KANU won a major triumph. We won just under half of the thirty-three open seats, but we polled 67 per cent of the votes cast, and KADU polled only 16 per cent. Other successful candidates included four of the New Kenya Party, three of the Kenya Coalition Party, three of the Kenya Indian Congress, one of the Kenya Freedom Party, and sixteen Independents.

Blundell's New Kenya Party played a clever electoral game by scraping through the first stage of the election in which they had to get a proportion of the votes of their own community in order to qualify, and then being returned on the predominantly African vote in the common roll election because its NKP policy was, by contrast with Cavendish-Bentinck's Kenya Coalition, more liberal. I was against KANU supporting Blundell's party candidates for the reserved seats on the grounds that Cavendish-Bentinck's party was an enemy we knew and could deal with. My apprehensions were confirmed when after the elections in which the New Kenya Party romped home on KANU support, it threw in its lot with KADU.

The post-election period was the time for the British Government to show true statesmanship to launch a united Kenya on the path of a new constitution. But in Britain a lobby in the Conservative Party was organizing against MacLeod's policies in Africa on the grounds that by turning the clock on so fast he was producing an explosion. There was no conciliation from Britain. The Governor broadcast on 1 March that there would be no release of Kenyatta until a working government had been found. The most he was prepared to do was move Kenyatta from exile in Lodwar to exile in Maralal—halfway between Lodwar and Nairobi.

As the Governor was broadcasting, Gichuru and Mboya of KANU and Ngala and Muliro of KADU were at Government House, being offered a visit to Kenyatta. This was no less than a pointer to a government effort to get four hand-picked men to negotiate some sort of coalition government, thus circumventing our pledge not to form a government without Kenyatta. The visit to the exiled leader would be exploited in the hope that the four would return with advice from Jomo to form a government as the best means of securing his release. The air was once again thick with manoeuvres and rumours of a bid for power by some of our officials. There were persistent reports in the press in Kenya and in Britain that KANU was looking for a formula to take part in the formation of a government. I summoned an urgent meeting of KANU's governing council. We vetoed Mboya's and Gichuru's participation in a joint deputation to Kenyatta. Once again we confirmed that KANU had irrevocably decided not to join the government until Kenyatta was freed. We urged the Colonial Secretary to come to Kenya to sort out the situation.

All around me people were advising that KANU should take its chance to enter the government and so get independence sooner. I was convinced that this would be a betrayal of our mandate from the people and that far from achieving independence sooner, we would bond ourselves to forces antagonistic to our freedom aims and so throw cold water on the fiercely burning fire of the struggle. Blundell had written of his hopes that a government would be formed of a coalition of KADU, the New Kenya Group, and 'some members of KANU'; his hopes of some members of KANU going over to his side to form a government were focussed on several leading members from our ranks. But the latter feared to go against the people and eventually decided to join on the side of those in KANU who stuck to the party stand on the Kenyatta release.

Post-election political stalemate continued. The Governor had a crisis on his hands but he seemed to welcome it and he sought no solution to make it possible for the majority party to govern. I wrote him an open letter in which I charged him with listening to advisers who were embittered with racialism and prejudice and responsible for the crisis hanging over Kenya like a swelling storm cloud. It was with relish that stagnation and doom were prophesied for Kenya. The Nairobi Stock Exchange recorded deep depression. Leading members of the administration including the Chief Secretary and the Minister of Internal Security and Defence threatened their resignation if Kenyatta were released. Colonel Grogan, the doyen of the settlers and their most tempestuous spokesman announced that he had given his life to developing perhaps half a million acres in Kenya, Tanganyika, and Uganda but he was selling his large sisal estate. 'Only a damn fool wouldn't sell,' he said. The pattern of emigration and immigration took a sudden swing: for the first time even more settlers left than entered the country.

KANU had refused to let the Governor choose the men to make up a delegation to visit Kenyatta, but KADU representatives had gone. Ngala returned to report that Kenyatta had at no time said that he wanted to be Chief Minister—a mischievous report if ever there was one. Not long after Kenyatta sent a message via his lawyer, Mr Dingle Foot, Q.C., that he would like to meet all the political leaders. As our organizations and not the Governor could choose the members of the delegation, KANU accepted.

Many of our leaders, among them Mboya, had never seen or met Kenyatta. On 23 March we were flown to Lodwar in two planes. At the dusty airstrip we had a taste of the dust and the heat of this place of exile where Paul Ngei, Bildad Kaggia, and Peter Kigondu, a leader of the Kikuyu Independent Church, were living with Jomo. Kenyatta and I greeted one another with great enthusiasm and we led the way to our meeting place. Our leaders in exile were optimistic and cheerful, and they had followed our activities fairly accurately.

It was a moving moment when Kenyatta addressed us. He apologized for having been unable to meet us as our planes touched down: the airstrip was out of bounds to the restrictees. He expressed his appreciation of the work the African leaders were doing and then went directly to the point: our meeting was to discuss the issues of African unity and Kenyan independence. KADU spokesmen had their say on their previous visit to Lodwar so Kenyatta urged KANU to put its case. We did this, going back to the existence of the Kenya Independent Movement and the Kenya National Party before the London conference, and to the Kiambu conference at which we forged unity for the conference. In London at the conference we had defeated all efforts to divide the Africans and had reached general agreement that a united movement should be built at home. But when KANU had been formed, men now leading KADU had declined office and the Kalenjin Political Alliance, the Masai United Front, and the Coast African Peoples' Alliance had been formed because, it was said, the Kikuyu-Luo alliance would dominate the minority tribes. The political movements' search for unity had foundered on the rocks of tribalism and personalities. At the London conference we all without exception told the Colonial Office that without Kenyatta's release the new constitution could not work smoothly, as the release was the one issue that all Africans were agreed was our priority demand. We regarded that constitution as deficient because it did not provide for an African Chief Minister, and this made one vital issue out of two demands: full self government and the release of the one leader who could inspire unity. Mr Nyagah said he saw an additional difficulty in the way of unity, namely, the factions in the Central Province of those who were in the forests and camps and the loyalists; each faction claiming it had Kenyatta's support. Kenyatta interposed at this juncture to say: 'I am not for those who have been in the forests or detention camps, I am for the African people. All of them. I do not support or fight for any particular individual, race, or tribe, but for all the people.' He said that he had read the policies of KANU and KADU and found them almost identical. He wondered where disunity came from. He was convinced it arose from selfishness among the leaders, each hoping to dominate, to be praised and to achieve fame. He condemned this attitude. The African leaders were contributing to his continued restriction by their disunity and quarrels. Every time a decision was made someone or some group undermined it and undermined the chances of effective action. This had to be brought to an end.

Kaggia, Ngei, and Kenyatta pressed firmly that the meeting had to give rise to a greater unity. Mzee Kenyatta said the world would be watching the outcome of these talks. He proposed a simple resolution, 'That from now on KANU and KADU work as one body on all national issues'.

Moi, for KADU, said the resolution was not new, and was vague. He wanted it to be known that KADU would under no circumstances consider a merger with KANU because within KANU there were personality clashes and lack of discipline; KANU had to clean up its house before it could expect unity with other groups.

We agreed to define the ground essential for unity: independence and Kenyatta's release. The meeting finally adopted a resolution:

This meeting of KANU and KADU delegates at Lodwar under the chairmanship of our national leader Jomo Kenyatta and attended by fellow freedom-fighters Paul Ngei, B. M. Kaggia and Peter Kigondu unanimously resolves:

1. That unity among all Africans is essential for our struggle towards independence and should be pursued relentlessly.

The author as Minister for Home Affairs with dancers at a meeting in South Nyanza.

Demonstrating the spirit of hard work for Uhuru.

A press conference in the Vice-President's office (*left*, Dr M. Waiyaki, Assistant Minister).

The author addressing a KANU rally at Kamkunji, Nairobi, September 1963.

2. That meantime it is agreed that KANU and KADU work together and in full consultation as from today on the immediate questions of

    (a) immediate and unconditional release of Jomo Kenyatta;

    (b) full independence for Kenya in 1961.

3. The meeting being convinced that personalities and selfishness, mutual suspicion and fears may be at the bottom of current misunderstandings and disunity, calls on all African people and members of Legco and party leaders to completely refrain from those negative and disruptive attitudes, and work together for the good of Kenya.

4. That to pursue the above, the meeting recommends the setting up of a joint consultative committee of the KANU Governing Council and KADU Supreme Council and their respective parliamentary groups to facilitate greater cooperation and collaboration and closer association.

As a first step a joint KADU/KANU meeting should be arranged immediately to facilitate further discussion.

Immediately the Lodwar visit was over the KANU delegation flew to Cairo where the Third All Africa Peoples' Conference was meeting. The day after both parties had signed the declaration of unity KADU leader Daniel arap Moi who had gone back to the Rift Valley, the settler stronghold, said: 'Our hands are not tied at all. The issue of the release of Jomo Kenyatta is a separate issue from that of forming a government. We cannot take the two together. Even as we concluded the Lodwar agreement some KADU leaders were negotiating with the Governor for the formation of a KADU government, and Ngala was pursuing the same matter in London.'

KADU was inhibited, in view of public feeling on this issue, from clutching too eagerly at government power so it was engaged in a desperate search for some face-saving formula on the Kenyatta question, together with promises of financial aid from Britain and the support of settler and

Asian members of the legislature. When finally the Governor made the announcement that KADU would participate in forming a government the formula was a damp squib: there was to be a 'phased' return of Kenyatta. The government was prepared to build a house at Kiambu for Kenyatta in readiness for his return. When? In due course. Would he live in the Kiambu house under restriction? KADU did not even know.

'Congratulations to KADU,' said Nairobi's *Daily Nation*. 'We can expect a return of business confidence as the new government gets down to work.' KADU's decision was enlightened, said the *East African Standard*, to which I retorted: 'We'll see this government doesn't work.' Ngala and his group, I accused, were now a party to the further restriction of Kenyatta. The detention of Kenyatta at Kiambu instead of Lodwar or Maralal was no concession whatsoever.

For its only chance to get into government KADU had to lean on the support of the New Kenya Party and the Indian Congress and even then the Governor had to nominate eleven members apart from the four *ex-officio* ministers. Blundell deserted his KANU-supporting electorate to go into the government. KANU was joined in opposition by the Kenya Freedom Party which had been formed to fight the reactionary policy of the Kenya Indian Congress (and which dissolved later when KANU opened its doors to non-Africans) and by two European national members, Derek Erskine and the former Minister of Agriculture, Bruce McKenzie. The latter two adopted a rather ambivalent stand: they were members of the KANU Parliamentary Group but as non-members of the party had reservations about their acceptance of decisions.

Kenya's government by mid-1961 was a government unable to keep in office a single day without the support of the government-nominated members. KADU, in nominal power, had become prisoner of the settlers and the Governor. Because of her obstinate resolve not to set Kenyatta free, Britain hoisted a minority government into power in Kenya. I was convinced this was no last-minute solution. The Governor had manufactured a deadlock over Kenyatta to get KADU into government, in the hope that KANU, in frustrated opposition, would splinter into quarrelling factions.

These were critical days for KANU. There were persistent reports that eight of our members led by Kiano were conceiving a plan to join KADU in government, by reviving KAU or starting a new party. Towards the end of April KANU Governing Council was alarmed by reports that Gichuru, then in London, carried a compromise formula for KANU to join a coalition government. We sent him a cable:

KANU position unchanged. No Kenyatta no Government. . . . Press reports here report you as saying that you carry compromise formula and that KANU ready for honourable retreat. We have discounted this as misreport since inconsistent our position. Urgently necessary you condemn press misreport.

Even more alarming was a set of cables brought to me by a 19-year-old Nairobi journalist, Ian Matheson, who was the son of the government's chief press officer, Alastair Matheson. The cables purported to convey explosive information about Mboya and Gichuru studying 'preliminary proposals' after talks with the Governor. In the offing appeared to be a deal for the continued restriction of Kenyatta and government sanctions against my activities in exchange for secrecy about stockpiles of nuclear weapons[1] and participation by Mboya and Gichuru in the government.

[1] The full text of the telegram from the Governor to the Colonial Office dated 16 March, as quoted in the *East African Standard* of 8 June 1961, read:

NEGOTIATIONS OVER MILITARY BASES

Talks on this subject should be concluded within a fortnight. Both Ngala and Muliro are studying preliminary proposals. Comprehensive government

I had copies made of the telegrams and returned the originals to Matheson. Were the cables genuine? If they were not their release could shatter KANU at this stage and the public's confidence in the party. I decided to defer a decision on them but meanwhile to alert the whole party to the danger of forces inside KANU making a deal over a new government. This had been our fear all along, but from the moment the election results had come in and the Governor had tried to manoeuvre a Gichuru-Mboya-Ngala-Muliro partnership to sound out Kenyatta at Lodwar, we had put our foot down. We would continue to do so.

When the existence of these cables was disclosed it was done not by me but, curiously, by Mboya. At the beginning of June he rose in the Legislative Council to expose the text of telegrams about 'negotiations over military bases' for the continued restriction of Kenyatta and action against me. The text of the telegrams created a furore. To me the text of the telegrams was most familiar, but the names Mboya and Gichuru had inexplicably been changed to Muliro and Ngala in the period between the time Ian Matheson had brought me the telegrams and their sensational circulation now. Four days after Mboya raised the matter in the House the government said that the telegrams were forged. Two days after that Ian Matheson confessed in court to forging the cables and told the magistrate who jailed him for eighteen months that when he had first made the forgeries

assistance in forming the new Council of Ministers and moral support for the continued restriction of Jomo Kenyatta. We would also guarantee the restriction of his movements towards political activity if he is released before the end of 1961. Direct government sanctions on the activities of Odinga and other African extremists. Immigration Dept assistance in cultivating lack of confidence in short term scholarships offered by Communist countries through Odinga. In exchange for these proposals I have demanded support for both the maintenance and continued restriction of information concerning the nuclear stockpiles planned for Templar Barracks and the Eastleigh Air Force base in Nairobi. I will advise when negotiations are concluded.

and handed them to me, as vice-president of KANU, the cables had contained the names of Mboya and Gichuru instead of the two KADU leaders. Mboya's denunciation of Muliro and Ngala thus boomeranged violently against him. Pursuing investigations about the telegrams the police raided my house, the Kisumu branch of KANU, the office of the Luo Thrift & Trading Corporation, and even searched me at the roadside where they stopped my car. Two months later Alastair Matheson, the father of the young man sentenced to imprisonment, was brought to court on a charge under the Official Secrets Act of failing to take reasonable care of forty-five official documents. His defence argued, according to the press report, 'You may feel that the inference that Ian Matheson got the documents which were found in his possession from his father's office is very strong . . . but that does not mean that the accused was not taking reasonable care'. Alastair Matheson was acquitted on all six charges.

The double mystery of the cables was never solved. If, as the government alleged, they were blatant forgeries, why the prosecution of Matheson senior? And who had switched the names of Mboya and Gichuru to Ngala and Muliro from the time that there was a danger of these KANU leaders compromising over the formation of a government, and KADU's actual sell-out over the issue of Kenyatta's release? Whether forged or not, the cable scandal greatly weakened the resistance of the Governor and the British Government on the Kenyatta release issue.

KANU's Parliamentary group took the offensive in the Legislative Council with a series of private members' motions which exposed KADU to the people. Our motion for the release of Kenyatta 'now and unconditionally' was debated for six hours and defeated by 43 votes to 26, KADU and its allies voting against. We demanded the repeal of the Outlying Districts Ordinance with its restriction on movement and ban of political meetings (three-quarters of the country was subject to these restrictions to stop inter-tribal and inter-district contact). We demanded independence in 1961, simultaneously with Tanganyika. KADU was badly discredited by her showing on all these issues.

The British Government and the Governor were playing for time. Their plan was to help KADU and Blundell hold on to office in the hope that they would seduce men from our ranks to cross the floor to join the government—only Bernard Mate did—and that there would be a public swing to KADU. Britain needed time for several reasons. Macleod was still under fire from Tory backbenchers over Central African problems and he dared not announce the release of Kenyatta; Britain was not ready to placate settlers with a land compensation scheme and there was Tanganyika's independence to be negotiated before the Colonial Office could take on the next Kenya round. Finally, the old guard civil servants in Kenya were obstructing a solution to the deadlock.

So the unreal contest went on in the Legislative Council, with the great mass of the people supporting KANU, but KADU gingerly holding the reins.

As the weeks went by, a new difference between KANU and KADU worked its way to the surface. Ngala, as Leader of Government Business, announced that Kenya could hope to achieve internal self-government by the end of the year; that there would be no need for a fresh constitutional conference but that the Lancaster House constitution could be stretched to accommodate the necessary changes. We had a totally different approach. We did not consider that the existing conditions could be patched up to provide a suitable independence constitution; we were not prepared to wait for independence in slow stages but wanted a new conference to thrash out constitutional questions. New talks were needed for a constitution that would dispense with the temporary expedients of a qualitative franchise, reserved seats, Governor's power to nominate, racial representation in the Council of Ministers and government veto powers. We also wanted a general election before independence because only a firmly based government would enable us to negotiate with the British Government from a position of strength. Government powers of nomination were the transfusion keeping minority KADU government alive: how could we advance to independence under such a constitution?

At this point Kenyatta asked for a consultation with political leaders and KANU and KADU went to Maralal to see him. Out of these talks came a formal agreement for joint action by the two parties, the Maralal Agreement. We defined common objectives and set up a working committee charged with the task of sending a joint delegation to the Governor and the Colonial Secretary to demand Kenyatta's release, to study the land question, and to report within one month on steps to be taken jointly by KANU and KADU on a new constitution and for independence in 1961. The Maralal Agreement read in full:

This meeting of KANU/KADU leaders at Maralal under the chairmanship of Jomo Kenyatta agrees that

1. The relationships between KANU and KADU should be improved to facilitate joint action on matters of national interest, i.e. the immediate unconditional release of Jomo Kenyatta and the true and immediate independence of Kenya.

2. To set up a joint working committee charged with the task of sending a joint delegation to the Governor and the Colonial Secretary to demand Kenyatta's unconditional release.

3. The Committee to study the Land problem.

4. The Committee further to report in a month's time on the steps to be taken on the constitutional question based on the Agreement today between KANU and KADU to work for the achievement of our independence in 1961.

The KADU leaders signed the Maralal Agreement but once again pressures on them of their partners in government undermined their adherence to it. The day after signing, Ngala made a statement that KADU was working for the next stage, which would be internal self-government. Here already were signs of a retreat from the undertaking that KANU and KADU would work out the next stage together, and that the next stage would be independence.

Not long after the signing of the Maralal Agreement, however, KANU and KADU leaders were in London for the East Africa Common Services Organization. I was to have been a member of the delegation but the government refused to re-issue my confiscated passport. After a prolonged discussion with the Colonial Secretary, Macleod agreed to come to Kenya if a workable solution for a national government could be found. The first round would be discussions between our two parties initiated by the Governor. In London our delegation formed the impression that on the release of Kenyatta the ice was beginning to crack. All the months that KADU had been in theoretical control, in a shaky alliance with nominated and White members, the focus of government had not been in Nairobi but at Maralal, because there, in the shape of the exiled Kenyatta, was the sole possibility for leadership of a united, majority African government.

At the end of July KANU and KADU opened their joint talks. We agreed to send a joint deputation to demand the release of Kenyatta, and on the constitutional questions to prepare papers that would not bind any party of participants but would explore the path to agreement between us. Our minutes said the meeting adjourned 'in good humour and high spirits'.

A week later KADU found a pretext for boycotting the talks. This was Mboya's speech at Machakos in which he said the existing constitution was a rotten sore which could not be cured by bandaging but only by excision. If charges were to be levelled, we replied, we would charge KADU with having already broken the Maralal Agreement not once, but five times. Our attempts at cooperation had to be suspended.

Meanwhile there were developments on the Kenyatta issue. The Governor and Britain had all along been conducting a nervous exercise in retreat. There had been the Governor's 'leader to darkness and death' broadcast; settler journals published repeated calumny of Kenyatta, using month after month the same phrases and paragraphs. 'Jomo Kenyatta,' said the *Kenya Weekly News*,

was convicted of the felony of managing one of the most debased and degraded illegal societies that has ever marred the record of mankind. This campaign for the release of Kenyatta to public life is no more than an election gimmick. If there be, which God forbid, surrender to this clamour, it is nonsense to suppose that confidence in the word or the probity of a British Government will remain in the minds of those who have given their lives to the building of Kenya from a waste of raw Africa to its present state.

Six months later the same columnist was eating his words.

Whatever may be the consequences of Kenyatta's release, I am now convinced that it would be wiser to face them than to allow him to continue the role of a Delphic oracle, whether at Maralal or Kiambu. . . .

What had happened in between? The attempt to work the Lancaster House constitution had failed. The attempt to use KADU in government to destroy KANU's support in the countryside had failed. It was realized that the attempt to get stable government in Kenya would continue to fail as long as Kenyatta was still in detention. By August it was announced that Kenyatta would be released by the middle of the month and settler circles pronounced their last furious

denunciations of appeasement of rampant African nationalism and sat back to watch events in a state of truculent
exhaustion.

At even this late stage the government temporized by not
removing the obstacle against Kenyatta taking a seat in the
legislature: Britain seemed unable to break the habit of
building renewed African hostility and encouraging the
rumblings of the most reactionary groups of settlers.

But we had achieved the impossible. Kenyatta was being
released. On 14 August I told a Mombasa rally: 'The
authorities say if they release Kenyatta it will be the end of
everything, but we say, far from being the end of everything,
it will be the start of the struggle for real freedom. Today is
the holiday of all holidays in the history of Kenya, for
Kenyatta is out.'

When the rejoicing at having Kenyatta back among the
people was over, Kenyatta presided, in his first visit to
Nairobi, over a joint meeting of the KANU and KADU
parliamentary groups. The day that Kenyatta came to the
Legislative Council building the largest crowd I had seen
in Kenya gathered to see him, to greet the father of the
nation back among the nation. In the Legislative Council
chamber I took the chair and introduced Kenyatta to all his
colleagues, and read the KANU-KADU agreement we had
concluded. By the time the Governor opened constitutional
talks at Government House, KANU and KADU had agreed
to press for independence by 1 February 1962.

CHAPTER TWELVE

Majimbo Gets in the Way of Uhuru

KENYATTA's release gave a new impetus to the KANU-KADU talks on our independence target and the formation of an interim government. We took a joint memorandum to the Governor which pressed that Kenya should move to full internal self-government immediately and that there should be a re-shuffle of the government, with a Prime Minister chosen by the elected members of the legislature. On land our formula was for the safeguarding 'in the interests of the people of Kenya' of land titles and private property rights, and fair compensation for land acquired by government for public purposes. 'Under all circumstances,' we recorded in a minute 'KADU AND KANU will work together to achieve independence.'

At one point in the proceedings I moved that Kenyatta be invited to join in these inter-party constitutional talks. I was apprehensive that there might be a move to keep Kenyatta out of public life, to relegate him to the status of an 'elder statesman'. The Governor ruled that he was ineligible as he was not a member of the legislature. KADU blocked attempts to reopen the matter and KANU's ten representatives walked out, but on Kenyatta's advice we went back; he was adamant that the conference should succeed and we should not insist on his inclusion if it proved an obstacle.

Other obstacles appeared. During a discussion on the framing of the agenda Blundell suggested, innocuously we thought, 'include the Somali problem'. When we reached this point of the agenda the Governor advised that we should meet the Somalis. There and then we were confronted by several score government-appointed Somali chiefs who had been moved from Wajir five days earlier in government jeeps and who threatened civil war unless they were allowed to secede at the time of the new constitution. There was also a strong move for Coast secession. 'See,' the government's unsaid moral was 'you ask for independence but you can't possibly manage your own security.'

Obstacles were erected at every turn. We agreed to form an interim coalition government. When it came to the composition of a coalition cabinet there were negotiations lasting four days over the allocation of places. While KADU agreed that the two parties should share equally the African-held ministries they refused to share the non-African seats. This would have left KADU with a ruling majority. We suggested that the Asian members should elect their own member but KADU blocked this solution. We were prepared to forego an Asian minister altogether, and to leave this seat vacant in a final compromise which we felt sure the government could not reject.

Mid-way through the talks, when the fate of the Asian ministry was still in the balance, Ngala met Gichuru at a party and showed him a pencilled sheet of paper. It was in Havelock's hand-writing and was a plan for regionalism. If the plan were not accepted, said Ngala, the talks would fail. By the following morning the plan had been typed, and now the ultimatum was official: without our acceptance of the plan for regionalism there would be no coalition. To our astonishment the Governor supported KADU. He bent over backwards to conciliate KADU. He did more than that. He said that the breakdown of the talks was KANU's doing, and the result of domination by the Kikuyu, Luo, and Kamba peoples. KANU abandoned the conference and prepared a large delegation to fly to London. The preliminary soundings should give way to full constitutional talks, we said.

Tension was rising in the country. Paul Ngei, one of the released Kapenguria leaders, made a strong speech on African land rights. The government reported that there was a recurrence of oathing and that the Land Freedom Army had been resurrected. I received personal threats. Elements in KADU thought I was the stumbling block to Kenyatta joining KADU. KANU-KADU relations were acutely strained. After a clash in Nyanza over a projected visit by Kenyatta that I was arranging, and as I was on my way to a meeting in Nairobi I was set upon in Harambee Street and rendered unconscious. From my hospital bed I appealed for calm. It was suspected that my assailants were KADU youths and this did not improve relations between the two parties.

As always when a constitutional conference was in the offing, there were energetic manoeuvrings, some open and others subterranean. For some weeks Kenyatta did not announce whether he would join either of the two parties (on one occasion he threatened to form a third if KANU and KADU did not find a way to cooperate). By the end of October, after the breakdown of our talks and the production by KADU of the plan for regionalism, he decided to join KANU and lead it. KADU let fly. Their leaders said that they would not accept Kenyatta as a national leader and he would not be allowed to address meetings in their areas while he advocated 'one party government'. In KANU, a Parliamentary Group meeting at which I was not present accepted a proposal engineered by McKenzie and Derek Erskine that Kenyatta should be asked not to demand a seat in the Legislative Council because this would raise dissension in KANU; no one was prepared to give up his seat and this would embarrass Kenyatta. Erskine telephoned me to say I had been elected to lead the deputation to Kenyatta. I said I would not go on such a deputation. At the same time I sent a private message to Kenyatta to tell him not to listen to this advice and that the KANU Governing Council was due to meet shortly and would certainly not agree to such a proposition. When it came to finding Kenyatta a seat in the Legislative Council party leaders seemed to have short memories of our election pledge to stand down, and they thought that perhaps it would be better for Kenyatta to wait until after the London conference. At a meeting of the Governing Council only Kariuki Njiiri, Angaine, Chokwe, and I offered to resign our seats. The Governing Council decided that Kenyatta should get the Fort Hall constituency seat of Njiiri. When the election was held Kenyatta was returned unopposed. At last he was a member of the legislature.

Kenyatta led the KANU delegation to London to press for a conference on a constitution for internal self-government. I had my confiscated passport returned, though it had to be surrendered immediately I got back to Nairobi. (I should here mention my warmest appreciation to Kwame Nkrumah and his Ghana Government who, when my passport was recalled, issued me with a Ghana *laissez-passer* that made me the most respected of travellers at a time when my own country was penalizing me.) The new Colonial Secretary was Mr Reginald Maudling. During a round table meeting that lasted fifteen days it was agreed that KANU would return to Nairobi to work out a plan for a constitution and Maudling would open discussions on the form of internal self-government. When we approached the Government of India for the services of a constitutional lawyer Nehru himself suggested Mr B. Malik, the eminent constitutional expert, and with his help a KANU sub-committee worked on a blueprint.

From about this time began a new campaign against me. Anti-national elements had been defeated in their bid to keep Kenyatta in restriction and out of political leadership. As they had failed to keep Kenyatta out of the way, they would try to keep him under their thumbs. The plan was to surround him with new advisers, new groupings, and at the same time to drive a rift between Kenyatta and me, to discredit me in public, to Kenyatta, in the eyes of Britain and Kenya. The nearer we got to the London conference the more virulent became the press attacks on me.

The *New York Times* wrote:[1]

Preparations for a London conference next month on a new constitution for Kenya are being hampered by bitter personal rivalries within the colony's largest political party, the Kenya African National Union.

Involved in the situation are:

A threat to leadership of Jomo Kenyatta, who became president of the party after many years of jail and detention. . . .

Charges that Oginga Odinga, the party's vice-president, has used large amounts of money received from Communist China to build a sizeable personal following. . . .

Reports that Tom Mboya, general secretary of the party, is preparing to lead about fifteen top members out of the party to form a new party that would ally itself with the Kenya African Democratic Union, the colony's second largest party, to form a powerful opposition to the Kenyatta-led party. . . .

From outside the party Masinde Muliro, vice-president of the rival Democratic Union . . . said 'once the British forces leave Kenya we will have the Communist onslaught upon us. . . .'

Political observers regard Mr Odinga as a threat to both Mr Kenyatta and Mr Mboya as well as a disruptive force at the forthcoming constitutional conference and in Kenya afterwards.

In that journalist's report was set out the strategy of the forthcoming attack against KANU and against my position

[1] *New York Times*, 7 January 1962.

in the party. Kenyatta and KANU were told that they were being undermined from two sides, by myself and by Mboya who was being driven into KADU's arms.

As the press slander campaign mounted it insisted repeatedly that I was the grave danger to Kenya. A report in the *Daily Telegraph* said:[1]

Mr Odinga is believed by security officials to be using Communist funds to make the first serious attempts to undermine the position of Mr Nyerere, Prime Minister of neighbouring Tanganyika. . . . This week there has been a polite exchange of telegrams between Mr Nyerere and Mr Kenyatta. . . . It is obvious that relations between Mr Nyerere and Mr Kenyatta are cool. . . .

When we got to the London conference the smear campaign continued and between members of our delegation there was most unfortunate strain. Even the way our delegation was divided in different hotels seemed to illustrate the stresses between us: Kenyatta and I stayed together; Mboya, Gichuru, and McKenzie (apprehensive of Kenyatta's influence and of mine) were working closely together, living at the home of the Aga Khan's representative in East Africa; and others were with Derek Erskine, dissipating their energies by isolating and disowning me instead of concentrating on the job we had in hand for Kenya.

There was a spate of private meetings: Kenyatta with the Colonial Secretary, Ngala and the Colonial Secretary, Mboya and the Colonial Secretary. Lavish entertainment was arranged for the members of the Legislative Council. Funds were flowing freely. Lobbying and caucusing was evident on all sides.

Kenya's *East African Standard* [2] carried a report of a KANU meeting in London at which I was the target of allegations of plans to take over the country by totalitarian

[1] *Daily Telegraph*, 12 January 1962.   [2] *Evening Standard*, 30 March 1962.

means. The persons who took part in this meeting were not named. The report read:

To Kenya the most startling news of the week was a sudden admission by KANU delegates in London. They spoke of a fear that some of their own colleagues planned to overthrow the very constitution that the conference at Lancaster House is laboriously trying to establish. The party's vice-president, Mr Oginga Odinga, the leader of a powerful faction within Kenya and a supporter of Mr Kenyatta and the Old Guard, was accused by colleagues of being the chief architect of the alleged revolution plan. 'We are fighting a battle against Mr Odinga's communist influence and the threat of revolution,' two delegates said.

The report added:

Inside KANU reaction varied from calls to prevent Mr Odinga taking part in any future government to anger at the disclosure of private party affairs. . . .

I believed, and I said publicly, that there were members of the legislature who had joined KANU not because they supported the party's policy but to cling to the coats of a few members of the KANU Parliamentary Group. Led by Derek Erskine they were revealing their motive in joining KANU, to sabotage the struggle of the people of Kenya. Mr Erskine's allegations, I said, revealed that

. . . he was the champion of the clique whose motive is to divide KANU into two groups, the so-called moderate (Mboya) group and the so-called extremists (the Odinga group). Mr Erskine alleged that I was training an army to usurp power when Kenya became independent. This is not the time to reply to these unfounded and baseless allegations which would divert our attention from the main issue which brought us to London. To the surprise of all except the instigators, the details of this private KANU meeting were given to the press. On the charge of the army, it would be unthinkable for me as a dedicated African nationalist to conspire against an African national government

225

in Kenya, because I know that the people of Kenya have no enemy other than imperialism and colonialism. . . . If the press is correct and the moderate elements in KANU have won the first round in the battle against Odinga, the question before the people of Kenya is: did you send us to London to fight Oginga Odinga or to bring independence? . . . The time has come for KANU to differentiate our foes from our friends. I and others worked for the admission of Erskine and others to the KANU Parliamentary group in the hope that they would be genuine supporters of our national aspirations, but like their counterparts in KADU these people are not with us. . . . I have always been accused of being a communist or an extremist when I speak of the will of the people for our rights and freedoms. I will continue to speak of the will of the people of Kenya . . . Kenya will not remain an island of colonialism in a free Africa. . . . The salvation of our country lies in unity. . . .

All this time the Colonial Secretary was studying our ranks closely and observing how vulnerable these attacks were making KANU. Some of our delegation were unable to withstand witch-hunting tactics; divisions created by them would be KADU's gain.

The battle for regionalism was in full swing. It was no secret that the authors of KADU's plan for regionalism were Wilfred Havelock, Michael Blundell, R. S. Alexander, and their associates, long practised in the art of political survival. 'The details of the plan', said The Times of London, 'were worked out by KADU's European associates.' Government House anticipation of the regional plan, at the talks which had broken down, was more than acute perception. We were convinced that the Governor had a hand in the development of the policy of *majimbo* and this scheme was a continuation of settler tactics to use KADU to block the formation of a strong African government. Regionalism was a development of the argument used by the settlers in the fifties when they argued that the Westminster parliamentary model could not be adapted to Kenya because it gave too much power to the majority. Havelock and Blundell convinced KADU leaders that an independent Kenya with a Kikuyu and Luo majority would be fatal. They could not stop independence, they argued, but they could divide Kenya into autonomous regions. Under such an arrangement KADU could control three states (the Rift Valley, the Western Region, and the Coast). The settlers of the Rift Valley would assist the finances of the Coast and the Western Region. This plan would ensure that Kenyatta would never be Prime Minister for there need be no head of state or prime minister, but a loose system of regional councils with rotating chairmen. KADU's P. J. H. Okondo, then parliamentary secretary to the Ministry of Finance and Development said about *majimbo*:

This idea of regional government is capable of unlimited extension and we hope it will be extended, with due consultation, to apply to Uganda, Tanganyika, Nyasaland and the Rhodesias and others that may wish to join. In this way we visualize a large state consisting of anything up to thirty or forty regions and to be known as the Federate states of Africa.[1]

To the authors of the plan for regionalism the need for Pan-Africanism was remote from their intentions; they wanted a new-sounding slogan for KADU that would rouse minority tribe support to prevent a strong centralized government. Feeling was worked up in the country by statements from Muliro that if KADU's regional plan was not accepted, KADU's leaders had a secret master plan. William Murgor said in Eldoret that if the plan were not accepted he would 'sound a whistle to my people declaring civil war'.

Ngala's opening speech to the constitutional conference married *majimbo* with the cold war approach. His party wanted, he said, to build a country in which dictatorship would be impossible. If that could be done Kenya would be

---

[1] *The Times*, 6 October 1961.

able to resist the menace of communism, already threatening it from within and from neighbouring countries. He made the blatant allegation that because KANU was in favour of a unitary system of government this meant dictatorship under Kikuyu-Luo domination.

KADU's tactics were to refuse to put forward its detailed proposals unless the principle of regionalism was accepted. Mr Martin Shikuku, KADU general secretary, threatened that his party would do without independence for another ten years if it did not get its way over regionalism. Throughout the talks KADU maintained this obduracy. The conference started on 12 February 1962 and lasted until May. The prolonged argument went on week after week, with an examination first of KADU's plan clause by clause, and then KANU's clause by clause. In a month of talking we made virtually no progress. The Colonial Secretary sat patiently waiting, letting everyone speak, waiting, seemingly, for us to reach a state of physical exhaustion as well as policy deadlock. KADU's generals in the battle for regionalism knew full well the dangerous effects this struggle could have. KADU's stand could give the British Government an opening to declare that since there was no agreement between the two African parties, the question of a date for independence would have to be deferred. This might force concessions from KANU. There was always the possibility, too, that the less resolute forces in KANU would be weaned away to an alliance with KADU. During the critical first weeks of the conference Blundell wrote a feature article in *The Times* in which he referred to 'many men in both parties who think alike', and he singled out Ngala and Muliro, Mboya and Gichuru. Then after attacks on me and warnings against the 'dangers of Communism' Blundell made an appeal for a 'regrouping together of the political forces dedicated to the creation of a modern country'. In case the meaning of this approach had not sunk in, *The Times*

228

followed with an attack on Kenyatta as 'the obstacle to national government', opposing the idea of him as Chief Minister and even calling for his removal from the leadership of KANU. 'It is suggested in official quarters that there can be no solution until Mr Kenyatta has been removed from his present position.' The article ended with the significant remark that Mr Tom Mboya, who is the only man who could lead the necessary breakaway from KANU, would be willing to serve in such a government (one led by KADU). Thus the talks were conducted under outspoken threats to KANU that if we made no concessions, we would be torn in two; and with settler influence in the Conservative Party and the press throwing the full weight of government and public opinion pressure against us.

KADU's constitutional adviser was a Swiss constitutional expert, the settlers' legal adviser was a Conservative M.P. associated with members of the right-wing Africa lobby of the Conservative Party, and they had the services of a man who had for years been the chief publicity adviser of the Conservative Party Central Office.

As the deadlock persisted, Kenyatta called KANU representatives together. Arguing, he said, was all very well, but we had to reach a settlement. If we failed government would be snatched from our hands. If we brought no government back with us, the people would regard it as an arch failure. We might be forced to accept a constitution we did not want, but once we had the government we could change the constitution. The Colonial Secretary must have perceived our eagerness to get into the government. All this time he had abstained from comment, acting as a quiet arbitrator while the parties engaged. With the KADU tactic of pushing their demands to the utmost limit, the Colonial Office was able to present itself as mediator. Now Maudling played his cards expertly. He made an extempore speech on a compromise plan for a constitution. It leaned over towards

KADU. There was provision for a central government, but a weak one, and the principle of regionalism was incorporated. There was to be a two-chamber parliament; six regions derived power from the constitution, not from central government; the regions were to have their own legislature, administration, financial and executive powers, and control over land and police. All Crown lands and trust lands came under the regional authorities. Scheduled land (including the White Highlands) came under a special central land board, but this board was composed of six regional nominees and only one from the central government, plus an independent chairman. Constitutional amendments required 75 per cent and in some cases 90 per cent of the vote in each of the two Houses. On many points there was no agreed constitutional formula and the way was left open for further argument and negotiation. The new constitution would start Kenya's government off under severe handicaps. No date was set for independence.

The KANU group voted, eventually, on our attitude to the constitution. Just over a third of our number (eight out of twenty) were against its acceptance. I was one of those who voted against.

Maudling delivered a virtual ultimatum to KANU and KADU to form a coalition government. We had each to produce a list of ministers. On Kenyatta's list I was Minister of Finance. The Colonial Office vetoed my appointment. The British Government refused to give a reason. I have no doubt that Governor Renison persuaded the Colonial Office (if persuasion were needed at all) that my visits to socialist countries made me unfit to take Cabinet office; I also know of behind-the-scenes discussions in London in which some KANU men hinted that I would be unacceptable not only to KADU but even to some groups in KANU. When the opposition of the Colonial Office was made known to him Kenyatta removed me from his list. I was neither consulted nor even informed by Jomo. It was Achieng Oneko, who had been in the dock of the Kapenguria trial with Kenyatta and had acted as his secretary, who came to me, greatly upset, to break the news. 'Kenyatta has agreed to form a government without you,' he said. I was taken aback, I admit. But I decided this was no time to make an issue of my exclusion. I did what I could to ensure that Kenyatta's final list included men who were genuine representatives of the people's cause. KADU's victory over the constitution had gone to Ngala's head and he was demanding three ministries; Constitutional Affairs, Administration, and Information and Broadcasting. Kenyatta accepted the Ministry of Economic Planning (not an important ministry at this time because planning was done by the Treasury). Here was yet another instance of the plan to divert power from the centre and from KANU, to KADU and the regions, and to divide KANU ranks this time by driving a wedge between Kenyatta and myself.

I said publicly that I had been the victim of witch-hunting aimed at dividing KANU and slowing down the pace of Kenya's independence, but I added: 'I am not going to allow myself to be provoked by these tactics, nor is KANU going to allow the pace of its programme to be slowed down.' Lure of public office was not my reason for joining in the national struggle.

The crowd of 25,000 that greeted our return from London roared its support for me. Posters said: 'Thank you, Odinga, for your heroism.' I had to explain to Nyanza meetings why I had accepted my exclusion from the Cabinet. There was, I said, a calabash with a very narrow neck and a snake inside it. If it had been for me to choose, I would have kicked the calabash over and smashed it open to get at the snake. Kenyatta's way was to drop a rope inside, to get it round the neck of the snake and to pull it out. Kenyatta told the country I would hold a key ministry in the independence Cabinet.

CHAPTER THIRTEEN

Harambee for Independence

As it happened I was in the Cabinet eleven months later—seven months before Independence—as Minister of Home Affairs under the fully self-governing constitution. This was after KANU's overwhelming victory in the May 1963 general election, and after a period of Coalition Cabinet government which was a crucial one for the country. At the time I was distinctly uneasy about many aspects and looking at events in retrospect it seems to me that our national struggle, at a time of promise and opportunity, lost ground in the battle against colonial influence and for full, unfettered independence.

Britain was reconciled to the fact that she had to grant at least formal independence to her East African colonies. An independent Uganda and Tanganyika would inevitably be followed by an independent Kenya. But while direct control would be surrendered, the strategy was to place in power elements which would be disinclined to effect a complete rupture from the old influences. Kenya has always held a pivotal position for Britain in East Africa. It has common borders not only with Tanganyika and Uganda but also with the Sudan, Ethiopia, and Somalia. In the pre-independence era Nairobi was in many ways the capital of East Africa; almost all the large capitalist enterprises of East Africa were centred in Nairobi. Nairobi housed the

main office of the East Africa Common Services Organization which controls the railways, air, postal, and telecom-
munications throughout East Africa. Uganda's access to the
sea lies across Kenya to the port of Mombasa. Our large
White settler population emphasized the British presence in
Kenya. A retention of British influence in Kenya, albeit by
devious and indirect ways, would leave Britain well placed
to continue to influence events in East Africa.

The joint KANU-KADU Cabinet was a thoroughly
uneasy coalition. Months of formal partnership between
KANU and KADU made the collaboration not less but
more painful. KADU was visibly a spent force and Britain's
insistence on her participation as an equal partner was daily
a greater affront to the overwhelming majority support of
KANU in the country. We knew that the alternative to
KANU-KADU agreement on the many questions that
cropped up was a solution imposed by Britain, but this did
not make agreement any more amicable.

Many important issues had been left unsettled by the
London conference which had set the course of regionalism,
and commissions were established to consider these questions. We had finally to grapple with one of the most
involved constitutions ever devised for Africa. It ran to an
overwhelming 223 pages. It has been called a constitution
of checks and balances, but I would say there were more
checks than anything else. Our population of eight million
had to carry a many-tiered government apparatus: two
central and seven regional assemblies (though the seventh
was born later because the Somalis boycotted the elections
on a demand for secession encouraged in earlier days), and
separate police forces, judiciaries, and public service commissions for each region. With this formidable complex
machinery of government came a heavy financial burden.
The Times commented that the constitution finally produced
out of the compromise hammered out between KANU and

KADU was a 'formidable instrument of government' and first requirement was a skilled corps of lawyers and clerks in the centre and the regions to explain to legislators what they were required, permitted, or forbidden to do under scores of legally worded clauses.

Kenya knew and the British Government knew that in any election KANU would sweep the polls with ease. This explains the ultimatum presented by Maudling at the Lancaster House conference to force Kenyatta, for KANU, into equal coalition with the minority party that had polled only a quarter of the votes. Prompt elections after the London conference would have enabled KANU to form a majority government instead of hamstringing it in the coalition, and would also have consolidated KANU ranks. Maudling visited Kenya but only to postpone elections for a further six months till May 1963, to be followed by a period of internal self-government and then yet another constitutional conference—the fourth in three years—to settle the final form of an independence constitution. It was a long exercise in delay, with decisions on key policy questions either deferred or taken by an uneasy coalition, decisions which KANU, as majority party entitled to the running of government, would have solved in a different way. Ngala as minister in charge of the administration was in a strategic position to dismantle the centralized machinery of administration and transfer it to the regions. Kenyatta was in charge of economic planning but it was linked with the Treasury run by British officials who were then hostile to Kenyatta and to KANU.

When we came back to Kenya from the Lancaster House conference Kenyatta had told the gigantic welcoming crowd that was silent and depressed at the start of the meeting that when KADU looked at the face of the constitution they would think it was a cow but when they tried to milk it they would find it was a donkey. Kenyatta's policy was to get KANU into government, to take for himself even a junior ministry, and to use our position in government not in office but in the country, to rouse the people against KADU and regionalism and in preparation for the next elections and the next constitution. It was KANU's work of organizing among the people during the coalition government that decisively won us the next round of the battle. As I had been excluded from the Cabinet Kenyatta allocated to me the job of building the party organization. My exclusion from the Cabinet was interpreted by the people as a surrender to the British Government. Many blamed Kenyatta for not having held firm on this question. The country was angry: it felt my exclusion was a betrayal of the struggle. It was necessary for Kenyatta to explain. He told the people that he would put me in complete charge of the party machine. For all this there were obstacles put in my way by the elements within KANU who had always feared a strongly centralized party organization and who thought I might use the party for the only purpose they had for it— the building of personal power. When finally the Colonial Office could hold back no longer our cry for elections, inner party strife over constituency candidate selection came to a head once more.

Paul Ngei broke from KANU to form the African People's Party when the Mboya group in KANU challenged Ngei's leadership of the Kamba people (Ngei and I were working closely together so this manoeuvre was in order to weaken the so-called 'Odinga forces') though after the elections Ngei's forces rejoined KANU. Party discipline collapsed in the face of rival claims for seats. In some seats strong KANU members were not chosen as candidates; but waverers and newcomers were; where some branches made an official choice of a candidate they were over-ruled by party leaders who didn't approve of the selection. Candidates who were over-ruled for indiscipline after an appeal to a higher party committee were told to stand down but they were not suspended if they declined; there were official and unofficial KANU candidates, and independents. A solution to the disputes was to let branches choose their own candidates, and branch elections were conducted with an official from headquarters presiding. Sometimes branches sent in the names of two or three candidates, and officials of the branches put up their own selections. In the case of the Kandara branch elections, Kaggia defeated his opponent by twenty-seven votes but the branch chairman submitted to headquarters the name of his defeated opponent, and it was suggested that Kaggia contest a KADU stronghold in the Rift Valley. Kaggia challenged the selection of candidate and after several rounds of arbitration and a second branch election under which I was called upon to supervise, Kaggia was unanimously elected candidate. In Nyanza Odede (by then Tom Mboya's father-in-law) appeared once again to challenge my seat. He had admitted to me in London during the constitutional conference that he had never forgiven me for defeating him in the 1961 election. His 1963 electoral intervention was not limited to his own candidature: he and five others appeared to challenge the official KANU candidates in Central Nyanza constituencies. Kenyatta himself was called in to mediate; all the names put forward by the Central Nyanza KANU branch were confirmed. Not one of the unofficial candidates was successful, and many lost their deposits. Unhappily there were physical clashes between the followers of the unofficial candidates and KANU youth wingers and KANU supporters John Martin Mito of Uyoma location and Owanga Oyola of Nyakach lost their lives. Personal rivalries criss-crossed with the battle of the militant and anti-national tendencies inside KANU. Tribal antagonisms were whipped up and I vigorously opposed the activities of a new movement called LUM (the Luo United Movement) which put up Luo candidates in

Nyanza against the official KANU candidates. All the LUM candidates were defeated.

As the date of the elections approached dissension subsided. KANU swept the boards. Although the constituency dice were heavily loaded against us, and we had to poll double the number of votes for the Senate and the regions to get the same number of seats as KADU, we won a triumphant majority in the Lower House, achieved a state of tie in the Senate, and shared the majorities in the six regional assemblies between us. In the period that followed, our majorities were increased by the APP forces of Ngei rejoining KANU, by many independents crossing the floor to us and later KADU members crossing too, and by a marked and continuous swing to KANU in all elections after that.

During my election campaign Kenyatta asked me to represent him at the African Heads of States Conference in Addis Ababa. There I introduced to the conference the statement made jointly by the non-independent African states. It was a great honour that I was chosen to make this statement on behalf of the still-struggling countries of Africa, and the statement was one of the most striking features of the conference. It was arising from this statement that the Committee of Liberation was set up to enable the independent states of Africa to assist the struggle in the still oppressed territories. I was not in my constituency to witness it, but I scored an easy victory as did other KANU candidates throughout Central Nyanza. I heard of my election victory in Mombasa on my way back from Addis Ababa and I hurried to Nairobi to join in our victory celebrations. This time we were able to form our Cabinet without interference. KANU had achieved the ascendancy and KADU the considerably diminished situation which years of settler and Colonial Office manipulation had tried to block.

Our new Cabinet reflected something of Kenya's freedom struggle but we took care to make it fully representative of the country, for tribal passions had been whipped to danger point in the year of *majimbo* and we had to show the different regions of Kenya that we had their interests at heart. We had Kikuyu, Luo, Abaluhya, Kisii, Taita, Kamba, Masai, Meru, Embu in the Cabinet. I was specially pleased with the recognition given to the men who had been in the dock, in prison, or in exile with Kenyatta, men like Achieng Oneko, Fred Kubai, and Bildad Kaggia (the latter two received parliamentary secretaryships). Paul Ngei was not included and I was conscious of his absence in the government until he was included in the Republic Cabinet of 1965.

After the swearing-in ceremony Kenyatta introduced our *Harambee* slogan. *Harambee* became our national cry from this time on but I remember it had first been used by Omolo Ongiro (who came to be known as Omolo Harambee) of Nyakach location in Central Nyanza. At every meeting he shouted 'Harambe-eeeh, Harambe-ee-eeh' and added 'Let us all go to Lodwar to pull Kenyatta from prison, pull together for independence.' *Harambee* became Kenya's slogan for national unity, for cooperation in the building of a new country. It stood for one country, one destination, one Africa, one party, one policy, the unity of all tribes and peoples for a united free country.

When the September 1963 talks on an independence constitution opened there were fresh battles. KANU wanted provision inserted for the easier amendment of the constitution; KADU fought this. The Colonial Secretary, Duncan Sandys, took the attitude that if the British Government imposed amendments acceptable to KANU, KADU minority tribes could resort to violent action aimed at secession. The British Parliament would then blame the government for provoking bloodshed and would probably refuse to pass the Independence Bill. Once again British Government tactics were to force a KADU policy on KANU, or to threaten to postpone independence. It was blackmail, and we said so. We had spent a fortnight in discussion and hoped we were on the verge of reaching conference agreement when we discovered that the Colonial Secretary had been meeting KADU (to give them the feeling that they were participating in the conference, he said) and their opposition *was* to be made the stumbling block to agreement. We put two alternatives to the Colonial Secretary: either we reached agreement on the amendments to the constitution we proposed which would remove the need to amend the constitution immediately after independence, or the British Government implemented only the technical changes needed for independence and left the future for the independent government of Kenya to decide. In this case we would declare in advance that we were not committed to the constitution. There was no question of our negotiating an agreement with KADU; to expect us to do this would be to make nonsense of the independence elections. As for the imaginary threat of KADU provoking violence, this meant that Britain was prepared to frustrate the vast majority of the population who were behind KANU: would not *their* frustration be likely to burst forth? We were still locked in disagreement when the KANU Parliamentary Group cabled us on 16 October to return to Kenya immediately with a view to declaring Kenya independent on 20 October. The cable signed by Joe Murumbi, Achieng Oneko, and all members of the Parliamentary Group said:

Throughout constitutional conference Colonial Secretary Sandys seeking to equate the insignificant KADU minority with the government of the country led by Kenyatta. The refusal of the Colonial Secretary to accede to the reasonable demands made by the KANU delegation in London will jeopardize the country's future relations with Britain, and force the government of Kenya to make a reappraisal of its previous commitment to join the British Commonwealth. KADU, having suffered a severe defeat at the general elections is, being encouraged to create semi-autonomous units within the regions it claims to control. All elections have emphasized the strong swing away from KADU and regionalism. The reluctance of the Colonial Secretary to accept the implications arising from the countryside and growing support for KANU and its policy of strong central government threatens to undermine the political and economic stability of the country.

This pressure helped to swing the balance of the agreement in KANU's favour. We won our point on the constitutional question of constitutional amendment, and achieved increased centralized control of the police and the public service commission.

We began work in our ministries with the trappings of power, only to find that it would be anything but an easy run. We inherited a constitution too complicated to be workable, and we found that many of our functions had been transferred to the regions without proper re-planning and there was a state of utter confusion in many departments. I was made Minister for Home Affairs. This was largely a new ministry. An aspect of its work had fallen previously under the Ministry of African Affairs, which before that was called the Department of Native Administration headed by the Chief Native Commissioner (this was in the days when the 'natives' were regarded as a separate policy, distinct from national policy!). The ministry thus covered administration. It also handled prisons and immigration. It should, like the previous portfolio, have included defence, internal security, and police. But when I joined the Cabinet I found that my portfolio had deliberately been severely limited. Internal security and police, the natural functions of the Home Minister for the proper control of immigration, had been reserved by the Governor, Malcolm MacDonald, as part of the Prime Minister's functions. It was reported that senior British police officers had threatened resignation if they came

The author receiving a gift from the people of Kisii after a Vice-Presidential tour of Majoge-Bass.

Kenyatta examining the author's Peace Medal presented by the World Peace Council in September 1963. (*below*)

The author with Premier Obote of Uganda.

The author with President Nyerere of Tanzania.

under my ministry and whether or not this was true—and if it was, how outrageous that civil servants should be allowed to blackmail their own government—here was the continuation of the process of penalizing me for my militant policies and of trying to reduce my effectiveness in our supposedly self-governing Cabinet. When I confronted Kenyatta with this limitation of my powers I found, to my surprise, that he was fully aware of this plan and in complete agreement with it with the Governor!

We had self-government at last, but not before thorough preparations had been made. A precaution taken by the British before moving out, I found, was the destruction, or perhaps just the removal, of records of their administration, especially of the vital Emergency period. There were blank spaces on shelves and empty drawers in the ministries where files had been removed. I found it amusing that I could nowhere trace the file on myself: I must have had a dossier? My friends in Nairobi told me that they had seen the chimneys of the Central Government building smoking for weeks before our government moved in: the record of the past was being burnt.

I was suspect but so was our entire government. Settlers and civil servants waited in apprehension for our first deeds and policy. The whole country waited. Just because I was the suspect minister I suggested to Kenyatta, and he agreed, that I should do a nation-wide tour to explain our policy to the people. I addressed regional assemblies, talked plainly to government officials, chiefs, and politicians. I told everyone they had to re-orientate themselves to a changed condition. Chiefs and civil servants had to accept the authority of the new government and carry out its policies wholeheartedly. I told KANU party members that they, too, had to change their attitude. It was now our police force, our civil service, even the chiefs were our servants, and the former attitude of hostility to an alien government had to make way for cooperation in the interests of the country. Chiefs or civil servants who did not change with the times would be promptly removed (some of our supporters demanded that *all* chiefs be removed on Independence Day);[1] for the rest the principle of *harambee*—working together—had to be carried out in local government.

Some people thought that independence meant the end of the struggle and all would be in order in a new Kenya. Some people in the villages thought that there was lots of money in the bank and Kenya would give it all to us, that money could be printed easily enough. I explained how we had to work to accumulate wealth, that much of the wealth our work had amassed in the past had been taken out of the country. 'Politics have changed,' I told countless meetings of KANU and the ordinary people. 'We must be busy now with reconstruction. It is your country now, don't shake it. It will take time for the government to fulfil its duty to the people. We will do our best to put Kenya on its feet.'

When our ministry came to look at the state of the country's administration we found there was almost no central control of administration. There were no estimates for the Commissioner for Administration. The administrative machinery of central government had been dismembered and given to the regions under the control of the regional assemblies. There could not be—and this was why *majimbo* was devised—effective central government with regional control and with regional financing enshrined in the constitution. There could be no question of refusing to delegate the administration to the regions; this would have been against the constitution. There was pressure from the British Government for schedules for handing over power to the regions. But we knew that the period of this regional constitution would be short-lived (it lasted for eleven months,

[1] (In January 1964 we announced that 205 of 423 Chiefs of the six regions would be replaced by more progressive men.)

until November 1964), and so we honoured the undertaking to hand over schedules but we improvized a new way of keeping as much centralized control as possible, ready for the day when strong central administration would be reinstated. Though we handed the services to the regions, the officials in the employ of central government were not automatically transferred to the regions, but were merely seconded to them temporarily. As they were our employees we had the final authority; we could recall, transfer, or sack them. Circular 55 said that all administrative officers above the rank of district assistant were to remain on the central government establishment, on the staff of the Ministry of Home Affairs, but would be seconded to the regions. This circular aroused much controversy but it was not challenged. In the result civil secretaries (formerly called provincial commissioners) of the regions assumed a dual role: they served the regional assemblies but they were also central government agents in the regions, and in this way we achieved continuity. At the outset regions protested. 'If you don't want our personnel, return them to us and use your own,' we said, but of course there was no administrative personnel to be found as replacement.

To ensure coordination our ministry issued a directive on the responsibilities of central government and the regions and the relationship between the two. All regions, we said, should refer to the ministry and all contemplated legislation to be submitted to the regional assemblies so as to enable the minister to give his advice in time. Regional Assembly presidents, especially from the KADU controlled regions (Havelock and Ngala were running the Coast region, and Moi the Rift Valley region) were regularly at our ministry protesting that we had usurped the functions of the regional assemblies.

For our part we convened the frequent consultations with the civil secretaries and the presidents of the regions. The latter charged that I was misinterpreting the constitution, but I stuck to my interpretation and we argued our case before the Governor-General and the Ministry of Legal Affairs. The interpretation in favour of the regions was over-ruled.

I undertook repeated journeys to the regions to face the elected members and outline their powers. These, I said, were barely larger than those of local government authorities. I asserted our authority to appoint chiefs and sub-chiefs. In replacing some of the chiefs who could not adapt to new times we adopted a method of part-election. We invited applications for chieftainships and asked the candidates to appear before public gatherings. We judged the public's reception and acclaim of the chiefs as indices of their popularity, and this was one of the factors taken into account when appointments were made.

This was a period of uneasy maladjustment, of tight-rope walking for our ministry. During the first year of transition funds for the regions had to come from central government, as the funds for the regions were to be drawn from tax collections which took a while to collect. Rational development would be undermined by regionalism, this we always knew. A regional system inevitably produced duplication of functions, erratic and uncoordinated planning. There was an additional danger that money would be spent not on essential administration and services, but on politics, on prestige spending. Fortunately regional assemblies had a duty during the transitional period to carry our schemes for which funds had been allocated in the previous period, so our ministry held a watching brief on the fulfilment of these commitments.

A serious danger loomed of border troubles. There was tension between Luo and Baluyha in the Western Region and Nyanza, and between Maragoli and Nyangori in Western Region and the Rift Valley. The Kitale Region was

to be transferred out of the Rift Valley and into the Western
Region and in exchange two sub-locations (Kapsengere and
Gimarakwa) were to be transferred from Maragoli to the
Rift Valley. The two Regional Assemblies of the Western
Region of the Rift Valley had agreed to this package deal
but it transpired that they had not consulted the local
inhabitants. The Maragoli would not accept a transfer to
the Rift Valley and their M.P.s—J. D. Otiende and Godia—
supported their opposition. We could not possibly carry
through the transfer in the face of such hostility. The two
M.P.s today accuse me of going back on the package deal,
but how could I streamline it through, ignoring public
opinion and their own opposition? Our officials stalled with
this plan, and there were other planned transfers that were
non-starters.

Our ministry's circular No. 1 laid down the relationship
between the regions and central government. Circular No. 2
gave me much satisfaction. It was headed 'Membership of
Clubs' and read:

I would like to bring to the notice of all managers of private and
non-private clubs that the government in keeping with its spirit
of creating a new national atmosphere in the country, wishes to
advise all clubs against any discriminatory constitution they might
have at present. The government is of the opinion that any
constitutions which bar membership solely on grounds of race,
colour, or creed, is out of step with the times. This advice is given
in order to avoid further unpleasant incidents, and it is hoped
that managers of clubs will cooperate with the government in
this matter. The government wishes this advice to be accorded
immediate attention. Managers of clubs are accordingly requested
to inform the Minister for Home Affairs of the action they propose
to take.

This circular was to outlaw the social colour bar. Bars,
hotels, and clubs sent in their constitutions to be scrutinized.
Some tried to wriggle by claiming that their exclusiveness

was based not on colour but on interest, but we were not persuaded.

The danger to our new standards came from old prejudices and discriminatory practices but also—and much more important—from the old hands in the civil service. Even where KADU was not running the regions colonial servants were at the right hand of the regional authorities, steering them in old directions. In Nyanza, for example, the former Provincial Commissioner was grooming the regional president in office. In the Eastern Region a former *aide-de-camp* to the Governor was running the administration. We transformed the provincial commissioners into civil secretaries but the old colonial ideas prevailed, and many expatriate officials had power in their hands. I told civil servants we demanded loyalty to the government. When I first took over the ministry there was serious unrest in KANU because many party members believed that all the former civil servants would be replaced by party members. They found it difficult to understand the call to cooperate with the service that had administered colonial rule. Overnight, I told the people, we could not make a clean sweep. If civil servants transferred allegiance to our policy there would be no need to replace them. Those who refused, or could not fit into the new pattern, would be replaced.

Some of the senior officials made no secret of their disrespect for our government. I took action in the blatant cases. The Provincial Commissioner in Mombasa was replaced at an appropriate moment when he was called to the capital to help with the Independence celebrations. When the Commissioner of the Rift Valley knew I was coming on a visit but absented himself and left junior officers in charge, I summoned him. 'You have tomorrow to pack', I said. 'You are being Africanized.' I removed this official not out of pique but because his action was a continuation of a series of activities undermining our government's authority. We had the power of deportation but used it as sparingly as we could. We had to make an example of those expatriate officials who stubbornly avowed open contempt. Kenya had changed but many refused to recognize this, and some deportations were necessary to bring home to the expatriates the reality of the transfer of power.

The civil service, I found, could frustrate the best plans of the best intentioned governments. Given a chance, top civil servants can direct a minister, not the other way about. An inexperienced, naïve, or unconscientious minister can be committed to a policy in flat contradiction to the overall policy of his government. The civil service resists change, even sabotages change. The ideal policy effected in Guinea where the party network of organizers moved in to take over the administration was not easy to operate in Kenya where independence was played out in slow stages, managed by the British and where KANU was never a strongly centralized party but an amalgam of many diverse tendencies and policies. Expatriate influence in Kenya was particularly strong in the police force and the army; only one year after the independence, for example, was there an African head of the police force.

I was warned when I took over the ministry that we would have no Africans to man our departments, and would not be able to train them. We had no difficulty. I appointed one of the few African District Officers to understudy the Principal Immigration Officer and after a month the latter recommended his understudy as highly qualified. The tasks which Africans are not supposed to manage they cope with very well as soon as they are given the opportunity. Except for cases where highly specialized knowledge and training are required it is not African incompetence that stands in the way of Africanization. It is the unwillingness of those in control to put Africans there. But Africans must have the encouragement that they will be supported by their superiors, and confidence in their own abilities and the importance of their work for their country. Decolonization is not a matter only of a new constitution and new faces in the government; it is a matter of liberating attitudes. The colonial order castrates one's mind if one is not strong enough. All his life the African has been groomed to believe that he must carry out orders which others will issue from positions of responsibility. There can come a time when the African civil servant is nervous to assume responsibility: he wants someone else to plan for him. The colonial system of education in our settler-dominated system created dependence. Attitudes of dependence have to be warred against. In the civil service bureaucratic tendencies develop too. Some senior officials do not promote juniors for fear of competition. Others go slow on Africanization in their own departments. Some seem to prefer to work with expatriates because they prefer strangers to know their weaknesses rather than their African brothers. This has grave dangers when expatriates are serving as advisers, for they are in an ideal position to learn the weaknesses of their ministers and departments and to exploit them.

I have always been convinced that training is one aspect of Africanizing our civil service but the other is the re-shaping of attitudes. There must be an orientation to national objectives. It is disturbing that the spreading tendency is to put promotion and salary above all else, including the national interest. The rot does not start in the civil service, but with the politicians. I have watched many members of my generation of political leaders thrown up by our colonial society, launch their offensive into the settler and White government citadel, but then succumb to the all pervasive influences of colonialism. The process begins a long way back to the stifling effect of colonial education and colonial administration on the confidence and self-respect of the African. Brought up in the presence of the White master, you are taught to defer to him, until this is ground into your soul. The 'reasonable' African is recognized by his quiet voice, speaking gently like a priest in church. He is discouraged from expressing his feelings forcefully. When he is taken into a mission boarding school the young educated African is intimidated by the wealth of the White world. At Makerere we used spoons, forks, knives, and plates; when I went home for the holidays I ate my food from a basket by hand. We were taught to be dissatisfied with the ways of the African world. In Church the preacher spoke against African custom. He might do it subtly, but many expressions of distaste for African society burned their way into my memory. A teacher at Makerere scorned the Baganda. They were the laziest people in the world, he said. 'They think they have a King. How can there be so many kings in the Empire? We have the King. They (the Baganda) sleep beneath banana trees and when they are hungry they open their mouths and hope bananas will drop down to feed them.' These things said to us in our childhood and youth are not easily erased. The African runs the risk of growing up haltered with an inferiority complex. I have watched many of my colleagues in Parliament, during Lancaster House discussions, in Government House, and there they are different men than when they are face to face with their own people: before Whites they become pleading, subservient, self-effacing and easily undermined in conviction. They are also, I have noticed, embarassed in front of Whites by their fellow African patriots.

A great change came over Kenya's Legislative Council with the entry of the African representatives: the Council chamber was charged with issues, antagonisms, battle. But as the African representatives were sucked into the processes of Parliament and constitutional conferences a change came over them. The more adept they became at parliamenteering the more remote they became from their own people. Of course those who were launched on a parliamentary career were an elite of the educated for only those proficient in English could qualify for the Legislative Council. This group was easily seduced by the trappings of power, overwhelmed by parliamentary traditions. The first post-Emergency generation of politicians was screened in other ways too. The Kikuyu, Meru, and Embu who were allowed to vote and stand as candidates in the first and subsequent elections were those who could produce loyalty certificates; not only had they taken no part in their peoples' political struggles, but their claim to political leadership had to be endorsed by the White man's government. All too easily members of these élites, the educated or the government-approved, fell victim to the lure of career politics. To the early generation of leaders, politics meant struggle, keeping close to the people to maintain their confidence, building unity to overcome the powerful enemy of colonial rule. To the later generations of leaders, especially those of the post-colonial era, politics can mean public standing, handsome salaries, shiny motor cars, and the manipulation of party branch and government office to stay in power because it brings personal advantage.

The opportunist or career politician can be the ruin of his country. External forces, for their own ulterior motives, are waiting to exploit the susceptibilities of politicians. The object of neo-colonialism is to change the alignment of independence forces in favour of imperialism, to place power in the hands of those who will forsake the national interest to advance themselves. Manipulating office for self-interest —using a civil service post to acquire land and property, an M.P.'s salary, perks, and opportunities to launch on a business career—is a short step to corruption. The spirit of national reconstruction is killed. An inner core of party leaders accumulate office inside the party and in government, a vast edifice of self-interest is erected while the people wait for lands, jobs, schools, and hospitals. The man in the street or in the field is called upon to work hard, to sacrifice for freedom; yet he sees the ostentatious display of wealth by government leaders and administrators who earn salaries of astronomical sums compared with his earnings. The people begin to ponder the meaning of *uhuru*.

The prostitution of our independence aims for self-interest is not an inevitable development. But it can happen. When the era of formal independence begins, this is not the end of our road, but only a new beginning in the fight for full freedom.

I could complete no description of my political life and our struggle in Kenya without writing about Pio Pinto who was assassinated outside his house early in the morning of 24 February 1965. Pio Gama Pinto was a great Kenyan patriot. He leaves a gap in our political struggle for full freedom that few men—none that I know—can fill. I first met Pinto in 1952 when he worked as an official of the Kenya Indian Congress to try to break the pattern of its conservative policies and get the Asians of Kenya to throw themselves fully into the African liberation struggle. Pinto might have been a Goan but he was as African as the truest Kenyan nationalist. There is no phase of our struggle in which he did not play an invaluable part. When the repression was launched against KAU, Pinto organized political defences. When fighting started from the forests Pinto maintained political liaison and supplied arms and money to the fighters from supply lines in Nairobi. When the authorities caught up with his activities, he served his term of detention. When he was released and free from restriction he devoted himself to the campaign for the release of the other detainees and the support of their dependents. He was a brilliant organizer and resourceful political leader. He threw himself into helping KANU win the 1961 elections, into founding our independent press, into the campaign for

East African Federation, into the struggle against imperialism, especially in a cause dear to his heart, the liberation of Portugal's colonies. He was a conscientious member of the Central Legislative Assembly and one of Kenya's delegates to the Afro-Asian Solidarity Conference at Moshi in 1963. Elected to our parliament in July 1964, he had but a few months of work there, but he set to it with the vigour and devotion that made Pinto a special man. He was a dedicated and intelligent socialist, prepared to sacrifice to the limit for our people, but determined that we should not lose the battle to build real Kenya independence and a social and economic system that would lead to real advance for our population. At his funeral, when the country was shocked and angry at his killing, I said that just as Lumumba had been murdered during the course of his heroic activities, so did Pio Pinto die. It may be some years before Kenyans see the full worth of Pinto and the part he played in our struggle before and after independence but there must come the time when this is well understood. Who were his enemies, if he were such a genuine patriot? The forces that knowingly or unwittingly are helping imperialism keep a grip on Kenya, those who have sacrificed the national advance to sectional or personal interests.

CHAPTER FOURTEEN

Obstacles to Uhuru

DECEMBER 12 1963 marked the end of sixty-eight years of colonial rule. Kenya was Africa's thirty-fourth independent country. At midnight Nairobi's Independence Arena was plunged into darkness while the Union Jack was hauled down; at one minute after midnight, in full floodlighting, our black, red, green, and white flag of Independent Kenya was hoisted to the standard to the shouts of the people. It was Uganda's Premier Obote whose speech made the telling point: 'Today,' he said, 'is the day on which Kenya formally joins Algeria at the high rank of being the hero of colonial Africa. The struggle in Kenya was bitter. Many people lost their lives. May they not look backwards. May they make their hard-won independence a reality. The past cannot be forgotten but must be forgiven. It cannot be forgotten because it is the past not only of Kenya but of world history.'[1]

Kenyatta's own speech inexplicably made no mention of the people who had laid down their lives in the struggle, the fighters of the forests and the camps who have been in danger in Kenya of becoming the forgotten men of the freedom fight because it suits the ambitions of the self-seeking politicians to divert our people from the real freedom aims of our people. In independent Kenya old colonial attitudes

[1] Daily Nation 13 Dec. 1963.

253

whipped up against the armed struggle persist, and this struggle led by Dedan Kimathi has not been recognized and honoured as the turning point in the advance towards *uhuru*. In a debate in our Parliament[1] on charges levelled by Kaggia of discrimination against freedom fighters, Ole Tiptip (today Assistant Minister for Commerce and Industry) is on record as having said 'I believe we obtained our independence in a very nice way at the instigation of the British Government but not through fighting in the forest!'[2]

Most politicians have not been as foolish as to openly denounce the forest fighters but rather have they connived at letting this period sink into forgetfulness. I have written this book because the present generation must learn from the total experience of the *uhuru* struggle if it is to save itself.

During the Emergency years the struggle was intensely bitter, but it was open conflict. Without the forest fighters in the so-called 'Mau Mau' period, Kenya's independence

---

[1] Govt. of Kenya, House of Representatives, Official Report, 26 November 1964, Col. 4661.

[2] Tragically in the statement in January 1965 (published in *Kenya Digest*, 18 Jan. 1965, as 'Minister Warns the Outlaws') by Kenya's Minister for Internal Security and Defence, Dr Mungai, forest fighters and *shifta* (the Somali fighting the Kenya Army on our northern frontier) were lumped together as 'outlaws who will be pursued and brought to punishment by the force of law'. By the time of independence some forest fighters had become used to a life beyond the law and could not easily adjust to normal conditions. Many of them came out to join the independence celebrations, and Munywa Waiyaki played a leading role in the talks that led to their return to normal life. But, for these men—and those who stayed in the forest to become raiders until two of their leaders were tragically and pitifully shot by our security forces—the Government has had no sound rehabilitation plan. The freedom fighters were thrown on to their own resources. Many of them found their land had been confiscated in their absence and they are among the worst sufferers from land shortage today. One of the reasons I had pressed so hard for the release of the camp detainees was that it was vital to begin their early rehabilitation and absorption into the national life, and to give recognition to their contribution to *uhuru*. Even when the detainees were released from the camps, the old colonial regime treated these people as outcasts and left them landless, jobless and homeless; our *uhuru* Government inherited this policy of neglect and far too many of the rotten and wrong attitudes.

would still be a dream in the minds of a few visionary politicians, for the rising in Kenya brought independence nearer not only for Kenya but, in precipitating an adaptation in British colonial policy, for the whole of East Africa.

But freedom for Kenya came not at victory point, as in Algeria, at the climax of the military rising, but only five years later, in staggered stages after the administrators of the colonial system had made preparations for the timing and the manner of the independence take-over. I have tried to describe in detail how every type of local separatism and tribalism was encouraged to prevent a strong national movement; how, when settler groups could no longer protect their interests in the names of White parties, from the benches of the legislature, they switched to lobby, caucus and backroom activity, and then used African political movements, especially KADU and *majimbo*, to project settler policies. By the time it became clear that KANU could not be stopped from heading the first independence government, the ground had been laid by settler activity and by careful Colonial Office planning, for the slowing down of the full achievement of our independence aims.

Some of us were, perhaps, slow to realize that the time when accession to independence was progress in itself has passed. Only the political and economic content of that independence can reveal whether it will have real meaning for the mass of the people. President Nasser has been foremost among those who have warned against the leaders of popular movements who give themselves up to deceptive constitutional façades while imagining that they have truly attained complete freedom.

The stage following on independence is the most dangerous. This is the point after which many national revolutions in Africa have suffered a setback, for there has been a slide back into complacency after the first victory over external control and pressure, and national governments have left too much in their countries unchanged, have not built for effective independence by transferring power and control to the authentic forces and support of the national revolution, and have forgotten that internal elements of exploitation are closely related to reactionary external pressures.

Neo-colonialism, after all, is not centred in a vacuum. It is built on to the previous colonial history of the country in which it operates, from foundations that the colonial regime lays before its ostensible departure. The object of neo-colonialism is to ensure that power is handed to men who are moderate and easily controlled, political stooges. Everything is done to ensure that the accredited heirs of colonial interests capture power. This explains the pre-independence preoccupation of the colonial power with the creation of an African middle class and the frenzy to corrupt leaders at all levels with the temptations of office and property and preferably both. Throughout Kenya's colonial period the colonial government, aided by the settlers, concentrated on infiltrating the nationalist movement and creating and encouraging divisions and splits within it. The constitutions that were devised incorporated provisions that gave institutional form to the forces of distrust and disunity which had been fostered.

Independence was on the way in East Africa, and Britain had reconciled herself, in the first instance, to the attainment of independence by Tanganyika and Uganda. But though Britain was reconciled to the fact of surrendering direct control over former colonies, she was by no means prepared to withdraw her influence completely. The strategy was to place in power in Kenya those elements that would be favourably inclined to Britain, and would safeguard her economic and military interests. This explains the never-ceasing efforts to foster moderate elements and to try to weaken the genuine progressive nationalists who recognized the forces of neo-colonialism and would not cooperate with them.

256

Silencing the militants and encouraging the moderate political spokesmen was one aspect of neo-colonialism; another aspect was the economic burden with which Kenya was saddled from the start of *uhuru* and the economic directions that were laid down irreversibly for us. As independence approached we were saddled with ever-increasing financial obligations arising out of Britain's subsidization of the exodus of settlers and civil servants and the land compensation policies established for us. Britain seemed more concerned with arranging compensation for those who were leaving Kenya than the state of things they would leave behind for the people of Kenya.

The period of the KADU Cabinet of 1961, in which there were four influential settler Ministers, was used to open negotiations with the British Government for the rescue oi settler interests. Two thorny questions went hand in hand through the protracted negotiations of the Lancaster House Conferences: the timing of self-government and independence, and the cry of compensation for the settlers and British civil servants. By the time we achieved fresh national elections and the independence constitutions under which KANU's government came to power, settler compensation schemes were well sewn up. We must admit that KANU pursued without question land and compensation policies embarked upon before we were in power.[1]

The Maudling scheme, for instance, fixed the purchase of settler acres at 1959 prices. 1959 was the last year of unchallenged settler rule and therefore of boom prices for land. Land bought by settlers for a pound or two when the White Highlands policy placed the country wide open for settler acquisition was bought back from them for £10 an

[1] More than that, KANU inherited the old evils of land consolidation programmes carried out during the Emergency which deprived of land many who had been detained. It has been largely due to the efforts of Kaggia to have this injustice corrected, that, for example, the Fort Hall area is being reconsolidated.

acre. During the pre-independence period I was totally against our concluding policy commitments with the British Government. A poor man cannot negotiate equally with a man of property, and dependent Kenya could not negotiate equally with Britain, her ruler. We hear, incidentally, a good deal about the massive economic aid from Britain. I have always considered Britain's 'golden handshakes' given on independence as more glittering than golden. The amounts of aid given Kenya are more impressive on paper, as book-keeping entries, than as the wherewithal to meet poverty and pay for development. The great bulk of this aid[1] was earmarked for payment of compensation to settlers and compensation and pensions to British civil servants, for the buying out by Kenya of British military installations, for the cancellation of a loan which Britain made to Kenya to prosecute the Emergency. Of this so-called aid an in-significant amount generated economic activity in Kenya itself.

The first settlement schemes prepared under Britain's guidance and executed by a Ministry top-heavy with old style civil servants (the former settler-owners were employed as settlement officers) was rushed through in anticipation of independence to take the steam out of the land issue, ever a raging grievance in Kenya, and as an overture to African political forces. The Coalition Cabinet in which the KANU Ministers were Kenyatta, McKenzie, Mboya, Gichuru, and Chokwe sanctioned the Kinangop Scheme which has proved

[1] 'The United Kingdom is providing Kenya with more than £60,000,000 in money, equipment and services as an independence settlement. Money given exceeds £36,000,000, whilst loans and services are valued at £23,000,000. Over £12,000,000 is to be spent on land settlement, £10,000,000 to assist the Kenya Civil Service in recruiting technical experts from overseas and £8,500,000 on development. Military aid is worth £10,000,000: Kenya has already made a start in creating a Navy and Air Force. Existing loan repayment obligations worth £6,000,000 have been cancelled, and £14,000,000 will provide compensation and pensions for expatriate civil servants who are prematurely retired.'—Overseas Survey, 1965, page 96.

virtually a write-off: the planners of this settlement ignored the basic ecological deficiencies of the area, so it is not surprising that production dropped sharply under the settlement scheme. There have been other settlement schemes, of course, not all as disastrous as Kinangop.

Our government's land policy was hobbled from the start by wrong policies inflicted on us during the negotiations for independence. The country's Bill of Rights, negotiated as part of the Constitution, contains the key clause on property rights which obligates us to pay compensation for settler farms. When land settlement is completed it will have cost Kenya £26 million to accommodate 36,000 families on the land.[1] Compensation must be paid in cash and not by bond: this is laid down in the Constitution. The economic implications for the country's economy of the settlement schemes are extremely serious because the compensation sums being paid the settlers—and prices paid for settler farms have been excessively high—are drained from the national resources. It is one thing to borrow and repay for productive assets, but quite another to borrow huge sums which are promptly lost to our country when they are paid to the settler-sellers at the source of the loan, Great Britain. These settlement schemes are included in Kenya's development vote, but they are not real development except where new assets are created on the farms, because the cash paid the settlers has left the country. (It was a condition of purchase under the settlement schemes that payment be made in Britain.) The entire settler compensation exercise has been mounted on borrowed British Government and World Bank money (plus some direct grants from Britain) and has made a huge addition to Kenya's national debt. The 36,000 families are being settled on one million acres of land formerly owned by European settlers. But when settlement schemes were inaugurated, European farmers

[1] Most of the high-density settlement schemes are in a bad way.

owned eight million acres of land. The settlement schemes thus cover only one-eighth of the land formerly held by Europeans.

Land settlement was an unprecedented opportunity for Kenya's government to do some drastic re-thinking and fresh planning in the field of cooperatives and even in the sector of state ownership. The division of valuable economic units into small individual holdings must inevitably hinder mechanisation, and without dynamic guidance by an active Ministry of Cooperative Development, the re-settled farms could quickly relapse to something hardly better than subsistence farming. As it is, much of the land acquired by Africans was already run down by the time it passed into African hands, because the European settler-owners were guaranteed 1959 land prices and they were not concerned to keep their farms in condition.

Cooperatives have to make a down payment of 50 per cent of the purchase price, and only then do they qualify for loans from the Land Bank and Agricultural Finance Corporation. The rate of interest is very high and there is no moratorium for repayments: repayments must start six months from the date of the loan, which puts a heavy burden on new farmers trying to develop.

The Government is clearly not trying to develop the cooperative sector of Kenya's economy. The few cooperatives that do exist have been left to struggle along as best they can. The country's Development Plan provides for the transfer each year of 100,000 acres of land,[1] out of which 80,000 acres will go to large African farmers, and 20,000 to peasant settlers. There is no provision among the 100,000 acres for cooperative development. Of over £2 million advanced by the Land Bank for land purchases since *uhuru*, only 6·7 per cent was given to cooperatives; of over £1½ million advanced by the Agricultural Finance Corporation

[1] Development Plan 1966–70, pp. 156–7.

for development purposes, only 5·3 per cent went to co-operatives.[1]

An even more disturbing trend emerges from the figures of land transfer (outside the settlement schemes) since independence. Of the total land transfers, more than half of the farms have been acquired by Europeans! Of the 1,185,299 acres of land transferred, European individuals and companies acquired 635,182 acres. Of the total land area sold to individual purchasers (excluding companies) 70 per cent was acquired by Europeans. The figures are given in the table below. Since *uhuru* European settlers have cashed in on the highly inflated prices paid for their land when it was bought for resettlement schemes. Then, their London bank balances swollen, they turned to apply for

LAND TRANSFERS OUTSIDE THE SETTLEMENT
SCHEMES SINCE INDEPENDENCE[1]

	African	European	Asian	Total
Individuals	62,502	159,777	5,503	227,782
Cooperatives	122,297	—	—	122,297
Partnerships	171,860	38,000	17,087	226,947
Companies	110,596	437,405	60,322	608,273
TOTAL	467,205	635,182	82,912	1,185,299

A racial breakdown shows, therefore, that Europeans acquired 54 per cent of the total, Africans acquired 39 per cent, and Asians acquired 7 per cent.

Kenya Government loan facilities, given freely, to borrow sums to buy new land in Kenya in the areas that were not marked out for re-settlement by Africans. When there was criticism in Parliament and elsewhere against the transfer of land and the granting of loans to non-citizens of Kenya and it was decided that only Kenya citizens would qualify for loans,[2] the British Government passed legislation

[1] *Cooperative Farming in the Former Non-Scheduled Areas of Kenya*, by Dr N. Newiger, 1965.
[2] House of Representatives Official Report, 5 May 1965, Col. 1874.

guaranteeing to Kenya citizens of British origin that they would automatically re-acquire British citizenship on their renunciation of Kenya citizenship.[1] This gave them the opportunity to become Kenya citizens for purposes of land and loan applications, and the privileges of Kenya citizenship; and the possibility of changing their status again when it suited them.

No one tried more conscientiously than Bildad Kaggia to put our government on the road to a land policy that would be good for Kenya's expanding economy, the interests of the landless, and the confidence of the poor people in the *uhuru* government. For his devotion to the needs of the landless in whose interests, after all, our independence revolution was fought, Kaggia was forced out of the Government. At the time, from mid-1963 to mid-1964, when he pressed for a revision of our land policies, Kaggia was Junior Minister of Education. As Member for Kandara he raised with the Ministers of Agriculture and Lands and Settlement the issue of the land confiscated from the freedom fighters who were then known as 'terrorists'. He wrote:

In my daily work in my constituency I have encountered a very difficult problem—the confiscated land—which was formerly owned by the freedom fighters who were then known as 'terrorists'.

The question now arises in the Fort Hall district more than in any other district because we are reconsolidating our land in the whole district. This does not mean that the confiscation affected Fort Hall alone. It in fact affects the whole of the Central Province.

The problem is a bit difficult because the land so confiscated was absorbed into the public purpose land and cannot be found now. But the whole question is very serious because our freedom fighters in the whole province expect a complete change of policy on the question. In my opinion, land must be found for these people somehow and somewhere.

---

[1] British Nationality Act, 1964.

To do this, I am sure a Cabinet decision is needed and I shall be glad to discuss this question with you.[1]

The reply of the Minister for Lands and Settlement (Mr J. H. Angaine) said

(1) I do not know to what extent the allegation of confiscation of land can be substantiated but no doubt the facts of the case could be established by a searching inquiry through the old administration.

I believe that any attempt to disrupt the present consolidated areas in the Central Province would lead to agricultural chaos, a grave set-back to the economy and be *in direct contravention of the spirit of Harambee whereby past differences are to be forgotten.* (my emphasis).

Kaggia wrote a memorandum[2] to draw attention not only to the problem of freedom fighters' land that was not being re-instated to the former owners, but also the plight of the evictions of African squatters from White farms. The evictions were as a result of a ruling that only those Africans who had been on a farm for a period of four years could be settled there. Some 50,000 African workers with their wives and children were liable to be displaced by the evictions and their misery was horribly reminiscent of the 1953 Kikuyu repatriations by the Emergency Government. Kaggia argued that all those who were working on farms, for however short a time, should be given priority in settlement plans.

Kaggia wrote:

Everyone in this country is very well aware of the landhunger that has existed among Africans as a result of the robbery of their land by the British Colonial Imperialists. The logical method to solve the problems passed by this robbery would have been to

---

[1] Letter dated 5 September 1963, to the Minister of Agriculture and the Ministry of Lands and Settlement.
[2] Kaggia's memorandum dated 14 April 1964.

nationalize all big estates owned by Europeans and make them either state farms, so as to alleviate unemployment, or hand them over to cooperatives formed by landless Africans.

Every day we hear of hundreds of poor helpless African families evicted from farms on various excuses. Many of these victims have lived in the farms for years with the knowledge and permission of the farm-owners. Even many of the so-called illegal squatters settled in the farms as contractors: given contracts to clear the bush or as charcoal-burners. Many of these contractors were also given pieces of land to cultivate by the settlers themselves. But now, whenever a settler wakes up from his daydream and reports to the police, these poor Africans are termed illegal squatters and physically thrown out on the roads. These inhuman settlers are not only evicting the TRUE SONS OF THE SOIL FROM THEIR OWN SOIL, but are also destroying their crops, making our poor brothers beggars in their own country.

To mention only a few instances of these daily occurrences in European farms: four farms in Naivasha—Cedar Mount Dairy, Marura Estate, Medlleton Karati and Munyu Estate—have evicted over 400 families in one month, and one farm (Munyu Estate) has also destroyed crops belonging to 200 families. The 200 families evicted from Munyu had over 100 school-going children schooling in the neighbourhood. All these children had to leave school to lead a life of wanderers. Where could these poor families and many others go? Who is going to look after them?

In another farm the manager of the farm decided to take over a piece of land from an African employee who had been cultivating it for years with the permission of the manager's predecessor. He gave the employee seven days' notice to remove all the crops from the shamba. As the employee had some semi-permanent crops such as sugar-cane, bananas, and arrow-roots, it was not easy for him to do so in seven days. However, before the seven days were over, the manager put his tractor into the shamba and uprooted all the crops.

As a result of these deliberate evictions, our Government is now faced with a very big problem of resettling thousands of poor, helpless and homeless families.

Six days later Kaggia wrote a letter[1] to 'All Cabinet Ministers'.

I have come to understand that my press statement of the 14th April on evictions from European farms has been misunderstood by some members of the Cabinet as an attack to the Minister for Settlement or to the Government.

This is a terrible misunderstanding because my statement was an attack to the unrealistic and unreasonable attitude of the settlers towards Africans who have been living in the settled areas for years.

I think the misunderstanding was due to the drastic 'editing' of my statement by the newspaper, which completely removed the 'body' of the statement, leaving only my views on what was taking place. To correct this misunderstanding, I take the liberty to circulate copies of my original statement to you all.

One thing I do admit is that the statement was strong. This is because I feel very strongly on this question and it is my personal view that the Government must rethink on the whole of the Settlement Scheme, if we are to solve the problem. The intention of the Settlement Scheme was primarily to relieve landlessness. But, today, with the prevailing craze on the part of the settlers, to sell their lands to the Board, every settler is trying to get rid of African squatters from his farm at the earliest possible time, which means that, every time a farm is bought by the Board, *more* Africans are made not only landless but homeless than can be resettled on the land. This exercise is not only creating more and more homelessness but it is also ruining the agricultural economy of the country, as the small fragments under individual farming cannot equal the big estates in production. I, therefore, think it is high time the Government changes the emphasis from small holdings to cooperative farming.

A month later Kaggia received the following letter from Jomo Kenyatta, the Prime Minister.[2]

Dear Kaggia,

I would be grateful if you could refer to the Press Release signed by you and dated 14th April 1964, and to your circular

---

[1] Letter dated 20 April 1964.   [2] Letter dated 22 May 1964.

letter PARL/SEC/PERS/11 dated 20th April 1964 addressed to all Cabinet Ministers.

1. Having carefully considered the contents of both these documents, I regret that I can draw no conclusion other than that the Press Release is a general criticism against the Government's policy of discouraging illegal squatting on private property and that it was issued in flagrant disregard of the instructions contained in my letter of last March, which I addressed to all Parliamentary Secretaries, concerning the issue of statements at variance with the Government's policy.

2. The circular letter addressed by you to Ministers was inaccurate and misleading. Settlement is not, as you state, ruining the agricultural economy and creating homelessness; the statistics available show that Settlement has not only given settlers higher incomes and better homes, but it has also resulted in many schemes, with agricultural production being much higher than it was in pre-Settlement days.[1]

3. Furthermore, I am seriously concerned at your repeated attacks on the policies of the Ministry of Lands and Settlement, and with your interference with land consolidation at Fort Hall.

4. I felt it necessary to repeat to you what I said in my letter addressed to all Parliamentary secretaries. If a Parliamentary Secretary is unwilling to support and accept collective responsibility for any of the Government's acts or policies, the only course open to him is to resign. It is a condition of your appointment that you recognize and accept this principle of collective responsibility, and I shall be glad to receive your personal assurance that incidents of the type to which I have referred will not recur.

In June 1964 Kaggia resigned his Parliamentary Secretaryship in the Ministry of Education, explaining as follows:

As a representative of the people I found it very difficult to forget the people who elected me on the basis of definite pledges,

[1] Subsequent statistics showed that this assertion was incorrect and production had indeed fallen. In any case, the total market produce revenue of smallholder re-settlement farms in 1964 amounted to only 2 per cent of the gross value of marketed produce in the small farm sector. The small farms contributed only 25 per cent of the gross value of marketed produce in Kenya. Two per cent of 25 per cent is an infinitesimal yield.

or to forget the freedom fighters who gave all they had, including their land, for the independence we are enjoying.

I, therefore, decided not to give the assurance required of me, especially as there was no indication on the Government side that the grievances listed in my Press statements, and the lengthy correspondence I carried out with the Minister for Lands and Settlement, would be satisfactorily solved. I felt that to give such an assurance and to be prepared to remain muzzled I was betraying my innermost convictions for the sake of a salary or a position.

Kaggia did much to detail a positive approach to relieve landlessness. In a statement 'Settlement Schemes or Cooperatives',[1] he argued the case for cooperatives.

It is my firm conviction that the answer in this struggle of resettling our landless Africans, without endangering the agricultural production is cooperative farming. There are two kinds of cooperatives. The first is a cooperative formed by farm workers in conjunction with their employer. The second is cooperative by Africans by themselves. I, myself, am against any kind of cooperatives where Europeans will be able to continue to exploit Africans . . . The settler owning the land would continue to be partner No. 1 in the cooperative and the African would be subject to his exploitation.

African cooperatives are the ideal solution and the Government should do its best to encourage Africans to pool their resources and strength into cooperatives, ready to work hard on the land for their own benefit and for the benefit of the country as a whole.

Today, many Africans have seen this light and are daily trying to band themselves into groups of one form or the other of cooperatives. The main difficulty facing them is how to get the land.

Without disputing the so common saying of the Minister for Lands and Settlement that there can never be 'free land' for

---

[1] Mimeographed statement dated 6 May 1964.

anyone, I think it is high time that the Government reconsiders this, if the economy of this country is to be maintained. One can recall the time when Colonial Governors were inducing new settlers from Europe to farm in Kenya by giving them free land. The aim was not to offer free land gifts, but to boost the agricultural production of the country and they succeeded. Now, as we all agree that Kenya will continue to depend on agricultural economy for many years, could there be too high a price to pay for increased production?

With a view to increasing the agricultural production, the Government must be prepared to set aside farms to be handed over to properly organized cooperative societies without asking the cooperatives to buy the land first. The Government should provide managers and experts to direct these cooperatives, and development loans, so as to ensure proper management and the highest production.

These cooperatives must be formed by not all landless Africans but Africans interested in farming. They must be people who are prepared to work hard on the land.

They should form themselves in the following manner:—

    (i) people who have been working in one farm;

    (ii) people who have already any other binding factor, such as partnership in a company or even clanship.

In this way, the Government will save all the money now being spent on splitting the big farms, survey and settlement officers, etc. These cooperatives will be able to farm well and will experience no difficulty in paying back their loans and, ultimately will do a lot to increase agricultural production in the country. They will also be able to employ workers.

The Government finally accepted that the 1959 prices paid in the early purchases against which Kaggia and others had protested strongly were too high, and in subsequent schemes the valuations were more realistically based, although the British Government, through the British High Commission exerted pressure for higher prices.

Kaggia resigned his government job. I remained in the Cabinet (where it seemed to me my relations with Kenyatta

were strained because he knew I supported Kaggia on the
land issue, and because he also knew I was critical of his,
Kenyatta's, acquisition of large farms, as were Achieng
Oneko and Pinto) but I was convinced that, despite all the
difficulties, our Government, with KANU behind it, could
set a course for full independence, political and economic,
and a foreign policy of non-alignment, as set out in KANU's
Constitution.

*   *   *

KANU, the party, it seemed to me, was the key to our
advance. If the party could be associated with policy-making
at all levels, including the Cabinet level, the whole national
effort could be galvanized for advance. No popular policy
would be possible without a strong and vigorous party.
Where there was no united and powerful national movement
neo-colonialism moved in and thrived.

The one-party state has become a feature of very many
parts of independent Africa. The party political system of the
Westminster type grew out of a highly stratified society of
conflicting power interests. We regarded the *uhuru* period as
a culmination of the struggle for independence, when
national mobilization was needed for a set of political and
economic *uhuru* aims—expressed as 'African Socialism'—to
which all forces and economic groups in the country would
subjugate their efforts. But a one-party government could
be democratic only if the mass of the people were associated
with policy-making at all levels, if the people were drawn
into the running of the party, if national issues were discussed in the branches, at public meetings, at conferences,
in our newspapers, among the women and the youth; if
careful thought was given to the role of the party in relation
to the administration so that civil servants trained in pre-
colonial attitudes could not, in the day-to-day running of the
country, undo the best plans made by the political leadership.

The existence of one party, an umbrella party, meant that all policy decisions and differences had to be hammered out within the party. There could be fierce controversy, but once majority decisions were taken through democratic process they had to be accepted. Differences of opinion there would inevitably be, but they would have to be resolved within the ranks of the party, by full and open discussion, not by intrigue and manoeuvre, or the rousing of local or tribal support. Discipline was essential to unity. The man who appeared on a party platform one day to take part in open discussion, but met the next week in a caucus of his personal or tribal followers to plan counter decisions sabotaged our national cause.

The party, as I saw it, was the guardian of our *uhuru* aims. A vigorous party organization that made public representatives subject to discipline and whose organisers were trained in the spirit of sacrifice for *uhuru* was the only guarantee against politicians jockeying for position to further their own ambitions. Since the formation of KANU in 1960, during the general elections of 1961 and 1963, we had been pursued by the devils of personality rivalry, tribal allegiance, and the undermining of party discipline.

Two things were essential for a strong party: an independent party press and a training school for party officials. Pio Pinto was a moving spirit in the establishment of Pan-Africa Press which published a weekly in Dhluo '*Nyanza Times*', a weekly in Swahili '*Sauti ya Mwafrika*' and a bi-monthly in English '*Pan Africa*'; and in the formation of the Lumumba Institute. Kenyatta performed the opening ceremony of the Lumumba Institute at the end of 1964 during the *Jamhuri* Celebrations of the declaration of Kenya as a Republic. The Institute, he said, was a training centre for KANU party cadres, teachers, journalists, and civil servants. It was to act as the party school of KANU, 'to define, teach and popularize African socialism in the context of universally accepted principles and practices of socialism to instil the spirit of *harambee*, nationalism and patriotism'. Kenyatta and I were joint trustees of the Lumumba Institute, which was run by an eight-man board including the men of the Kapenguria trial imprisoned with Kenyatta. The Institute, built on a 20-acre plot seven miles from the centre of Nairobi, off the main road to Kenyatta College, was made possible by aid from socialist countries. Requests for help and teachers were made to Western countries too, and some gifts were received. The Lumumba Institute was to be the vital centre for the training of party officials who would function at the grass root level of KANU party organization. Indispensable to *uhuru* was a live and dynamic party to serve as continual reminder to government and administration that they were in office by virtue of the peoples' decision.

But others in the Cabinet and in the party did not share this view of the role of KANU. For two years no meetings were called of the national executive or of the Governing Council. No annual delegates' conference was called after the one at the party's inception at Kiambu in 1960 and a special conference called in 1962 to draft a constitution. The new constitution stipulated that the post of party Secretary-General should not be filled by anyone holding a government post. Mboya served as Secretary-General and retained his Cabinet post; KANU affairs were conducted according to the new constitution with the exception of the clause that did not accommodate Mboya's ambitions. After the Kiambu Conference there were no further elections. Branches in most parts of the country were allowed to die; or at most were used at election time as election machines or to hang out the flags, usher the crowds and cheer an M.P. or Cabinet Minister at a public rally. Membership was not recruited, membership dues were not collected. Head-quarters and branch rents, office post office box rentals and telephone accounts went unpaid, and telephones were disconnected. As an arm of the government for popularizing development programmes, for encouraging the discussion of policy, for keeping the people alive to the aim of *uhuru*, or the government alive to the needs of the people, the party was paralysed.

The party was marking time, but the spirit of *uhuru* still beat strongly in other quarters. The KANU Parliamentary Group, in which the back-benchers were very vocal, became a live-wire centre for policy pressure and initiatives. The first major test of the strength of the peoples' elected representatives came on the issue of Federation.

*   *   *

East African Federation was an old concept that went back to the 'twenties, but the closer union of Uganda, Kenya and Tanganyika that the settlers wanted was one they could dominate, something like the Central African Federation. A Royal Commission inquired into Federation in 1929 and explicitly recognized in its report that a closer union of this type would be unacceptable to the African people. The Joint Parliamentary Select Committee of 1931[1] recommended that such allegations as discrimination in allocation of revenues unfavourable to the African people and the land problem ought to be first investigated, and the notorious 1934 Carter Commission on Land arose out of this. In other words it was recognized at this time that glaring differences in land policy in the three territories had to be eliminated before a common approach would succeed. After the second world war a more restricted approach to the problem resulted in the creation of the East African High Commission to administer certain common services, but in all important respects the three colonial territories were run by three

[1] See Statement of the Conclusions of His Majesty's Government, as regards closer union in East Africa. CMD 3574.

(above)
The author is received by Premier Chou en Lai in Peking, 1960. Wera Ambitho, then secretary of the Kenya Office in Cairo, is on the right.

Pio Gama Pinto cheered after his election to Parliament in 1964. (left)

Joe Murumbi and the author at Nairobi airport after returning from a mission to the Soviet Union, 1964. (right)

Independence Day celebrations, December 1963: (*left to right*) the author, Kenyatta, James
Gichuru, Tom Mboya.

The author welcomes to Nairobi (1964) Mohamed Fayek, President Nasser's adviser on
African affairs. In the background to the right is Pio Gama Pinto.

separate colonial administrations. In July 1961 the East African Common Services Organization was established to centralize the administration of East Africa's customs, excise, revenue, currency, land, sea and air transport, posts and telegraphs and radio communication, and education. A Central Legislative Assembly grew out of the existing nominated advisory council so that there was the nucleus of a federal parliament as well as joint administration of services.

Federation became a totally different proposition once the period of *uhuru* began. In the colonial era Federation would have meant tighter control over the African people of the three territories and the extension to Uganda and Tanganyika of Kenya's most virulent form of settler domination and racialism. Under *uhuru* the political unity of East Africa would have enormous repercussions from the international point of view. The united strength of the millions of Uganda, Tanganyika and Kenya would make East Africa a force to be reckoned with in international affairs, and would make it the largest political unit in Africa after Nigeria and Egypt. Of course, Federation involves tricky questions like the division of powers between Federal government and regional governments, the determination of the relative strengths of central government and the degree of autonomy of the constituent units of the Federation, but the interests of freedom for Africa demanded that the three territories put their heads together to solve these problems. For there are the enormous economic advantages of Federation in a continent where colonialism has led to balkanization and the creation of African countries that cannot be economically viable, whose boundaries were artificially drawn by contesting colonial powers to define their empires and did not necessarily correspond with ethnic and other realities, like the division of the Masai between Kenya and Tanganyika. Federation could dramatically accelerate the impetus for development in all three countries. Our economic needs cry out for a federation of the three territories which between them have a common market of 27 million people. Inter-territorial planning, development of industry and trade could enormously raise the level of all our people and bring incalculable economic benefits to all three countries. Industrial or other facilities that a country of seven million could not afford would be economically feasible for a unit of 27 million. The scope for mutual planning and cooperation would be endless.

Nyerere's recognition of the importance of Federation for the peoples of East Africa was shown by his willingness to postpone independence for Tanganyika, so that *uhuru* day for all three countries would correspond, and with it their ability to enter a Federation.

On 5 June 1963, the Heads of State of the three countries signed a formal Declaration of Intention to Federate and set up a working party to prepare the constitutional instrument for East African Federation. Uganda, in mid-1964, took a policy stand with which Kenya and Tanganyika were not in agreement, on the powers of two Houses of Parliament and questions of citizenship and external affairs which Uganda could not agree should fall under federal jurisdiction. But it was in Kenya that the progress of Federation gave us most anxiety. For, despite the bold declaration of our commitment to Federation on an official level, there were critical signs of back-pedalling in certain quarters. The KANU Parliamentary Group went into action. If delays in the formation of a Federation were coming from high places in government, the backbenchers felt that the people were solidly for Federation and that their wishes should be honoured. Together the backbenchers of two Parliaments, Kenya and Tanganyika, met under the auspices of the KANU and TANU Backbenchers Associations to draft resolutions calling strongly for

274

Federation.[1] On 15 August 1964, in a vote in Kenya's Parliament, the backbenchers instructed the government immediately to table instruments for the ratification of Federation and against the background of a major back-bench revolt against those in government and administration who were dragging their feet on Federation (and other questions) out-voted the government.

I was a member of the Cabinet and supported Kenyatta on the Federation issue, recognizing that there were many problems to be sorted out between the three territories. But as time went by the real problems were over-shadowed by personality and political manoeuvres. Nyerere had warned that the longer Federation was delayed the more difficult it would be to achieve, and his warning was borne out by events over the months. We watched a year of deteriorating relations go by as one cold war manoeuvre after another began to work in East Africa and we were forced to recognize that powerful agencies were in the field to subvert our national and Pan-African interests.

*   *   *

During 1963 and 1964 I was becoming increasingly uneasy that forces were at work trying to drive a wedge between Kenyatta and myself. The attempt to divide us and sow suspicion between us began, as I have described, at the London Constitutional Conference of 1962 at which the British Government vetoed my appointment as Finance Minister in the Coalition Cabinet, and at the time of *uhuru*

[1] The resolutions of the joint meeting at Nairobi on 7 May 1964 of the Parliamentary Groups of TANU and KANU were signed by:
  B. M. Kaggia, J. Odero Jowi, J. D. Kali, Henry Wariithi, C. M. G. Argwings-Kodhek, F. M. G. Mati, Z. M. Anyieni, E. Omolo Agar, Senator D. O. Makasembo and J. Gatuguta—for Kenya.
  Bi. Titi Mohamed, Al Noor Kassum, R. K. Mwanjisi, E. B. M. Barongo, K. R. Baghdelleh, R. S. Wambura, C. M. Kapilima, P. S. Siyovelwa, H. E. Sarwatt—for Tanganyika.

when my Ministry of Home Affairs had its most important departments placed directly under the control of the Prime Minister, and its powers clipped. Rumour and insinuation seemed to pop up at every corner. They reached a climax in mid-1964 when Kenyatta was leading our delegation to the Commonwealth Prime Ministers' Conference and it began to be whispered in places where rumours of this kind flourish that I was planning a take-over bid and would seize control of the government while the Prime Minister was away. (During his absence Kenyatta appointed Murumbi, not me, acting Prime Minister.) I campaigned through the country to speak at meetings in Ukambani, Central Province, the Coast and Nyanza to denounce these reports as mischievous and slanderous and to declare 'Kenyatta's Government is Odinga's Government'; that I had no reason to work against the man I had fought so hard to have released so that he could head our *uhuru* government.[1]

The campaign of slander and undermining was only a taste of what was to come. During 1964 there were two disturbing sets of tendencies. The first was that the Cabinet did not seem to be its own master. When we came to Cabinet meetings we were faced with decisions that had been taken outside by a group of the Ministers acting as a caucus, with or without outside advisers—we were never told. A curious example of a decision taken out of Cabinet was the occasion when we were all invited to go to the airport to meet the Commonwealth Secretary, Mr Arthur Bottomley, and there Kenyatta took me aside and said 'We are accepting Mac-Donald as High Commissioner.' (Malcolm MacDonald had been Governor-General, and, most unusually, stayed on after *uhuru* to become the High Commissioner.) The decision told me at the airport had clearly been taken in advance.

The second thing that disturbed me was that I seemed

---

[1] Kenya's daily press carried reports of my speeches at this time, as in the *East African Standard* of 13 July 1964.

repeatedly to be the victim of manipulation from forces within our country whose tactics, if not planned in conjunction with external, neo-colonial forces, nevertheless managed, with astonishing accuracy, to coincide in intention and effect. The strategy seemed to be to make my position so embarrassing for the Prime Minister that he would be forced to dismiss me.

Instances of this kind of insinuation continued steadily. The deportation in mid-1964 of Ian Henderson, the head of the C.I.D. Special Branch, and of the Assistant Commissioner of Police in Nyeri, was one such occasion. The deportation of the Nyeri Police Chief was carried out on Kenyatta's instructions. When it came to Ian Henderson, key man under Richard Catling, the Police Commissioner, but notorious in his own right and hated throughout Kenya for his role during the Emergency, the government was being made uncomfortable by the pressure put on it by Africans who could not understand at all how we could tolerate Henderson's continued presence in Kenya. Kenyatta was in a dilemma. Catling had said 'If Henderson goes, I go too.' Kenyatta asked me to take the matter in hand. I agreed to take responsibility and when the opportunity came I deported Henderson at the same time as we took deportation action against two Europeans who were making a practice of anti-African talk in hotels and other public places. The Henderson deportation brought the wrath of British expatriate circles on my head, as though I had acted independently of the Prime Minister and the Cabinet.

Another cause of misunderstanding between Kenyatta and myself was over the military training of students in socialist countries, which we had agreed upon because, before Independence, Britain would not agree to grant facilities for the training of African officers. When the trainees started to return, the slander was spread that they were 'Odinga's boys' and that I would use them against the government. All this was poison dripped into Kenyatta's ear.

Suddenly I found myself the so-called evil genius of a ruthless plot to overthrow the government. Several British newspapers carried reports in November 1964 that I had smuggled communist arms into the country, had used my office as Minister of Home Affairs to arrange their secret transport to my Ministry, and had stored the arms in the basement of the building. I knew, Jomo Kenyatta knew, and Joe Murumbi, the then Minister for External Affairs, knew, how those arms had come to be stored in the basement of my Ministry building; that they had been ordered by us before Britain handed over control of the police force to Kenya's independent government and when the Prime Minister wanted to be able, if necessary, to equip the police independently of Britain; that the arms had arrived at Nairobi airport as a shipment consigned to the Prime Minister Jomo Kenyatta; and that it was by arrangement among the three of us that I had used the vans of the Prisons Department, which fell under my Ministry, to have the consignment conveyed for storage in the building basement. (Part of the consignment was in the safekeeping of Kenyatta himself.) But no explanation was forthcoming from the Prime Minister, no statement of protection of one of its Ministers issued from the Government, and the country was left with the impression that there might possibly be some truth in these reports about my plotting. Worse than this, the removal of the arms from the basement, organized by the Ministry of Defence, was leaked to the press and reporters gathered in the early hours of the morning—while I, away from Nairobi, was not even informed of the proposed removal.

I reacted as coolly as possible to the provocations. For the most part I let them slide, watching the manoeuvrings about me as politicians curried favour with the Prime Minister, and he himself sometimes followed a policy of ignoring the insinuations about my supposed political ambitions and, occasionally, to my bewilderment, appearing to be influenced by them.

Doubts seemed to have begun in Kenyatta's head from the time of Zanzibar and the army mutinies at Colito Barracks, Dar-es-Salaam, Lanet near Nakuru in Kenya, and the Jinja army barracks near Jinja in Uganda. There is no doubt that the Zanzibar revolution of 12 January 1964 was a watershed in East Africa. This was the start of the cold war scare in East Africa on a large scale. The effects on Tanganyika and Kenya of the events of Zanzibar and after were dramatic by contrast: Tanganyika moved towards bolder, more independent pan-African policies; Kenya took a sharp turn towards reaction.

I had been to Zanzibar more than once. On one occasion I tried to mediate between the Afro-Shirazi Party (ASP) and Zanzibar Nationalist Party (ZNP), following a Pafmesca resolution that this should be the direction of pan-African influence. Another invitation was during an election campaign when Babu invited me to address meetings for the ZNP campaign. When I arrived on the island I spoke instead for Karume's Afro-Shirazi Party because I discovered this was the party that the masses followed; Babu's break with the ZNP signalled a decisive shift of alignment during the crucial period of 1963 leading to formal independence. On one occasion Babu came to Nairobi and he stayed in my house. I knew he was the force behind the new Umma Party and for all I knew he and his supporters were planning for a revolution at that time but I knew nothing definite, was told nothing, and if I had been asked my opinion anyway, would have told Babu that I would have preferred him in the leadership of the Afro-Shirazi Party. So much for the press reports that I was behind Babu, who was behind the Zanzibar revolution. As for the telephone calls that I

279

was supposed to be getting in quick succession from John Okello, these were non-existent. Zanzibar's revolution was planned by her own leaders and no others—not by me in Kenya, or by Castro in Cuba or anyone anywhere else— when the constitution was arranged in such a way that the African majority could not remove Arab domination through the ballot box. I did make a telephone call to Zanzibar but this was later to intercede with Karume when the reports circulated that the new Revolutionary Government was planning to shoot all the members of the former Cabinet. I argued against such a step and Karume assured me that he would reconsider, which he subsequently did. The press reports were more reckless and inaccurate than ever at this time because the imperialist forces received a tremendous shock and setback at the armed seizure of power by the Afro-Shirazi Party and the young men and trade unionists of the Revolutionary Council. Zanzibar's revolution, left isolated, could have been destroyed. The British and Americans were trying to persuade Kenya to intervene to restore the Sultan. (I understood that at one point British troops were at Nairobi airport ready for embarkation to Zanzibar, but Murumbi acted as a restraining force and the troops did not leave.) Instead Kenya was the first African Government to recognize the new Zanzibar Government. Tanganyika which had always advocated unity between the island and the mainland—and TANU, after all, had taken the steps that led to the formation of the forces of the Afro-Shirazi Party—came to Zanzibar's aid and asserted not only Zanzibar's right to full *uhuru*, but Tanganyika's own determination to strike out on her own independent policies, uninfluenced by the imperialist denunciation of the Zanzibar change.

The press reports insisted that I must have had a hand in the revolution because, after all, they said, John Okello was a Luo. (The press reporters who were so free with their sensational reports did not bother to find out that I never met Okello until *after* the Zanzibar events. He might be called Okello which is a common Luo name, but he is actually a member of the Lang'o tribe, and comes not from Central Nyanza, but from Uganda.) I laughed at these reports, but they became serious when I heard rumours that a certain number of Chinese had disembarked at Nairobi airport, had been put in a van and been driven to Kisumu, where they had disappeared (little wonder, since there were no Chinese arrivals) and that I had been engineering this.

A few days after this the army mutiny broke out at Lanet. I was in my house in Nairobi when Kenyatta rang me. He told me that trouble had broken out at the barracks, and requested me to stay at home, and not to leave for Kisumu. The road to Kisumu was blocked by the British army, he said. This was how I learned that Kenya had called on the British army to put down the soldiers' mutiny. We were not called to a Cabinet meeting to discuss what steps to take.

Perhaps it was the highly imaginative and slanted intelligence reports that were delivered to the Prime Minister daily by British or British-trained or British-influenced intelligence officers that were responsible for this suspicion building in Kenyatta's mind. He seemed not to recover from the shock of the army mutiny and he seemed to be plagued by a fear that the government was not safe from internal revolution. Those whose plan it was to surround the Prime Minister and find favour with him took advantage of his suspicions and there was competition within a little group to appear the man most concerned with bringing the head of the state the most impressive proof of his loyalty, even if the reports were inventions from beginning to end.

Zanzibar and the army mutinies and the use made of them by the imperialist forces had disastrous effects on Federation. The very political advantages that were so important an aspect of an East African Federation seemed to be what anti-Federation forces were trying to avoid. Nyerere went personally to Nairobi to plead for urgent progress towards East African Federation. He pointed out that unless immediate steps were taken by the three countries to set up a political and economic union, the economic imbalances existing between Tanganyika and its two neighbours, to the grave disadvantage of Tanganyika which was the poorest of the three countries, would force Tanganyika to take protective economic action. The statistics proved his case: Tanganyika had a £10 million balance of payments deficit between the goods imported the previous year from Kenya and Uganda and the Tanganyika products taken by these two countries. Under political union, Nyerere argued, it would be possible to find ways of balancing this growing economic disadvantage, and the allocation of new industries could be done on the basis of an over-all plan for the three countries. Without Federation Tanganyika would be forced to take steps to protect her own industries and her own economy, such as imposing quotas on Kenya imports and so on. Tanganyika would have to have her own currency, her own independent central bank. She had hoped for Federation and still desired it.[1] In Kenya, Tanzania found few responses to her overtures. The fading hopes of Federation did not make for better relations between the three East African countries and their leaders, and relations reached an all time low in 1965 when Kenya seized Uganda's arms convoy, as I shall explain. Some top civil servant advisers in Kenya were always against Federation, and as Federation was blocked month after month it became apparent that many politicians were afraid that though they

[1] As late as 8 July 1965 Nyerere said that Tanzania was still ready for Federation, no matter that outside influences had interfered in the hope of blocking its formation. He said, 'If we listen to foreign influences we should be made to quarrel with Kenya and Uganda but this we will not do.' He had already told President Kenyatta that if his country was ready to unite, Tanzania was also ready.

were prominent in the political hierarchy of our country, they might be small fish in a larger political unit, and they were not willing to forsake office, and to put the interests of their country before their own ambition.

* * *

As *Jamhuri*, the first anniversary of our independence, approached in December 1964, and Kenya was to become a Republic with Jomo Kenyatta as President instead of Prime Minister, I was anxious that we should achieve political party unity in the country. Surely, I argued with KADU leaders, the time for an opposition party and opposition policies was past? I used my tours to different parts of the country, whilst on administrative business of my Ministry, to sound out the leaders of the different KADU regions on their willingness to join KANU for one-party unity. Konchellah, one of the Masai leaders, was one of the first to cross the floor to KANU and as time went by there was a steady trickle into our party. In the constituencies KADU's support was being weakened by the hold of our central administration. On the eve of *Jamhuri*, KADU's hard core, led by Ngala, Masinde Muliro and Martin Shikuku crossed into our party. I worked hard to have KADU absorbed into KANU; I hoped that an augmentation of strength would ginger up the party, and, most important, would end disunity and tensions among the people so that our united national energies could be harnessed in the building of the country.

I must admit that I calculated falsely; that the merger of KADU with KANU, far from strengthening the party, introduced dangerously divisive policies and forces into KANU and made possible the dilution of KANU's policy

283

from within. Instead of KANU's policies triumphing over KADU, Ngala and his lieutenants began to work changes on KANU. I had always said that the KADU leaders and their party machine and policies were the instruments of external, settler and colonial forces; I had not foreseen that these same forces absorbed by KANU would strengthen that wing of our own party that had shown tendencies in the past to waver and to compromise on issues of pan-African advance and real Kenyan independence.

*   *   *

A year after *uhuru* several tendencies, then, were taking place simultaneously. A group in the Cabinet, growing alarmed at the strength of back bench and popular pressure, was resorting to caucus forms of procedure and was excluding some of us in the Cabinet from decision-making procedures. The party, as the expression of the will of the ordinary people, was not being allowed to function, and despite repeated requests by branches for the holding of a conference and new elections, head office stalled on this demand. KADU's joining the party gave the party officials a prolonged pretext for delaying national elections and a national conference, because all the KANU branches had to hold elections to absorb KADU members at their local levels.

It seemed to me that our leaders in government and party were retreating from the people, that every excuse was being made to avoid consulting them, and that government by a small circle of leaders could too easily be influenced by forces against the national interest. This is not something I have ever had to learn from books; it is the experience of my accumulated years in political life. I have frequently had the experience of being manipulated by political forces, but where I have judged that national unity is the prime need, I have put up with the slander and the intrigue, the rumours and the manoeuvres, because it is my conviction that in the long run the people will decide, and as they have not prestige and office to protect, but their right to land, jobs and social services, they are the best judge of policies and leaders.

I believe in making the democratic process work in the party, in government, among the people. We fought for *uhuru* so that the people may rule themselves. Direct action, not underhand diplomacy and silent intrigue by professional politicians won *uhuru*, and only popular support and popular mobilization can make it meaningful. This is one of my convictions repeated with, to some, monotonous regularity over the years. My second conviction is that at this time in history if Africa is to be really free, if we are to attain true economic independence—and let us remember that this stage is crucial for if we fail to attain true economic independence we will rob our political freedom of its lasting guarantee—we must follow a policy of non-alignment, of relations with both 'east' and 'west', with both capitalist and socialist countries. If our aid and investment come from one source only we can banish the prospect of pursuing an independent policy, for we will be brought under control by the withholding of aid, or by some other economic pressure. As an African nationalist I cannot tolerate an African regime dominated by either the 'west' or the 'east'. If non-alignment is used to justify relations with one of these worlds alone, it is not non-alignment. Kenya is still today largely part of the western sphere of interest and investment. To reach the non-aligned position we must break this predominantly western influence, and develop relations with the east. It was with the deliberate intent of making Kenya less dependent on the colonial powers that I have worked for

relations with the socialist countries, and this, not the development of relations with the west alone, is the true policy of
non-alignment for Kenya. The fiercer the attacks on the
socialist countries—and on me for visiting them—the more
convinced I became that we in the colonial countries
struggling for full freedom can find much in common with
socialist policies and economic planning, and that if the
colonial powers that have tried for so long to keep us inferior
are so alarmed at our efforts to seek friendly relations with
the socialist world, this must be the true path of non-
alignment. Non-alignment, let us remember, means that we
shall tie ourselves to no power bloc; and that while we shall
not necessarily opt for neutrality on every issue, ours will be
the freedom to decide.

The danger in Kenya has never been communism but
imperialism and its remnants. I told the Pafmesca conference at Addis Ababa that the snake in the bush is less
dangerous than the snake in our house, which is imperialism.
Why seek a non-existent enemy when we already have a
fight on our hands against the remnants of imperialism? If
communism were to prove a problem in the future we would
deal with it, I told the conference. Nothing had happened in
Kenya between the 1963 Addis Ababa Pafmesca Conference
and the end of 1964 and *Jamhuri* to make me change my
mind that no communist forces were actively plotting against
Kenya. I am convinced that the external vested interests at
play in Kenya are not Communist forces, but the result of
the involvement of an increasing number of politicians in
British, American and West German commerce and big
business.

*   *   *

Political intrigue, caucus decisions and ambitions for
office cannot thrive side by side with a vigorous, popularly-
based party machine, or democratic decision-making of any

kind. KANU itself was being left to wither but the KANU Parliamentary Group was hard at work, though far from being welcomed by the Government as a ginger group to keep contact with the people, it was resented and frowned upon.

The life and soul of the KANU Parliamentary Group, of the pressure for Federation of the attempts to build a KANU press and the Lumumba Institute to train grass-root organizers, was my close friend and associate Pio Pinto. On the morning of 24 February 1965 as Pio drove his car down the drive of his home, with his year-old daughter on the back seat, an assassin hidden behind the fence called out 'Jambo, Bwana' and shot Pio in the stomach. Moments later he was dead. Achieng Oneko told the press that day that the shooting was 'a deliberate and cowardly move in what I believe to be a planned assassination.' Two teenagers, Kisilu Mutua aged 18 and Chege Thuo aged 19, were brought to trial in what the Deputy Prosecutor described as a murder 'well-planned and efficiently executed.' A third man had been involved in the shooting, according to the witnesses, but he was never brought to trial. Thirteen hours before he was killed Pinto had told his house servant 'a man has been offered money to kill me, Kaggia, and Kali' (Kali was then Chief Government Whip).

One of the accused was sentenced to death, later commuted to life imprisonment, and the other was acquitted. During the court proceedings the names were mentioned of numbers of persons who were never brought to court to give evidence (among them Mak'Anyengo, the trade union organizer who said he wanted to be called), and the Judge, Chief Justice Sir John Ainley, commented on this:

'We may not have all been involved in the crime before us', recalling that it had been asked in Court why 'the prime mover of the whole affair' had not been more thoroughly investigated.

The car used by the assassins was never traced: the investigating officers in the case were baffled by the difficulty in finding clues to the crime. Careful plotting had been behind it.

The shock at the killing reverberated through Kenya. Parliament adjourned immediately. The day after the shooting an anonymous leaflet was distributed to all M.P.s— a demonstrably clumsy forgery designed to put us off the trail of the plotters behind Pio's murder but also, more significantly, a clue to the next phase in the conspiracy against Kenya. The leaflet said that Pinto had been getting in the way of the Chinese Communists, and the implication was that he had been a victim of the Chinese-Soviet split. It said

It is well known that the Hon. Pinto favoured the Communist cause and handled money for them, acted as their printer and spoke the words of the Communists. Recently he has been in trouble with both his Chinese and Russian bosses, and tried to satisfy both sides. It is well known that Pinto was in financial difficulty at the Pan-African press and that the debts were covered only by help from the Communists. It is also known that his friends in the Chinese and Russian embassies were constantly fighting to gain the upper hand in guiding and paying him. Only a week ago Pinto was told by the Russians that he must not work for the Chinese. When he protested that all communists must work together, he was told that it was impossible in Kenya and that he must take Russian guidance only. When he reported this to his Chinese contact, the Chinaman got furious and said that he would not allow Pinto to listen only to the Russians. Pinto became so disgusted that he threatened to go to our President Jomo Kenyatta to tell him the truth about the communists. Today he is dead.

This obvious plant was posted from Uganda. Its purpose was to distract the House from an investigation into the real forces behind the murder of one of their Members and to set them to fight a bogus 'Communism'.

A far more revealing document in the same anti-'Communist' conspiracy was a set of notes of a secret meeting of a clique of politicians that has come to be known throughout Kenya as the 'Corner Bar' meeting. The notes were compiled by someone who had been present at the meeting. The following is an abridged version of the report of the Corner Bar conspiracy:

Ronald Ngala was on the Chair at an urgent meeting held in the Corner Restaurant which was attended by the following Members of the National Assembly: Malu (Machakos); Mbesi (Kisii); Lubembe (Nairobi); Odero-Jowi (Labour); Kubai (Labour); Gachago (Settlement); G. G. Kariuki (Laikipia); Kiprotich (Kericho); Kerich (Kericho); Tipis (Narok); Senator Koinange (Kiambu); Bomet (National Member); J. Nyagah (Home Affairs); Mbogo (Embu); Malinda (National Member); Senator Kago (Nyandarua); Okwanyo (C. Nyanza) . . . at 7.30 p.m. until 11.00 p.m.

Convenors: Kiprotich, Malu, Gachago. The reasons for the meeting was said to be set-backs and defeats for the democracy loving people as shown during the period since independence. This was a meeting to find out the workable way in order to defeat the common enemy. The convenors made it clear that everybody in the group must come openly and fight an open fight without care of losing life, property or victimization.

MALU:

drew up a declaration which he said must be signed by any member of the group so that confidence among members of the group must be maintained. Each one of the people present signed this declaration. After this Malu went on enumerating the weakness of the group when faced by a few 'communists' with loud mouth. He asked why are we shaken by these few people among them Anyieni and Oduya? Suppose they were heckled, jeered and opposed in every ground, would they continue as they are doing now?

KIPROTICH:

A review must be made on the enemy strength if at all this group is to win the fight. Kiprotich said he had been a Policeman

289

and had been doing a bit of investigations as to who are responsible of spreading Communism in Kenya. He gave figures of Members of National Assembly who are communists in each Province as follows: Rift Valley 3; Central Nyanza 4; Western 2; Central 3; Eastern 1; N. Eastern 1; Coast 2; Nairobi 3. He said most Members of National Assembly are put in the pockets by accepting monies.

GACHAGO:

He knew most Ministers would support this group and every effort must be made to acquaint them with this groups move. It should be a duty of each member of this group to capture those members who are known not to side the with 'communists'. He thought Ngala was a strong leader of Kenya. He was not shaken by the might of Mzee[1] and KANU and nobody can forget what hard time he gave to KANU leadership and for this reason he thought Ngala was the right person to take the post of Vice-President and replace Jaramogi and eventually lead the country after Mzee. This suggestion was unanimously accepted by the group.

TIPIS:

He was sure the group would be supported all over the country and that every effort must be made to capture the leadership in the Parliament and the Cabinet.

ODERO-JOWI:

Every endeavour must be made to bring together all M.P.s in this group to work together with the Ministers who support this groups' principles and that whenever a member of this group has a public meeting all members of the group must attend. After discussion this was unanimously agreed and a start would be made by a meeting which will be held at Mombasa on 27/3/65.

J. NYAGAH:

Attacked Lumumba Institute and said this was intolerable since there are two Russian teachers. After a lengthy discussion it

---

[1] Kenyatta.

290

was unanimously agreed that a motion be tabled before the Parliament tomorrow demanding the Government taking over of Lumumba Institute at the same time dissolving the Board of Management. Motion was drawn up by Gachago and would be tabled by Mr Mbogoh and at same time the same motion be tabled by Senator Koinange in the Senate.

MALINDA:

brought a suggestion that Mr Ngala should table a motion calling on the nation to accept Mzee Jomo Kenyatta as a life President of Kenya so that Jaramogi's efforts be curbed. This was agreed and further agreed that all members should start working up Ngala as future President of this country.

Other tactics adopted by this group were as follows: Heckle and oppose any member or Minister who supports communism. Members should not leave the house in Parliament or Parliamentary Group meetings as this had been giving communists chance to elections. Organize the group and demand new election for the Backbenchers so that all communists be swept off the leadership. Chief Whip and Assistant Whip must be swept off. Support, applaud when member of the group is speaking in the House. Each member must subscribe to the group 10/-. A working Committee was elected—Ngala, Kiprotich, Malu, Nyagah, Mbogoh, Tipis, Gachago, Malinda, Okwanyo, Bomet. Drinks and food were served and the group looked satisfied with the progress made.

Step by step those who master-minded the Corner Bar meeting—and who knows how many other such meetings were held, and at what level of party and government?— began to put their plan into operation. We were subjected to several months of intensive but devious 'anti-Communism'. Men were judged not by what they said in Parliament or did in their constituencies, but by what the rumour-mongers said about them. Thomas Malinda, one of the specially-elected members, now Assistant Minister of Natural Resources, moved a motion in the House alleging that Communist money and arms was being smuggled into the country.[1] Challenged to substantiate his charges he left the debate in the House and did not return for the rest of the day when the motion had fallen away. The Lumumba Institute was attacked as a hotbed of 'Communism' and the attacks finally resulted in its closure. The KANU candidates for the special seats (elected by Parliament) vacated as a result of Pinto's death were defeated—on the grounds that they were under my political influence—and 'independents' were elected.

Again and again I was charged with seeking to replace the President and undermine the Government. What I wanted, I said in reply, were changes in Kenya's policy, not in the Presidency.

The same group of politicians who had opposed me when I advocated the release of Kenyatta from detention were now telling the President 'Odinga wants to overthrow your Government', I told a public meeting[2]

the imperialists have sucked our blood for a long time and even now the sucking tube is still connected to Kenya. The imperialists still have influence in the country through their stooges.

On 16 May 1965 Kenya security forces suddenly seized a convoy of lorries carrying arms—Chinese arms, the press said—that were consigned to the Uganda Government. The convoy should have been travelling up the west side of Lake Victoria but heavy rains had made the road impassable, and the convoy had diverted to Kisii bordering South Nyanza where I was that weekend addressing a KANU rally. Kenya's refusal to hand the arms back to Uganda led to an open breach between Kenya and Uganda. The Central Legislative Assembly was meeting at the time but was suspended on Uganda's angry insistence. The Kenya Government pretended that it knew nothing about the consignment of

---

[1] House of Representatives, 31 March 1965, col. 1083.
[2] 2 May 1965.

The author campaigning in 1966 after his resignation from KANU and the formation of the Kenya People's Union. (*above left*)

Achieng Oneko announces at a press conference (April 1966) his reasons for leaving the Government and joining KPU. (*above right*)

The author and Bildad Kaggia are interviewed by Mr Coward, Registrar of Societies, in connection with the registration of KPU.

Bildad Kaggia, Vice-President of KPU, with the author.

Denis Akumu, Administrative Secretary of KPU, addresses a rally in Nairobi in May 1966.

arms bound through Uganda for the rebel forces in the Congo. Uganda was shocked by this attitude of double-cross, for she said (her Attorney General and six Ministers descended on Nairobi to protest) the arms convoy had been cleared with Kenya's Minister of Defence. Some of our Cabinet members told the Uganda delegation that they believed the arms were mine and that the Uganda military were trying to cover up for me. The Uganda Ministers were shocked. They repudiated this at the meeting of representatives of the two governments called to discuss the arms fuss and demanded the return of the arms to their government. The arms were returned but not before Kenya's military heads—all British officers—had taken photographs of all the arms for their own intelligence purposes. Kenya's Minister for Defence never had the courage to admit that he had given consent to Uganda for the movement of arms through Kenya. During this arms scandal—and the previous one over arms stored in the basement of my Ministry—General Service Units (the tough para-military police unit created during the Emergency)—were posted to Nyanza. The insinuation was that if arms were discovered I would be connected with them. There was a rumour that I had stored arms somewhere in Nyanza and houses were searched. Need it be said that no arms were found?

The arms plots were not yet over. A Soviet ship docked at Mombasa with a consignment ordered officially by the Kenya Government. Soviet arms for Kenya? The suggestion was too much for some circles and the very government that had ordered the arms sent Ministers Mungai, Bruce McKenzie and Murumbi to Mombasa where they examined the shipment and reported that the arms were second-hand. Mboya said in Parliament that Soviet aid was not worth getting. The arms were turned back.

The Kenya Government made a fool of itself in both this and the Uganda arms convoy incident but the pressure was on, from certain unseen forces, for Kenya to join in the cold war and, significantly, it is from this time that Kenya's policies on the Congo and on non-alignment began to change and her relations with her immediate African neighbours took a sharp turn for the worse. The Uganda arms had been meant to reinforce the Congo nationalist forces of Gbenye and Gaston Soumialot; the timing of the arms plot was intended as a sign that Kenya could be relied on not as an ally of Pan-African liberation forces, but as a bulwark against them in the centre of Africa. Kenya's foreign policy began to be sharply reversed from this time. Ugandan and Tanzanian foreign policy was based on the strengthening of Pan-Africanism and aiding anti-Tshombe forces, for militant Pan-Africanism is the strongest bulwark against imperialist pressures on independent African states. Kenya's policy by contrast, was to copy British and American foreign policies in Africa and to undermine African unity.

Kenyatta's speeches on non-alignment from now on began to say this kind of thing:

Some people try deliberately to exploit the colonial hangover for their own interests, to serve some external force . . . To us communism is as bad as imperialism . . . It is a sad mistake that you can get more food, hospitals or schools by crying communism.

Madaraka Day, 1 June 1965

The allegation 'communism' has always been a convenient weapon. During the colonial times Kenyatta was termed a Communist, and the freedom struggle was labelled Communist-inspired. Politicians have made use of the anti-communist smear not because they hold confirmed political views but to use a stick to beat those campaigning for real consultation with the people and against corruption in public life. I ought to know. I am not a Communist but I have been a constant target of anti-communist forces for all the years of my political history.

294

I am incensed at all these declarations of 'fighting communism' when the target is really African liberation, African independence, and the right of Africans to make policies for their own countries.

In the midst of all the hullabaloo about arms plots and Communists in Kenya I read in the press a statement by the Secretariat of the Western European Union that a detailed survey of 'Communist' activities in Africa had been carried out and that the Western powers should make preparations to 'fight Communism on African soil.'[1] Whose soil is it, after all? Why should Western powers—or any powers for that matter—fight for or against any policy on African soil? Foreign countries have no right to declare their determination to make Africa a battlefield of their ideological differences. It is an insult to our dignity that a foreign power should tell us what is right for us. Nobody would quarrel with the members of the Western European Union if it determined to fight out differences of ideology within their own countries, but we would consider hostile any country that declared to the world the issues it would fight on our continent. I issued a warning at a public rally in Kisumu that it was the Americans and the British who were creating tension in Kenya, that the British High Commissioner and the American Ambassador went frequently to the President to tell him they were his only friends. I said that if the people of Kenya did not stand firm they would lose the independence they had already gained; that what was spoiling Kenya was the money given to persons to create confusion among the people, for those giving the money were determined to create trouble. I reminded the people that when we were fighting for independence the British called us 'communists'. Now the British were working through influential politicians who had taken over the cry

[1] I issued a press statement 'Western European Countries Take Heed' on 16 March 1965.

of 'communism'. If the people of Kenya elected perhaps Mr Mboya or Mr Ngala to lead the country I would have no objection, but it was not for the Americans and British to say who should be Kenya's leader. 'These people should stop working for their foreign masters', I said. As for cries of 'Communism', I was sick and tired of them for I had been hearing them all my life. I understood that in Communist countries the emphasis was on food for all. If that was what Communism meant then there was nothing wrong with that objective.

The newspapers headlined the speech 'Communism is Food.' This is the speech that created a furore throughout Kenya and was a convenient occasion for an attack against me—though this attack had been mounting for some time, and the speech was merely a convenient pretext for its intensification.

Before the Kisumu speech it had been announced in the press that I would lead the Kenya delegation to the Commonwealth Prime Minister's Conference in London. After the speech all the Cabinet Ministers except Achieng Oneko met in caucus and signed a letter to the President demanding my removal from the delegation. Some Cabinet Ministers came to me later and said they had been pressured into signing the letter; they did not say who had applied the pressure.

The next stage in the campaign was the manoeuvre to unseat me as Vice-chairman of the KANU Parliamentary Group—which was by now a shadow of its former self, and had become a tool of those who were conspiring to fight imagined 'Communism'. When I saw that there had been preliminary caucusing to edge me out of the office I left the meeting of the Group, and the country was treated to the spectacle of Ronald Ngala, former leader of KADU, arch-opponent of all KANU policies, and always one of the most obedient protégés of the colonialists, handed the vice-chairmanship of our Parliamentary Group.

The provocation continued. On United Nations Day 1965, I was present at the commemorative meeting when a Minister appeared to represent the President and to take the salute in the presence of myself as Vice-President. Next there was yet another shuffling of my functions as vice-president. Responsibility for elections was removed from my portfolio, and given to a civil servant. Then came the incident in the House when a motion of confidence in the government—then under fire, significantly, for its policy on Rhodesia as expressed by the Minister for Finance, James Gichuru, in Lagos at the time of the Commonwealth Conference on Rhodesia—was introduced by Tom Mboya, Minister for Economic Planning, but without my knowledge; and at the time I was Leader of Government Business in the House.

These provocations were clearly not accidental. They were deliberately mounted to isolate not only me but the forces I represent in the country. I tried to understand them in this light.

In the Cabinet I was being excluded from decision-making, and at one and the same time my membership of the Cabinet was used to silence me and to hold the allegiance of my supporters, not only in Nyanza but throughout the country. I was being held hostage in a Cabinet carrying out wrong policies and this was worrying me more deeply than anything else in my political life.

*   *   *

Meanwhile, in the Party things were going from bad to worse. The conference was postponed time and again while the party bosses led by Tom Mboya endeavoured to get branch executives that would accept their leadership. A series of coups was held that created crises in KANU branches in many parts of the country. Aspirant candidates would put themselves up in elections organized by their supporters, would declare themselves the new branch leadership and send their name in for registration as the new executives by the Attorney General who controls the Department of Registrar-General. (All party and trade union officials have to be registered under the Registration of Societies Act.) The leaders of the coups were inevitably recognized as the branch leadership by Tom Mboya, the KANU General Secretary. A battle to control the party was thus launched by these methods. Kaggia was one of those whose leadership was challenged in the Murang's branch.

Discontent was brewing in the KANU branches and on one occasion it boiled over when delegates from 17 branches gathered in Nairobi passed a resolution for the immediate convening of the party conference and the election of new office bearers, and carried the resolution to the party headquarters. The officials in the office called in the police and the delegation of 27 was arrested and its members subsequently charged and sentenced to one year's imprisonment for taking action liable to cause a breach of the peace. (The normal judgement for this offence would have been to warn and bind over the offenders but in this case the Court refused bail, so that the accused waited nearly three months in prison before trial, and the Attorney General personally appeared to prosecute and made a political speech alleging that the operation was 'masterminded' by someone in high circles in the country.) I appealed to the President against the stern handling of party officials who were trying to get the party headquarters to return to democratic procedure and pointed out that the Attorney General had not seen fit to act against party members who had organized coups against recognized and constitutionally elected branch officials in various parts of the country. Kaggia was among those refused licences to address meetings, even in their own constituencies. Some of my meetings were cancelled by government order, and restrictions were placed on some of my vice-presidential tours.

Suddenly, after years of delay the KANU party convention was on top of us. It was summoned without the necessary constitutional notice, and without certain other constitutional requirements being observed. Ministers, M.P.s and officials signed a protest against the hurried calling of the conference, but it was pushed ahead by the Secretary General and the President. A new KANU constitution, approved not by the Conference as required under the functioning constitution, but by the KANU Parliamentary Group, was rushed through. It replaced the party vice-presidency (the post I had held) with seven provincial vice-presidents and one for Nairobi. This KANU conference held at Limuru in March 1966 took on the pattern of a closely stage-managed American-type political convention. The delegates were accommodated in hotels (who paid the bills?), lavishly entertained (including air-trips over Nairobi, a State House banquet and a trip to a game park), and were driven in hired transport to the conference sessions which were held about 18 miles from where they were accommodated. Before the Limuru Conference KANU's bank account was overdrawn, yet someone paid these bills.

In the elections for vice-president of the Central Province, Kaggia was elected by a majority of voters; but that election was declared null and void, a new election was held in which more delegates arrived to vote and James Gichuru became the new vice-president.

I made a speech in which I charged that the conference had been hand-picked, some delegates picked by Moi, some by Ngala, and that while some accredited delegates were not present, men had been brought overnight from Central Province to defeat Kaggia. I warned that if the President allowed the conference to continue in this way he would succeed only in dividing the country.

Round the Limuru Conference was whipped as much 'anti-Communist' feeling as possible. This was a preparation for my demotion in the Party, and final exclusion from the Party. To lend weight to the rumours and whispered allegations that I was a stooge of the 'Communists', the Government ordered the expulsion of eleven members of the diplomatic staffs of several socialist countries and some journalists. It was alleged that they were engaged in subversive activities, but the country was not told the nature of the subversion.

*   *   *

This account of events is an attempt to explain the background to my resignation from the KANU Government and the formation of the new party which I lead, the Kenya People's Union (the KPU). In my letter of resignation to President Kenyatta I wrote about the series of pin-pricks to which I had been subjected and that I had tried always 'to remain calm and cool' because I was 'aware all along that my appointment was after strong public pressure against your will.'

But I added:

You have not given any consideration to me as your number 2 in State matters. I have a conscience and this in fact does prick me when I earn public money but with no job to do. I consider this a waste of public money and I am worried lest the future generation questions my sincerity, when they would learn that I allowed myself to hold a sinecure post in the midst of poverty and misery in our country. With this realization, I cannot continue to hold this position any longer and I hereby tender my resignation.

In his statement of resignation from the Cabinet, Achieng Oneko recalled the years he and Kenyatta had spent in detention together under the colonial regime. He said it

300

would have seemed unbelievable at that time that he and Jomo Kenyatta would ever part company, but this was a fact of life which had to be faced. He said that his continued presence in the Government was proving an embarrassment to his remaining friends and that he was concerned lest it might further the interests of 'a small clique of individuals' who formed a caucus within the Kenya African National Union. It was they who had been the cause of the disunity within the Cabinet, which was not only regrettable but could have been avoided. He explained that he disagreed with present policies on foreign affairs, land, agriculture, federation and foreign loans, and accused the Government of failing to carry out its promises made in the KANU election manifesto. Under its present construction Oneko said, Kenya was not non-aligned. Kenya was a capitalist country with military arrangements with Britain and the Government had taken no effective steps to meet its obligations of achieving social equality by the nationalization of various private concerns and the limitation of private property. Among the concerns he listed that should be taken over by the state were the East African Power and Lighting Company and Kenya Bus Services. Oneko accused some Ministers of being motivated by the desire for personal gain. Personal gain had become the guiding star in the Party. He said that he had been considering his position for some time, but decided that when the radio network of his own Ministry (The Voice of Kenya) was being used daily to attack him personally through innuendo he had finally decided 'enough is enough'. He had found it intolerable to work in an atmosphere polluted with political 'ganging up' and intrigue by certain leaders—a practice based not on personality as many people were made to believe, but on the general policies of the Government and their implementation.[1]

[1] Achieng Oneko's resignation statement of April 1966.

We had been strong advocates of the building of one party for Kenya's independence era. But one national party must grow out of national unity, for national reconstruction, and had to have a policy forged in common understanding and directions. In KANU it was quite clear we were not agreed on the directions. Everyone advocates 'African Socialism' but in the case of most party and government leaders this has become a cloak for the practice of total capitalism. These politicians want to build a capitalist system in the image of Western capitalism but are too embarrassed or dishonest to call it that. Their interpretation of independence and 'African Socialism' is that they should move into the jobs and privileges previously held by the settlers. If Kenya started *uhuru* without an African élite class she is now rapidly acquiring one. Ministers and top civil servants compete with one another to buy more farms, acquire more directorships and own bigger cars and grander houses.

False standards are set with salary scales for M.P.s, Ministers and top civil servants that the country cannot possibly afford in a time when examples not of extravagance but of austerity and sacrifice should be set. In 1963 M.P.s earned £620 a year. This was increased to £840, then to £1200 a year, making three increases and a doubling of salary in less than three years. (And the £100 a month is augmented by a daily sitting allowance, plus mileage and other allowances.) Junior Ministers earn £2260 a year. The President's salary has been fixed at £15,000 a year tax free and including other emoluments. KANU's present over-weighted government of 46 ministers and junior ministers earn between them something in the region of a quarter of a million pounds sterling a year, enough to provide housing for 500 families. Civil servants are still paid according to the old colonial salary structure. In six months an M.P. receives more money than the average peasant earns in half a life-time. This salary scale reflects nothing like the true economic standards in the country, and can only encourage the emergence of a governing group that is almost as remote from the mass of the people as were the former colonial administrators.

High salaries are not the whole of the story. Gradually political control and business interests have begun to inter-twine. Many have begun to use their positions in politics to entrench themselves as a propertied economic group. A self-entrenched class of politician-businessmen is growing up in the cities, and in the countryside a large land-owning class. When the Sessional Paper on African socialism was debated in Parliament the Government undertook to set up a committee[1] to look into the question of fixing a ceiling on individual land-ownership, in other words, limiting the number and size of holdings by individuals. Kaggia proposed a motion to the effect in Parliament, but this didn't seem to have made any difference. The issue has been quietly forgotten. As the KPU manifesto[2] says:

The Government and KANU are unable to take drastic action over land for many obvious reasons. Its ideological commitment to capitalism is reinforced by the ownership by many individual members of the Government of hundreds and even thousands of acres of land. Most of the ministers and assistant ministers own big estates, some of them more than one. This being so, they cannot issue policies which will benefit the *wananchi*.[3]

They have become the allies of the settlers who fully appreciate the position. It is an irony of history that European settlers' organizations should be swearing loyalty to the Government. They have good reason to support their friends.

The *wananchi* cannot tolerate this situation. Not only are many European settlers still sitting on big farms, but we are getting a new class of Blundells, Delameres, and Briggs, deliberately created.

[1] House of Representatives Official Report, 5 May 1965. Col. 1860.
[2] The first instalment of the policy of the Kenya People's Union, on land, agriculture, the constitution, education, and socialism, was published on 19 May 1966.
[3] The masses.

A radical change in land policy is obviously necessary. The *wananchi* shed their blood to secure it. They will not tolerate the present position. The KPU is fully committed to secure this change, to correct the highly unjust and inequitable present distribution of land. It recognizes that the issue is a complex one, but it cannot be evaded. The KPU's land programme includes the following measures:

1) Distribution of free land to the neediest, including squatters and those who lost their lands in the struggle for independence, either by expropriation or through land consolidation. The KPU recognizes that consolidation in areas affected is now an accomplished fact and it would be undesirable to disturb it. Those who are now owners of consolidated land will be left in undisturbed possession. Compensation will, therefore, take the form of land acquired from European settlers.

2) Settlers who are not citizens cannot be allowed to continue in ownership of vast areas of high potential land. The KPU will take measures to restrict ownership of such land to Kenya citizens.

3) Cooperative farming on land taken over from European settlers will be preferred and encouraged, in line with the socialist policy of the KPU.

4) The KPU will fight for a reduction in the size of farms held by individuals. It believes that this is an absolutely necessary measure. In this way, more land will be made available to the *wananchi*. We do not want a new class of big landlords.

5) Once all farms are reduced to a size consistent with democracy and socialism, all individual owners will be given maximum assistance to develop their holdings.

6) Land consolidation will be promoted but only in a democratic manner, according to the wishes of the people in particular areas. In the pastoral areas, particular care will be taken to ensure that individuals do not grasp too much for themselves, to the detriment of the rest of the population in these areas. KPU will honour the rights of tribes and clans to their land.

Under the KANU government the peasant has for the most part remained as he always was. The wealth of the privileged few in government has had a demoralizing effect on their poor countrymen called on to make sacrifices for *uhuru*. The politicians have clung to position and been prepared to abandon principle because they have developed an appetite for power and for property that grows with each new farm or promotion. This is a leadership that has not shown the moral or the intellectual strength to withstand the pressure of civil service advisers trained in the old ways of colonial administration or the external economic and political pressures working against true Kenyan independence.

* * *

Workers looked to *uhuru* with confidence and have slowly been losing hope that this is a government for the working people, and one in touch with their needs and grievances.

In 1961 there were 615,000 in employment in Kenya; by 1965 the figure had dropped to 586,000. Africanization in industry has been painfully slow and artisan training schemes half-hearted. Each year, for all the propaganda about its housing record, the *uhuru* government has spent less on housing; and of the amounts for housing voted in the estimates, housing planning authorities are lucky to get half. In the towns the workers are as over-crowded as they were in colonial times, three or four families sharing a house, and beds all around the walls. Workers would wait with patience for the fruits of *uhuru* to mature if they had confidence tha this government was composed of leaders genuinely concerned with their future. But the history of the trade union movement in Kenya is one of attempts from external forces to infiltrate the unions and subsidize them to follow tame policies. Let us first look at a brief outline of the development of the trade union movement since *uhuru*.

The affiliation of the Kenya Federation of Labour to the western-orientated and controlled International Confederation of Free Trade Unions (ICFTU) resulted in a series of breakaways led by Ochwada, Gachago, Kubai, Mutiso, Wachira and Ohanga. Continued ICFTU domination of the KFL led to a fresh and major split, this time spearheaded by Akumu, Gichohi, Oduya, Makanyengo, Wachira and Mutiso. This was in 1964. The new Federation was called the Kenya Federation of Progressive Trade Unions, and later renamed the Kenya African Workers' Congress. The Congress was registered and rallied workers behind it. Numbers of unions broke from the KFL, including the dockworkers, the oil workers, the Common Services Union, the railway, building and construction union, the quarry and mine workers, the Salaried Workers' Association and it was clear that KFL was losing heavily to the KAWC. The KAWC started with a minority of the unions affiliated to it, but it had mass support even in the unions affiliated to the KFL. It held enormous workers' rallies in Nairobi and Mombasa, and in Kisumu during 1964 and 1965. Both union federations were registered, and they functioned side by side, with the KAWC continuing to rally most workers' support. Minister of Labour Mwendwa was demonstrably sympathetic to the KFL and went out of his way to give it facilities. Examples of this favouritism were the recognition in Kenya of the KFL as the only representative body of Kenya workers at the ILO; and the admission of the KFL as the only trade union body allowed to sit on the Labour Advisory Board, a statutory body.

The Tripartite Agreement, under which government, employers' and workers' organizations not only declared a moratorium on retrenchment but also on strikes, was done with KFL connivance. The KAWC was opposed to the Tripartite Agreement because it arrested wage advances when wages were still very low, and when the government should have made the employers absorb more workers without employing any wage restraint. The KAWC maintained that the workers should have been the last people penalized to cope with unemployment, and this was a policy of being soft with the employers.

A number of unions affiliated to the KAWC broke the Tripartite Agreement, followed by some of the unions affiliated to the KFL. By the time the Tripartite Agreement ended there was no ground to refuse the KAWC recognition; it had proved it had the mass backing of the workers.

The President was under strong pressure to intervene to force unity in the trade union movement. He appointed a Commission of Inquiry of Ministers, but they were all pro-KFL. The KAWC informed him that it would take no part in the inquiry unless some Ministers known for their Pan-African outlook were appointed, so Oneko and Murumbi were included. This was mid-1965. The commission recommended the dissolution of both the KFL and KAWC. The two bodies were to come together in the Central Organisation of Trade Unions (COTU) and were jointly to elect a leadership. The three names that led in the ballot were those of Lubembe (KFL) Denis Akumu (KAWC), and Kioni of the Teachers' Union which had been independent of both the KFL and the KAWC. The names were sent to the President, in accordance with the procedure recommended by the Commission of Inquiry, but because there was the fear that the selection of one of the names as Secretary would revive the fight from the other side, a compromise was hit upon and Lubembe was appointed COTU general secretary, Akumu Deputy Secretary and Kioni Assistant Secretary. COTU then tried to settle down to work, but it ran into difficulties immediately. The KFL seemed determined to continue clandestinely its association with the ICFTU. One example of this was the amount received each month by the Transport and Allied Workers' Union from one of the ICFTU transport secretariats abroad. The next difficulty, and a major one, was that the COTU unions that had been part of the KFL seemed to be dependent not on their workers' and union leadership assessment of policy but on the kind of guidance their officials seemed to think the government would like them to give (maybe they had direct hints or instructions?). These unions seemed able to commit themselves to strike action, for instance, only if the government agreed.

At this time the country was waiting for the government's national wage policy which was being prepared during 1964 and 1965 but which was not published because of the division in the trade union movement. By the time it could be published the former KAWC-led unions in COTU said that there should be a new commission of investigation because workers' conditions had changed in the intervening period and the feeble wage policy of the former KFL unions was completely out of touch with the needs of the workers. So, even as the two sets of unions existed side by side in COTU there were sharp splits in approach. The KAWC unions wanted militancy but the former KFL unions, led by men who were being pushed by the Minister for Labour into silent directorships and farm-ownership, seemed to think they were leading unions so that they could keep the workers in control, whatever the labour policies of the KANU government might be. When KANU started on the path towards meaningful African socialism the trade unions were enthusiastic and ready to put the national interest foremost in their calculations, to make sacrifices if the conditions of the country demanded them. But when KANU and the government showed no interest in the conditions of the workers and all evidence showed that the leaders of the country were looking after their own interests while the workers stood in the streets waiting for jobs, the workers got impatient and demanded a militant lead from their unions. This the former KFL leaders would and could not give. In

most instances these union leaders have not organized the
hard way for years; one effect of regular ICFTU subsidies
was to make union organizers lazy; they didn't go out to
organize the workers but waited at their office desks for the
subsidy cheque to arrive. (Apart from ICFTU money which
was siphoned to several countries in East and Central Africa
through agencies in Kenya, the AFL-CIO opened the Afro-
American Labour Centre in New York which is financing
unions to wage 'anti-Communist' campaigns.) KAWC-
supporting unions got money too, from the All African
Federation of Trade Unions, but AATUF aid was insignificant compared with the amounts from the western-domi-
nated unions and it came in with the full knowledge of the
government.

Finally the break with government policy came on the
political front. Thirteen trade union leaders decided that
they could no longer support KANU if it was no longer
interested in the welfare of the workers, had no wage policies,
had not attempted to grapple with the unemployment crisis,
and was prepared to defend the interests of employers or
potential-employers rather than those of the workers.

The 13 trade union leaders resigned from KANU in
protest and, under government pressure, Lubembe called
an emergency meeting of the COTU executive, and suspended the 13 from COTU leadership, though the government interpretation of the law is that the unions are obliged
to stay inside COTU. (The government through COTU
now began to take a hand in union elections, as for instance,
Kiano's journey to Mombasa to campaign in the dock
workers' elections. This pressure failed completely and the
dockers returned a militant leadership.) Once again the
future of the trade unions is in a state of flux, but though
approved unions may get official recognition, the mass of the
workers of Kenya are demanding the protection of their
interests and they will, in the long run and despite all

difficulties, follow the trade union leadership that will give them a militant lead.

*   *   *

When we hang out the national flag for *uhuru* meetings and rallies we don't want the cries of *wapi uhuru* (*where is uhuru?*) to drown the cheers. Our independence struggle was not meant to enrich a minority. It was to cast off the yoke of colonialism and of poverty. It is not a question of individuals enriching themselves but of achieving national effort to fight poverty in the country as a whole.

Kenyatta's cry to Kaggia before a vast crowd at a public meeting

'What have *you* done for yourself?'[1]

is a sign of the depths to which our spirit of national sacrifice for *uhuru* has sunk. Is there no need for national sacrifice? Has *uhuru* given the people what they need? The landless don't think so, nor do the unemployed. There are fewer people in jobs today than there were in 1960. Between now and 1970 400,000 new jobs will be required for school-leavers —this apart from the existing population of unemployed. We have come to understand that *uhuru* is a matter of dealing with poverty.

Government's policy guidelines are contained in the Sessional Paper on African Socialism and the Development Plans for 1964–70. The Sessional paper outlines an economic policy wherein a private sector, cooperatives and a state-owned sector are supposed to complement one another. The only industry nationalized by the Government since *uhuru* has been the Kenya Broadcasting Corporation (now the Voice of Kenya), and this by Achieng Oneko when he was Minister of Information and in the face of strong opposition by some members of the Cabinet. A critic of the Sessional Paper on African Socialism wrote in Tanzania's *Nationalist*[2]

[1] *The Times*, 11 April 1966.   [2] The *Nationalist*, 28 June 1965.

that it sounded as if it had been drafted by neither an African nor a socialist. Its drafter turned out to be an American professor-adviser. Before it could be properly debated, the paper was pushed through Parliament; the very few worthwhile clauses it contains have been overshadowed by economic planning and direction firmly founded in capitalist control.

The role of the public sector is visualized only in a very minor sense (as one of KANU's critics said 'the State sector of ownership is still in the mouth).[1] Many pages are taken up in a valueless argument about the respective merits of capitalism and so-called socialism. Throughout the confused talk about African Socialism for Kenya there is the basically false assumption that there can be a harmony of interests between private capital, including private foreign capital, and Government as the representative of the public interest in Kenya. The cooperative movement is dismissed in one paragraph in the Sessional Paper. Nothing is said of the force cooperatives can become in breaking the circle of poverty on the land by helping the farmers, organized collectively to improve production, enjoy better yields, and thus provide not only domestic savings for economic expansion,

[1] From time to time and with a flourish of trumpets, the government announces the formation of companies in which the country has a share. One such was the Development Finance Corporation of Kenya. But the corporation was launched with a third British government capital, a third West German and our Government held the remaining third. The impression is given that the Government is enlarging the state sector of ownership but in reality this is not so.

The Agricultural Development Corporation is heavily financed by Britain, West Germany and to some extent by the United States. Britain made her participation conditional on the employment of British officers to run the Corporation. The Kenya Government might have money invested in the corporation but, subscribed by loans with strings attached, she is not an independent agent. When the National Assurance Company of Kenya was established Parliament was given the impression that it is a state-owned company. But Kenya holds under 10 per cent of the shares and the balance is held by overseas British insurance companies, all of which are also active as private companies in the insurance market in Kenya.

but also national enthusiasm for development and mass participation without which no building of socialism is possible.

The targets for Kenya's Economic Development Plan for 1964–70 (both the original Plan and the revised) are modest, taking into account Kenya's potential economic resources. There is major emphasis on the agricultural sector, whereas what any underdeveloped country needs is an industrial base, and a meagre allocation to industry under the public capital expenditure programme, meaning that the Government as such is evading responsibility for the development of this sector. Private ownership was the vital force in the past; under these plans it will continue to be so under *uhuru*.

Relying so heavily on agriculture has grave dangers for the economically dependent country. The prices of raw materials have fallen steadily in the world market and the prices of manufactured goods have risen. The imperialist countries, as under colonialism, have the whip hand over our economies. There is much talk in the Sessional Paper about 'economic growth' but nothing about the forces of imperialism which inhibit the economic growth of all African countries, and how only our independence of external forces will remove the restraints on real planning for socialism and hence on our economic growth.

*   *   *

We have frequent examples of our continued dependence on external forces and the inability or unwillingness of Kenya's government to assert our independence. The power of outside pressures and aid constantly influence our foreign policy. The most tragic recent example is Kenya's appeasement of Britain on the Rhodesian crisis.

Imperialist tactics in southern, central and east Africa are clear. They are to hold back the assault on the southern strongholds of colonialism and White domination for as long

312

as possible; to protect and preserve strategic and economic interests in the Congo; and in East Africa, using Kenya as a base, to keep a careful watch on and if necessary to isolate and undermine the new state of Tanzania which is making rapid progress in building socialism and is the cutting edge of the revolutionary forces of Pan-Africanism for the total liberation of our southern half of the continent.

Yet when Kenya was represented at the Accra OAU Conference, her policy at that crucial juncture was influenced not by the needs of strong anti-colonial policies in Africa but by her nervousness to hold on to the £18 million loan being negotiated with Britain for the purchase of settler farms in the latest scheme of the Agricultural Development Corporation.

Kenya's instructions to her representatives at the OAU conference at Accra were not to support a call for the use of force by Britain to bring down the illegal Smith regime—but not to state this explicity lest Kenya and Kenyatta's stock fall in the Pan-African world. Murumbi who represented Kenya had been a member of the OAU meeting which was advocating the use of force by Britain. When the time came for the Lagos Commonwealth Prime Ministers' Conference, Murumbi was replaced by Gichuru who led the Kenya Delegation of behalf of the President. It looked very much as though it was Britain's pressure on Kenya that resulted in the replacement of Murumbi by Gichuru as leader of the delegation. Gichuru in Lagos appeared to fulfil the fondest hopes of the British Government when, in an interview on television, he is alleged to have said, when asked whether he thought that Rhodesia was ready for immediate majority rule:

It would be very stupid if we were to ask for an immediate take-over. The Africans in Rhodesia are not as well organized as they are here in West Africa or in East Africa, if I might claim that much.[1]

[1] House of Representatives Official Report, February 1966, cols. 875–879.

Gichuru denied in the debate referred to that he had made this remark; Parliament, however, rose in protest at this policy.

At the OAU Addis Ababa Conference, Kenya broke the front of Pan-African unity on the question of severing relations with Britain in protest against Britain's Rhodesia policy and her action was largely responsible for the subsequent inability of the OAU to act decisively on Rhodesia.

Kenya's stock has therefore fallen in Africa. It will fall even lower if these policies and this dependence on external forces are not reversed.

Inside Kenya the struggle before us will be stern and exacting. We are struggling to prevent Kenyans in black skins with vested interests from ruling as successors to the administrators of colonial days.

What form will the struggle in Kenya take? Is our country to see government and high office riddled with corruption and men in power using force and manoeuvre to block the expression of the popular will? But in the long run, the wishes of the people must prevail.

Kenya's problems in the age of *uhuru* are formidable. We have to deal with landlessness, combat unemployment, give the children more schools and the people more hospitals, push up living standards of the poor in a world where the gap between the rich countries and the poor is daily growing wider.

A Kenya government backed by popular enthusiasm and national mobilization would have a chance of finding a way to solve these problems. A government that is isolated from the people, because government and wealth are in the hands of an elite that is taking power to itself, will plunge our country into pain and tragedy.

Every year that passes swells the throng of those who will not put up with the policies of our government as they are now operated. School-leavers become the unemployed and

314

the unemployed become the bitter men of the streets. The jobless, the frustrated, the peasants starving on the land, will endure much hardship, but how much more and for how long?

I do not imagine for a single moment that these formidable problems are easily solved; but to begin to solve them, one must recognize that these *are* the key problems—and the Kenya Government turns its eyes away from these questions to examine private bank balances and the lists of vacant company directorships.

I do not delude myself that now that I have broken with the government in power and launched a party that will seek for a really just solution for the people of our country, that it will be an easy struggle and that we will not face great difficulties. But it will not be the end of what I stand for if I do not score immediate victories. For our cause is the cause of the people of Kenya and so must triumph, however long and hard the struggle.

Sources and Acknowledgment of Illustrations

The publishers are grateful to the following for the use of photographs:

East African Newspapers (*Nation Series Ltd*) for eleven photographs as follows:
One of Mrs Odinga facing page 17, for two photographs facing page 144, for the bottom photograph facing page 145, for the lower photograph facing page 209 and the lower photograph facing page 240, for the two photographs facing page 272 and the lower one facing page 273, for the photograph of Mr Pinto facing page 292 and the lower photograph facing page 293.

Kenya Information Services for eleven photographs as follows: The two photographs facing page 176, the lower photograph facing page 177, the two photographs facing page 208, the top photograph facing page 209, the top photograph facing page 240, the two photographs facing page 241, the bottom photograph facing page 292 and the upper photograph facing page 293.

The files of the late Mr Pio Gama Pinto for five photographs as follows:
The two photographs facing page 49, the upper photograph facing page 96, the lower photograph overleaf, the photograph of Dedan Kimathi facing page 97.

Mr Ambu H. Patel for the middle photograph facing page 145.

The author for nine photographs.

The Reporter (*East Africa*) for the photograph of the author and Mr Kaggia facing page 273.

Index

INDEX

Nairobi District African Congress, 145, 158, 183
Nairobi War Council, 128
Naivasha police station raid, 117, 119
Nasser, President Gamal Abdul, 191
Nationalist movement, beginning of, 24–9
Nationalist press, 80–2, 191–2
National Assurance Company of Kenya, 311
Ndewga, George K., 96
Nehru, Jawaharlal, 128–9, 222
New Kenya Party (NKP), 164, 176, 204, 210
Ngala, Ronald, 142–3, 145, 150–1, 167–8, 171, 181, 184, 193–5, 205–6, 209–10, 212–4, 216, 220, 224, 227–8, 234, 283–4, 289–91, 296, 299
Ngei, Paul, 82, 110, 112, 114, 206–8, 221, 235, 238
Nigeria, 273
Njeru, Paulo, 116
Njiiri, Kariuki, 222
Njogu, Pratt, 114
Nkrumah, Dr Kwame, 165–6, 185, 222
Nomiya Luo Church, 68–9
Non-alignment, policy of, 285–6, 294
North Kavirondo Central Association, 71
Northey, Sir Edward, 28
Nuhu, Bishop Lucas, 69
Nyagah, J., 159–60, 168, 207
Nyahera, meeting at, Christmas 1921, 27–8
Nyanza Alliance Boys' Fraternal Society, 37
Nyanza, Lake, 4, 17, 38, 133
Nyanza Times, 79, 99
Nyerere, Julius, 131, 224, 274–5, 282
Nyende, Rev. Simon, 54–5, 65

Oath-taking, 97, 107, 113–5, 120–1
Obote, Milton, 253
Ochola, Jacob, 26
Ochwada, Arthur, 182, 185, 194, 201
Odawa, Gilbert, 50
Odede, Walter, 39, 51, 76, 87, 113, 128, 148, 203, 236
Odina, Chief, 52–3
Odindo, Chief, 25
Odinga, Oginga, family history, 5–6; his village, 6–15; boyhood, 30–6;

education, at Maranda Primary School, 31–2; at Maseno, 33–6; at Alliance High School, Nairobi, 36–8; at Makerere, 38–43; his religious development, 40–3; teacher at Maseno School, 44–52; his marriage, 52–4; baptism of his sons, 54–5; resigns from teaching profession, 60; organizes Thrift Association, 77–8; organizes Luo Thrift and Trading Corporation, 79, 81; opens store at Maseno, 83; builds Ramogi Hotel at Kisumu, 84; champions economic rights of Africans, 87–94; member of Central Nyanza District Council, 90–4; first meets Jomo Kenyatta, 98; talks with Kenyatta, 100; writes to Kenyatta, 101; chairs KAU meeting in Nairobi, 102; returns to Kisumu, 103; opposes tribalism, 127; visits India, 128; questioned by security forces, 129; reasons for immunity from arrest, 131; called popularly 'Jaramogi', 133; fights for seat on Legislative Council, 138–40; problems of dress as member of Legislative Council, 141–2; early experiences as member of Legislative Council, 143–5; policy as a member 148–50; negotiations with Lennox-Boyd for new Constitution, 151–3; visits London in 1958, 154–5; champions detainees in Legislative Council, 156–7; defends this policy, 158–62; sued for libel, 162; visits Ghana, 156; presides over AEMO, 167–9; helps form KIM, 170–1; attends Lancaster House Conference, 176–81; discusses Kenyatta's release with Governor, 182; helps form KANU, 182–3; visits China, 184–5; visits Guinea, 185; visits East Germany, 188; visits Yugoslavia, 189; visits Egypt, 189; visits the Sudan, 189; visits Japan, 190; visits China, 190; visits USSR, 190; returns Kenya, 191–2; arranges scholarships to socialist countries for Kenyan students, 186–8; allegations of communism, 192; concerned at disunity of KANU, 199; campaign

321

Glossary

ajuoga witch doctor, prophet, diviner
askari kanga tribal police
baraza gathering
boma village or local administration centre
duol elders' office in centre of circular village
jodong gweng clan elders who adjudicate land disputes
jobilo seer or prophet
kiboko whip from hippo hide, or strokes given with one
kipande registration card
kuon sorgum or millet flour bread, red in colour
kanzu long robe
milango an elder carrying messages

from a chief to his clan people
mkebe or *okebe* a tin
majimbo regions
ojuok euphorbia tree
okoche tribes at the coast speaking Swahili
posho maize meal
reserves area set aside for Africans
ruoth chief
simi double-edged sword
sim-sim sesame
shamba plot of land
shenzi ngombe scrub cattle
simba hut for unmarried young men
ugali bread made from maize flour
wimbi type of millet

DT434.E26 03 1967b   GEN
Odinga, Ajuma Oginga, 1911–   SCC
Not yet uhuru; the autobiography of Ogin
Hill and Wang [1967] [1st American ed.]
3 3666 00125 4936

Somerset County College LRC

3 3666 00125 4936

4304

DT
434
E26   ODINGA
03   Not yet uhuru
1967b

Evelyn S. Field Library
Raritan Valley Community College
Route 28 & Lamington Road
North Branch, NJ 08876-1265

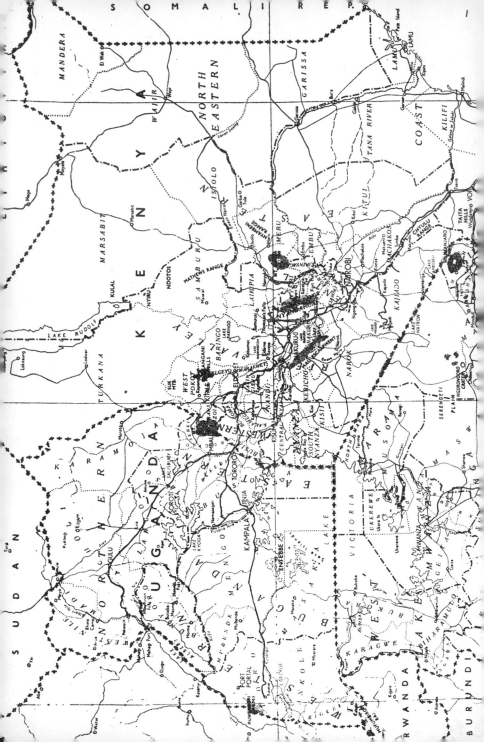